THE SPIRIT OF HUMANITY

FINDING THE FUTURE

LEON SPROULE

BALBOA.PRESS
A DIVISION OF HAY HOUSE

Balboa Press books may be ordered through booksellers or by contacting:

Balboa Press
A Division of Hay House
1663 Liberty Drive
Bloomington, IN 47403
www.balboapress.com
844-682-1282

Interior Graphics/Art Credit: Rick Singer Photography

Printed in the United States of America

ISBN: 979-8-7652-3699-4 (sc)
ISBN: 979-8-7652-3701-4 (hc)
ISBN: 979-8-7652-3700-7 (e)

Library of Congress Control Number: 2022951431

Balboa Press rev. date: 12/24/2022

DEDICATION

I was asked to submit a piece for an anthology and I wrote about my experiences with death. I thought that it would be available at the end of 2021 but it wasn't published. My hurt and disappointment in not having that piece available to share with friends lead me to the realization that I could publish an anthology of my own writing. This is that book. I have included some essays about my shamanic experiences and some pieces of fiction that I wrote with the idea of illustrating the concepts that I wanted people to know about. I also included some stories about my Dad. I hope you find it useful and interesting.

This book is dedicated to Virginia Carter, my wife and inspiration for over forty years. She always encouraged me and allowed me the freedom to explore my visions.

This book is dedicated to Michael Harner who has taught thousands of people around the world and created the possibilities of many people learning from spirit with all of the teachers whom he taught. I thank him for accepting me as a friend and student.

This book is dedicated to my Dad, Walter Sproule for all of the strength and wisdom he shared with me and all of the experiences he let me have as a child and my Mom and my brother and sisters who were a large part of my life and experiences without which I would never have been the Black Sheep of the family.

This book is dedicated to all of the fellow students of Michael Harner that I got to work with. Thank you for your acceptance, patience, caring, healing, and love that we shared, it was possible because of all of you who were there.

This book is dedicated to all of the people that I have had the opportunity to work with for teaching and healing. You made it all happen by creating the opportunities to share in caring and spirit.

A special thanks to Corey Hitchcock because whenever we are together something magic happens.

It also needs to be said that a lot of this would not have happened without the kindness and generosity of Maurah Kaunah who taught beside me and traveled with me.

Thank you all,

Leon

PREFACE

This book is basically my life's story told in different ways in order to fulfill what I have understood as my life's purpose. I have come to understand as I approach my final days of living with the rest of the humans on this earth that many of them have no idea that it doesn't have to be this way. There are right ways to live in harmony and peace. It is possible for humans to grow in understanding and learn the right way to live in peace and harmony. I hope to be able to explain through my experiences what some of those ways are. My message is, "It doesn't have to be this way. A peaceful way is possible."

My experiences during the last seventy four years have given me many opportunities to interact and learn from spirit directly. I hope to encourage everyone to have a personal relationship with their spirit helpers or guardian angels. There are many types and courses of study that can lead one to a personal relationship and a greater understanding. Choose a course that is suited to you and your experience. All paths can lead to opportunities for enlightenment and illumination. Choose a teacher that encourages your seeking without explaining your experiences to you. Realize that as your experiences lead you to a greater understanding your consciousness will learn that it is free to travel from the smallest particles to the farthest extent of the Universe. Light is slow compared to thought which is instantaneous.

To illustrate the power of the greater understanding consider the person who hits the triangle during the symphony, they don't have to know more than the right time to hit it. Each musician knows their part while the first violinist is responsible for the whole of the orchestra and the Conductor must understand the whole piece of music and the intent of the Composer. The Composer hears all of the parts of the music in their head before they write it down. The music is imagined in the realms of consciousness that connect across the galaxies.

You are not the form that you occupy or your history or your imagined limitations. You are part of the Spirit of Humanity and that connects you to every other human alive or who has existed for all time. You are a part of the Creator who continues all of this into existence and your thoughts and feelings affect the outcome of all of the realms of the Universe. It is my hope that humans will learn to behave responsibly with their thoughts and feelings once they have grown to a proper understanding of the right way to live in the Universe.

There is a certain urgency of need for the people fourteen galaxies away that face extinction if the humans on this planet don't learn to shut down the constant flow of addictive violence across all realms of human society in movies, television, and music. The daily death count from gun violence just continues to grow but our society won't even look at the harm that the proliferation of guns has allowed. The change to a peaceful nonviolent society is needed and possible once you learn that we are all one in the Spirit of Humanity.

I hope that you enjoy reading this collection of stories and experiences. If you are troubled by any of it, just think of it as a work of imagination and let your imagination see the possibilities.

May you be blessed by Love and Light,
Leon

Leon, is an exceptional man, one dedicated to serving others with compassion, and understanding. Leon's words tell the story of his adventures into shamanism. I studied with Leon and feel blessed to know him, he is a rare jewel of a person.

Love, Light and Happiness, Charles Lightwalker

I found this book to be a fascinating story of one man's journey to wisdom.

Sheila Thomsen

TABLE OF CONTENTS

CHAPTER ONE

———— ❁ ————

Imagine a universe in order. Everything that occurs is according to the laws of nature and the descriptions of that order are coordinated and uniform. The physics of the reactions are in harmony with the biological impulses that create the sustaining ever evolving changes in the structures of planets, stars and galaxies and nebulae. Consciousness connects across all of the layers of creation guiding the process. There is a rhythm and harmony to all of the various cycles in all the galaxies. There is no uncertainty or questions of motivation. No doubt limits the extent of imagination that envisions the ongoing continuing creation that unfolds.

In the millions of galaxies there is one spiral that wobbles as it passes through billions of other stars that are all vibrating to the celestial frequency. The wobble is caused by the vibrations that emanate from a small system that follows around a mediocre mid-sized star in one of the arms of the spiral. These out of harmony non-synchronous energies radiate in all directions from a blue planet. Periodic eruptions are accompanied by a continuous array of radiations that spew forth from the surface of the planet and spread out across the universe.

These vibrations began a few hundred thousand years ago and have steadily increased as the cycles around the mediocre star have accumulated. Violent ripples in the space time continuum that connects all parts of the universe began reaching other systems. The effect of the violent ripples was to cause concern in the galaxies that began to be changed as the continuous flood of energies grew and magnified. The energies were monitored and sampled. Information was gathered and analyzed. Plans were made to imagine a response and those imaginations were sent forth in an array that came from all of the areas surrounding the violent blue planet and the destruction that it was emanating at rapidly increasing rate.

The imaginations began to arrive in various ways. Consciousness has its way to express itself. Some of the manifestations of consciousness found human forms that were inhabited by weak or addicted souls that were easily convinced to leave. Others stepped in at the moment of conception and experienced a human birth. In any case they didn't all arrive from the same places or in the same manner. It would turn out that they didn't all have the same agenda or even the same concerns about the harmony of the universe being upset by one planet addicted to violence.

There are currently over eight billion humans on the planet. Most of which have little or no hope of living a life of peace and harmony. Only a small percentage of the people control the planet and keep the rest employed in waging war on each other. Each of the humans perceive themselves as separate individuals, discrete and tied to the form they see themselves as. In today's internet world it is only necessary to be famous to be some one of monetary value, therefore young people work to be famous and not a person of actual value. The little blue planet is lost in a confusion of belief systems with little regard to understanding how the harmonious universe actually works.

It doesn't have to be the way it is. It is not necessary to continue on this path of destruction as all of the required ingredients are available in the world. They only have to act with a correct understanding of the process of creation. It is possible to learn methods of experience that alter your perceptions without using any mind altering substances. During these altered states it is possible to directly experience the connection to the knowledge that is needed and use that knowledge to change the course of events. What is needed is enough people willing to learn a few simple truths through their own direct experience. The knowledge that has been withheld from many of the world's population is that they are not separate individual beings but are part of a greater consciousness that is the Spirit of Humanity. This spirit is hundreds of thousands of years old and is comprised of all of the experiences of all of the humans who have existed on this planet. Each person has their lifetime to make their contribution to what this spirit becomes. Over time if enough people cared and cooperated, the Spirit of Humanity could evolve into a compassionate caring entity that would be welcomed by the rest of the conscious realms in the Universe instead of our current status as the pariah of creation.

Understanding natural law means to be able to look at the life forms in the natural world and perceive the relationships between the various species and realize that they all are contributing to evolution of consciousness. Everything that is, is conscious and aware of its existence. I have been fortunate and I have met the spirit of the Andes Mountain in Ecuador called Imabura, which is a volcano. I was humbled by the vastness of its experience and knowledge but also by the willingness to teach me and show me its true nature. The visions I was shown and the answers I was given to my request were immediate and clear and brought me joy and laughter as they happened. Years ago and in a much different manner I met the stones that were cast within a concrete wall. Every stone of them down to the grains of sand within the concrete felt that their coming together meant that their existence had much more meaning and value as part of a wall that was something useful. They knew who they were and what their purpose was.

Humans are a mixed up bunch. Some of them know who they are and what their purpose is and many of them do not have any idea, have never had any idea and never will they ever have any idea about who they are or what their purpose is. Many humans work for the money and the things it can buy. A greater understanding of who we actually are would help us to learn about each other and how to get along. My wife and I recently returned from a short whirlwind tour of some of the main tourist destinations in Peru. Before I left I spent a lot of time watching movies that were made in Peru. The original idea was to give my ears practice in hearing the Spanish as it was spoken in Peru. I also got a lot of lessons about Peruvian history, customs, religious celebrations and how they work and get along. I noticed that the Peruvian people have developed ways of getting along that help them in their everyday life. One way is the exchange of little gifts when they meet. It is a ritual that says, "I know you. You are one of us. You are welcome."

Tour Boats in Puno

Virginia and I witnessed this every day that we were there. Watching the tour boats in Puno on Lake Titicaca maneuver as they filled with passengers was amazing. These boats are tied together in rows of ten or fifteen boats and there are four and five rows of boats on each side of the pier that sticks out into the lake. Some of the boats that were in the back rows were ready to leave first. The driver had a long pole which he used to slowly propel his boat as the other drivers used their long poles to move slightly out of the way. Little by little with no shouting and very few words exchanged they accommodated each other's needs. The passengers for some boats walked across the stern of four or five other boats. Each driver held the boats together and helped the passengers step from boat to boat. They do this every day. They have been doing it for years. It works so much better when everyone chooses to get along. Each of the tour boats is very much like the others. The available passengers are taken to islands made of reeds where each island takes their turn as the tourists are distributed among the available families.

This also happens with the tourists who stay with the host families on Amantani Island. The families take turns hosting the available tourists. In this manner everyone has the opportunity to share in the wealth that the tourists spend. I enjoyed the reaction of the host family that Virginia and I stayed with when I gave them my little gift as I had it tied up in little bundles like they would have done. Something I learned in watching one of my movies before going to Peru. The smiles and hugs that I got told me that I had passed the test. I was one of them and I was welcome to our home. While we were there we were a part of the family and participated in what they were doing. I had a greater appreciation for the quinoa flour pancakes because I had helped to grind the grain. I also figured out real quick that grinding corn between two stones has to be a lot more work than grinding quinoa.

Living on Amantani Island are about 5000 people, living where their families have always lived. On an island that is about seven miles in circumference and rises over one thousand feet above the surface of Lake Titicaca which is at an elevation of 12,700 feet. Nearly every part of the surface of the island is terraced into garden plots. They grow what they eat and weave or knit most of what they wear. They entertain tourists to earn money that they use to improve their living conditions. They are installing solar power and public water systems. A lot of the work that is done on community projects is shared as is the work between neighbors helping each other build their houses. They live without police and jails and take turns being the village president with a term of one year. They live with each other in trust and without fear.

What you still see in the more rural areas of Peru is that they still have hats and styles of dress that reveal who they are and where they are from. Each town of any size has a public square with statues that represent their history and culture. Each place also has variations of the societal rules that determine how people conduct their lives. One of the days that we were in Cusco, there was a dance festival in the public square. Schools from different areas got a turn at the center of the plaza and dancers with unique costumes were doing the dances that told the history of something that had happened in their own area. The variety and complexity of the dances and costumes was amazing.

Costumed Dancers with Virginia and I

All of the people we had a chance to talk to shared that while they may be Catholic in religion, their daily practice is to the spirit of Pacha Mama, the Mother Earth. In this way their lives are unchanged. Unchanged by the Spanish and unchanged by the Inca, the practices that guide the lives of the Quechua people date to civilizations thousands of years older. The fields are terraced with rock walls across every hillside where there is dirt and water enough to grow something. The methods have been perfected thousands of years ago. Irrigation systems over two thousand years old are still used to water the crops. The way the people live is as close to being sustainable as any that I have witnessed.

However, much of this way of living is threatened just by the number of people on the planet and the impact of busses, trains, boats, and automobiles. In Lima the traffic is just crazy at times and our taxi missed a bus by maybe two inches. The horns keep up a steady cacophony of sound but the flow continues as people yield a little and everyone keeps moving. Another adaptation of the Quechua means of getting along. We all do better if we help each other.

One of the Inca sites that we toured was Raachi where the Incas had a large annual festival to honor the sun. The temple that was built there was large enough to accommodate thousands of people inside but there was only one large round window on the south side of the temple. On the north end of the building was a large gold disc that was polished to a mirror finish. The people who were invited to the ceremony were the leading families of the tribes who had joined the Inca. They were brought together to build unity and harmony of purpose and to experience the power of the Sun. They were well fed and cared for during their time at Raachi. There are the remains of over 140 silos that were built to hold the food necessary to feed all of the people at the ceremony. All of the people were led into the temple were it was dark. When the sun aligned with the window on the south, the light went through the temple and struck the golden mirror which reflected the light and lit up the entire temple for the ceremony. The Incas had a different understanding that allowed them to achieve great things in a short time. They did not want the force of the people's labors but the power of their imagination. They inspired the people with the power of the sun but in the short one hundred years that they ruled the Quechua peoples convinced them to add Pacha Mama to their rituals. We could benefit from studying how they got large groups to work together in peace and harmony to achieve amazing things with imagination.

CHAPTER TWO

───── ❁ ─────

WHAT HAPPENS TO THE LOST soul of consciousness that was sent out on a journey past thirteen galaxies, past the star we call Polaris, the North Star to be conceived and born of a human mother in the year 1948? The individuals that are the dominant species of the fourteenth galaxy past Polaris are very intelligent and sensitive to the vibrations of some of the frequencies that are being transmitted by the blue planet. The energy that causes the most difficulty is a frequency that interrupts the secretion of hormones that regulate the reproductive cycles that are much different than a human could understand. The disruption in the pattern of reproductive behavior is such that the continuation of the species is at risk. There was an urgency to the mission that they imagined and sent forth. However, there were problems from the very start. The beings have a non-human form. They are not bipedal and do not actually have legs. The closest description of something similar on earth would be a cross between an anaconda and a crocodile. They are very long lived but do not remain reproductive in their elder years. The likely outcome of the current situation is that they will slowly die out unless some change could be effected allowing the reproductive cycle to return to normal.

The Child's parents were selected for intelligence but no thought was given to the economic situation that the Child was born into because economics was not known. The beings freely used what they needed much as trees in the forest do on the blue planet. Resources could be allocated to serve a particular need but they could not be owned. The idea of ownership does not carry the same importance when the relationship between all of the individuals is more like a hive than a clan or tribe. The unity of all was the reference guide by which ideas were valued. What is the benefit to us rather than what is my share? The Universal Standard for behavior between individuals does not allow for the monetization of what should be freely allowed to all. The proper way is to take only what you need and to share freely what you have to those others in need. The concept of economics is responsible for most of the conflict and violence that plague the people of the blue planet. The false idea of ownership is the root of the evil of economics. All of the concepts of economics are invented. Money does not exist on its own. It is an idea whose usefulness has been out grown. We need a new way to relate to material and needs.

The process by which consciousness condenses the imagined idea as a life form fourteen galaxies away involves understanding dark matter and dark energy conversion. The process did not include a solution to the problem of how different they were with regard to the mammalian human form. The Child was not able to nurse as it was allergic to the mother's milk. Every time that the mother attempted to feed her child, the baby started wheezing and coughing in asthmatic attempts to breathe. It was soy powder mixed with malt that feed the starving infant as no animal milk was suitable either. The tension and mistrust that was caused by the failed attempts at feeding haunted the relationship between mother and son.

The lack of any memory when human children are born was a further complication. This emissary that so much hope and effort had been invested in had no idea what any of this was about. There were deviations from the norm in the Child's life that left him confused and depressed as the Child was abused and bullied until he was in his teens. Incredibly skinny as he was, he was easy to pick on. However, he brought a lot of it on himself. He was moody and depressed, short tempered and impatiently critical of the slow minded humans he was living with. He only had a few good friends and was not socially adept.

The guardian angel that taught him to breathe when he was a tiny baby had a full time job keeping him alive as the Child would climb up on over under and jump off of anything. He was called the wild child and the Black Sheep of the family. His mother told the Dad every time she could, "Just take him with you." He liked being with his Dad but it meant being involved with the bees as they had a thousand hives of bees to care for. He was not like his Dad. The bees and his Dad were in love. His Dad could have whole piles of bees crawling on his face so it looked like he had a beard. His Dad hardly ever got stung and when he did he didn't even notice the sting. The Child's relationship with the bees was a mixture of fear and admiration. He got stung a lot and was stung on the inside of his nose once. That was the worst.

The advantage of working with his Dad was he got to do things that other kids did not. He learned to drive the two ton flatbed bee truck for his ninth birthday and learned to play pool and drink beer in a bar when he was twelve. He was tall and no one ever said a thing even when he drove into a truck stop and got out the gas station. Years later when he was sixteen and took his driver's test he drove the bee truck. When the instructor got in for the driving test, he saw a few bees flying around in the truck, had him drive around the block and said, "Slow down long enough for me to get out." and handed him the license.

A lot of what formed the character of the Child was the time spent hour after hour working with his Dad. There was not a lot of verbalization needed. When they were taking off the honey from the hives, his Dad would take the hive apart and sort out the combs that were full to make up full supers to extract. The supers were piled on a stand for him to carry to the truck. As his Dad finished each hive he yelled out a number between one and five that was the number of empty supers he was to put back on. He carried the full supers one at time back to the truck and returned with empties. He had to put the hive back together while not stepping in the pile of bees in front of the hive where his Dad had shook them from the supers of honey. On good hives there would be two bushels of worker bees in a pile in front of the hive. They would quickly return to the hive and resume their continuous flights carrying nectar to the hive. The numbers yelled out usually were the only words exchanged until they were driving away from the bee yard. He worked at a run most of the time in order to keep up. When he first started he had to carry the supers to the truck and then climb up on the truck to stack them to eight high. Eventually, he could run, jump, and throw the supers to the top of the stack so he did not have to climb up on the truck to stack.

The process was a routine that had been done again and again. The thousand hives were spread along the sides of the Cheyenne and White rivers in South Dakota. When the honey was flowing in the summer the pattern repeated every two weeks. The first week was working the Cheyenne River area, on Monday take off honey and on Tuesday it was extracted, on Wednesday take off honey and on Thursday it was extracted, on Friday take off honey and on Saturday it was extracted. The following week the first step was to drive 150 miles east to the White River area starting at three o'clock Monday morning. Dad rented a falling down old house that was used as a place to stay and they took off honey Monday, Tuesday, and Wednesday. Drove back Wednesday night and extracted on Thursday, Friday, and Saturday.

Sundays were always for going to church.

The Child had grown to an adult and went to college and got a degree in Mechanical Engineering. He had a facility for math and science. He became an Engineer for Westinghouse Electric and then the City of Spokane, Water Department and had many adventures. He began to read and study shamanism in order to understand his experiences and to learn how to have more experiences and to be able to direct the nature of those experiences. It was the now older man who started learning of the possibility of traveling in spirit when he became a student of Michael Harner and the Foundation for Shamanic Studies which Michael Harner started. These studies resulted in experiences that began to cause doubt in his understanding of realty.

In 2004 studying with Michael Harner, an experience of the death process in one of the shamanic exercises, set the spirit of the emissary on a journey straight past the Pole Star to the fourteenth galaxy where there was a home coming of sorts. Disappointment and fear rattled through the realms of their civilization when the realization struck home that the mission was stuck on go and the emissary that was sent had no knowledge of any mission. The meeting was short there was no time to explain it all. It became apparent that there was a need for communication so another agenda was prepared.

When the spirit of the emissary returned to the human form that lay on a mattress in the room where the shamanic exercise had taken place, it was difficult to get back into the form and the spirit had a longing to just go home to stay. Friends assisted him to get to his room half in and half out of the form. He struggled to relax and eventually fell asleep. He was completely back in his form when he awoke the next day. That next day he tried to talk to Michael to see if he could help him to understand what had happened. Michael told him it was his experience to figure out but that he should not doubt that it was real because that was what happened.

During the meetings at the Unity drum circle Debra Peterson started attending and through her influence a series of excursions to mountain tops began. Her emphasis was on repairing the ley lines and the energetic balance of the earth. She led a small band of warriors in the restoration project. Her influence and tales of intergalactic visitors started the emissary on a greater understanding than he was used to. Finding an intergalactic portal on Mt. Spokane not far from the emissary's farm surprised him. The emissary began to have doubts about his own origins that reinforced some of the feelings that he had been having.

It was the 21st of December in 2009 when a tutor in spirit form arrived on the back of a meteor that landed in the pond on the farm where the emissary and his family lived. The tutor focused on the urgency of the message and wanted the meteor announced in the news and the emissary on TV explaining the need to change now. His wife would not allow him to call the news media and no response was made.

Pond after Meteor Impact

Meteorite Found after Draining Pond

The tutor remained and did his best to communicate with whoever would listen. He haunted the dreams of the emissary passing on what ideas and information that he could and would appear in the emissaries shamanic journeys with visions of the home world that were meant to demonstrate the need to speed up the process of moving the earth towards peace.

The tutor learned that the emissary was a good telepath and would occasionally set up links to the elders who had sent him so they could express their hope that he would overcome his fear

THE SPIRIT OF HUMANITY

and act with some haste. The elders sent the emissary information about the Universal Standard of Behavior for Intelligent Species. The elders emphasized the fundamental of "you can have more only when everyone has enough," as the place to start.

The elders of the home world have no way to appreciate the very real threat of death that the emissary faces. The rich will kill any and every one that expresses a doubt to their right to be rich and own everything.

LETTER TO AN ELDER BROTHER

———— ❖ ————

A SHORT STORY BY LEON SPROULE

Over the years, I have usually had an annual meeting with Jesus Christ generally sometime before Christmas, we would talk about the things that were troubling me and discuss the alternative courses of action that I could take. This started when I was an altar boy in the services of the Lutheran Church. I felt then that I had a very personal relationship that allowed me to ask critical questions. We didn't always agree about all of the things all of the time. This is a reimagining and retelling of one of those times.

Dear Brother Jay,

I know we talked the other day but I wanted to write to you and try to express the things that I didn't say so well then. I know that you are the oldest and most favorite of Dad's children but you are not his only son. The rest of us are tired of you making

20

such a big deal about being begotten to a virgin mother. Ok, she was a great mom and she treated you so special that you think it is important to remember her in this way. But get over it. She was knocked up when she married. You got tired of the other kids teasing you at school and started this whole thing about being born to a virgin. Being a bastard is not a big deal and you shouldn't feel ashamed. We all are bastards. Dad didn't marry any one of our mothers.

I know that the rest of us kids are also part of Dad's creation. He has always been a busy guy and never sticks around long after he gets done making something new. He shows up occasionally to see how we are doing with what he gave us to work with. Right now, I wish he would come around and see what people are doing in your name. I wish you would do something about it but you don't seem to get involved any more either. This business of killing people over in your homeland is embarrassing to the rest of us. Couldn't you at least explain to those people that they are cousins and are descended from the same familial stock?

I know that you always talked a good game about love and harmony and loving your enemy like yourself but what these fools are doing now makes it seem like they never heard any of your words of wisdom. I don't want to seem ungrateful because you did always try to help the rest of us out. You said things like, "As I do, you can do also." I took that to mean that my powers for creation and healing were the same as yours. I have found that to be true.

You set a good example for the younger members of the family by healing the sick, helping the poor, and chasing the money lenders out of the temple. The problem is that the money people have chased the sick and the poor out of the churches that they have built to glorify your name. They have taken over the governments of countries and instituted policies that enable the rich to pay no taxes. I thought that you said that it would be easier for a camel to go through the needles eye than a rich man to get to heaven. Why are these people preaching that you want them to be rich and successful?

You made a big deal about being dead and rising up from the dead. Then you took off and left your followers behind to screw up all of the things that you claimed to care about. Let me tell you about that death and rising up again. People do it every day now. They call it a near death experience. I have done it myself. It was interesting and some of the people who have had this experience change their lives for the better and try to tell people about their visions of the other side. Most of them, however, go right back to living every day as if they expected to live forever. Why didn't you stick around and show people how to live in a manner that would indeed glorify your father?

One of the other things that have been bugging me lately is the idea that you found gays and lesbians to be less than human. It seems to me that you could take the time to point out that you hung around with a group of twelve guys. Twelve guys who were jealous of your relationship with the good looking redhead. They wanted you to love them as you loved her. How many of your friends were gay? You have never given me a straight answer. Don't you want to talk about it? Is it because you think that your friends are less than human? I don't think so. I think that you know that they are the most creative, imaginative, interesting, and most spiritual of the people. They have a connection to the powers of the universe that the ordinary straight people deny. I wish you had been more open talking about these things. You could have helped a lot of people who are suffering now. They do not deserve the persecution that they are receiving in your name.

I know that you and Dad have a big thing about judgment and the origin of sin but I think it is time to let the cat out of the bag. There is no such thing as sin. You inherit the genetics of your parents not the sins of your father. This idea that people's choices result in a debt of sin that must be repaid by death is false and you know it. You know that only the physical form can die. A person's spiritual form or soul can not die and can not be evil. You know these things and yet you let your priests go on and on about the evil nature of man. There is no evil. There are only choices and the consequences and experiences that result from those choices.

I know that you are busy with all of the demands of running your heaven and you aren't able to keep up with all of the requests that people make of you, but you could make it easier on yourself if you let the rest of us help. Tell your followers to be more tolerant of other's religious practices and beliefs. We all are here to help people get through the problems that they face. These problems could be minimized by including every human, every animal, every plant and all of the earth as children of God when you speak. All were created by the same loving creating universe of one whom we call Father.

Thanks for taking the time to read this, my brother, and know that I love you as I have always. Please think about these things and try to understand that all people want to feel good about themselves. If they feel good about themselves then they will do good things to and for each other. Please stop telling them that they are sinful and that they must die. Tell them instead that they are beautiful and they should live in love and glory.

Sincerely,
Your younger brother Al

SPIRIT OF HUMANITY

❖

THIS IS A CONCEPT THAT I think most people are not familiar with. Just as there is a spirit that is all the things that are the earth, Gaia as we call her, there is a Spirit that is all of Humanity. This spirit is the sum of all of the experiences, knowledge, feelings and emotions, talents and abilities of all of the humans on the planet. It has been growing and learning since the beginning of homo sapiens as a species. I began to work with the Spirit of Humanity when I was taken by one of my spirit helpers to meet the Spirit of Humanity in response to a journey that I did after the massacre in the Colorado movie theater trying to understand why such things happen. What I learned then about the Spirit of Humanity is that it is the sum of all of us and when something happens that causes an emotional compassionate response in a large number of people as they hear the news, the Spirit of Humanity grows in the compassionate direction.

I experienced the shift in the balance of humanity as we responded with caring. This has happened too many times already since with a school in Connecticut and the Boston Marathon. We have been slowly growing and moving forward as a species since we began sitting around a fire. As our experience and knowledge grew so did our ability to change the world. There has been an exponential growth in everything during my life time. The time is ripe for an exponential shift in our conscious awareness of what humanity really is and for us to learn to choose where we are going as a species.

The real benefit to current humanity is that they can learn directly from the knowledge that is held within the Spirit of Humanity. The technique is to contact a spirit that has the knowledge that you want because of their life's experiences. You can ask them to show what they have learned. In this way it is possible to learn all kinds of useful skills.

The experience of connecting to the Spirit of Humanity opens one's eyes to the realization of unity. Once you have felt the connection it is hard to say I think we should bomb those people over there because you feel that you would be bombing yourself. If we begin to think of ourselves as connected and whole, we can begin to solve the problems that we face with the climate crisis and the endless wars.

It is possible to change to a peaceful world if we begin to help those that need it most and allow the billionaires to have no more than they need to live in peace and safety. If you are not part of the solution then you are the problem. In Buddhism there is the understanding that evolution proceeds by death. The old ideas will die away as the old people who have them die away. It is the young who will learn to utilize these possibilities and create the future by connecting their minds. They are already doing it.

CREATION STORY

———— ✲ ————

THIS WAS WRITTEN AS AUTOMATIC writing following a meditation.

In the beginning there was light and the light was free and clear. It shone and illuminated all around it but there was nothing around the light to shine back or reflect the light. So the light had no way of knowing what was happening. The light wanted more and began to break off pieces of itself that condensed and became solid. Each piece then could reflect back the light and the light saw the pieces moving and changing as they went about their way.

Each piece of solid light became more and more evolved and broke into other more complex shapes. The shapes formed and grew and became more shapes. Each shape reflected the light in a new way. So the light became fascinated by the possibilities and kept creating more pieces of itself to become solid.

As the pieces became more and more complex they learned that they were light and some wanted to go back and become light again. As this happened the light was disappointed in that then the pieces were no longer reflecting the light. The light caused the particles to forget that they were light and they continued to grow and be more and more complex.

As time went on the pieces started living as separate beings and they saw the light and were glad for its warmth. As they came together and joined more pieces of light were created and they never knew that they were light. The forms became more and more evolved and began to see and think and plan and dream. I was born from one of the dreams that two beings had. I was meant to be a special being that would remember the light and tell others of the light.

The light is all there is. It is the nature of rocks and trees and hills and birds and people. We each have this light and we can share it between us. When we let our own light shine and the glow warms those around us, we are also warmed and enlightened.

I was created by the love of two beings who wanted me to express this love. And all of this for love. What do I call the light who created me? How do I know the light? I would know that which is as **SHAGAWAY NEUMANA**. I am a being of light. I am love and the act of creation. I am light. I am **SHAGAWAY NEUMANA** the power which is all.

I came from the sun. I came from this world. I came from my parents and grandparents and I came here to bring light to those around me. I came because I was needed to help and I came because I was wanted. I came because the light shines and all is.

DAD AND I

❀

THESE ARE STORIES ABOUT MY Dad and I. They have occurred over my lifetime and continue through what is left of time. The relationship between my Dad and I was special. I got to spend a lot of time with him as he worked and taught me how to work. I must warn you that this is an amalgamation of my memories and thoughts and experiences and is distorted by seventy-four years of living at this point as I write this. The memories do not occur sequentially or in any kind of planned out sequence. I'll do the best I can to explain the stories as I go along but don't forget that I forget a lot of the details.

I was born in Lander, Wyoming in May of 1948 on the 18th at 11:45 pm. I was nearly late for my own birthday. My parents lived on a small farm south of Riverton, next to the Big Wind River. I grew up with plenty of time to wander alone to explore the natural world. My mother and I never really connected as I was allergic to her milk. As it turns out I am allergic to all milk as even the minutest amount will set off my immune response. I am a genetic defect who only lived because of powdered soya, which was available at the time. The result of not bonding with my Mom meant that I was always afraid of her, because of her not bonding with me meant I experienced harsh consequences at times for my wild behavior.

I was a wild child who would wander off at every chance to explore whatever there was. I had no concept of time when I was in the world of bugs and rocks and sticks and I never remembered what I was supposed to be doing. At the age of two I was found to have crossed over the slough of flood water to get to the island, where I had left some jacket I was supposed to be wearing. I was spotted coming back climbing across the box wire fence that was hanging across and in the moving water. They were more upset than they were when they found out that I was climbing on the corral fence and waiting for a horse to come over so I could climb down onto its back. The horses were used up in the mountains for hunting and were not known to be tame, but there was a big old white horse that would let me sit on it as it walked around the corral and then bring me back to the fence. My Dad took the horses back to where he had borrowed them and that ended my career as a cowboy.

When it was decided that I needed something of a task to keep me out of trouble, it became my job to herd the sheep. Some of the time the sheep would be corralled in the orchard so they could clean up around the trees, but other times my Dad liked to have them clean up along the road and irrigation ditch and I became responsible for making sure they were ok. There was not a lot of traffic on the dirt road that ran through our place, but some of them went fairly fast. The sheep liked to lay in the road in the shade of the cottonwood trees that grew along the river. They liked the soft dust of the road and the old ewes would nap as the lambs cajoled around. I was supposed to keep them out of the road but keeping them out of the shade on a hot afternoon was next to impossible. I wasn't any bigger than the lambs. There was only so much you could do by throwing rocks and shouting.

One day I was not paying attention to the sheep but was floating things down the irrigation ditch and watching to see which was fastest. A car came flying down the road at a high speed and before I could get the sheep out of the road, the car had hit and killed a lamb. They never even stopped to say anything, they just kept on going. When I went to the house and told my Mom, she was furious about how I had cost them the value of the lamb and all of its future earnings. When my Dad came home, he listened to my story and then picked up the lamb and put it in his pickup. There were not that many people who lived on the road and my Dad must have figured out who it was from my description of the car. He drove down the road and was gone for a short while. When he came back he didn't have the lamb. He gave my Mom a handful of money and said, "They decided to have lamb for dinner."

The sheep and I were stuck with each other. I learned to be more careful but I am always easily distracted. For many years we didn't have electricity, which also meant that the only running water we had was the river and the irrigation ditch. The well was several hundred feet from the house on the west end of the garden. It was an old cast iron hand pumper. Next to the garden was a fenced pasture for the sheep and there was a water trough next to the well. If you didn't hang a bucket on the well pump the water would fill the trough for the sheep as you pumped. I was not very old when my Dad bought me a red wagon. It would hold two five gallon buckets. Because the ground was level I could fill the buckets and drag the wagon back to the house where someone else would carry them into the house. I was standing there one evening as it was just getting dark, pumping water into the sheep trough after filling the buckets. The sheep were milling around the water trough as I filled it, drinking the fresh water. I didn't notice that we had a visitor until it was too late. The skunk let fly and I was swamped in odor but the amazing thing was that the skunk missed me and the entire spray soaked the side of the well pump. I didn't get any on me. The well smelled for a long time after that and the sheep thought the water tasted funny.

I guess I should back up to the beginning. My Dad wasn't always my Dad. He was born in 1920 and named Walter Sproule. He was the second son, as his brother John was born two years earlier. One of his first adventures in life was that in 1922 he and his brother got smallpox. The town of Riverton, Wyoming was where they lived. The town's people ran them out of the area at gunpoint. My Grandmother, Kiva Sproule, took her two small children and spent the winter in a sheep wagon up in the Rocky Mountains. How she survived and kept her two sons alive is a mystery. She never would talk about that time. When they weren't dead the town let them come back in the spring.

As near as I can tell from the little either my grandmother or my Dad said about his Dad was that he was a shepherd and a horse trader. He wasn't often home. I asked my Dad once how old he was when he last saw his Dad. My Dad answered that he thought he was around twelve or fourteen but wasn't sure. The place that Grandma Sproule had where I lived my first six years was bought by her at a county tax auction. At some time in my childhood I learned that she was able to afford the place because no one bid against her. The story I heard was that the people took pity on her because she couldn't get any help from her husband.

I have an H and R .22 caliber seven shot pistol that was my grandmother's. It is worn out and not much use but it has a lot of history. Grandma made beer during the depression. It was how she fed her kids. I don't know when she stopped but she still had a lot of large stoneware crocks when I was a kid. Mom made sure the evil items went to the dump after Grandma's passing in 1964.

My Mother and my Dad did not come from similar backgrounds. Mom was a child of several generations of German potato farmers. They had settled in Arkansas, some of them moved to Colorado, and then my Grandpa Dierks decided to go to Wyoming and claim one of the first places when they put in the irrigation project. He and Grandma Dierks had nine children and while he worked in town at the grain elevator of the Farmer's Union which he helped to found, Grandma Dierks and the kids did the farming. The German famers still spoke German and had their own Lutheran Church where the hymnals were in German. This ended when Hitler started to rise in Europe. The German was stopped and my mother never spoke the language. Everything was in English and no one wanted to be considered German. The Lutheran Church however was the mainstay of my Mom. She was devoted and questioned the morality and personal worth of any one who was not similarly as devoted and pure.

Mom never got along with Grandma Sproule and considered her a heathen because she was member of the Order of the Eastern Star which was a women's auxiliary to the Masons. I don't know how my Dad managed but he remained calm through it all. Mom was four years younger than my Dad and they met because Dad and Mom's older brother Bud were drinking buddies. According to Mom her brother had tried to introduce them several times, like the time he tried to take my Mom into a bar to meet him. Mom turned around walked out and said she didn't want to know any man she had to meet in a bar.

Eventually they did meet and as World War Two was well along my Dad was drafted into the army. He finished basic training in Texas and was being sent by train to Seattle to be shipped out to the Philippines. Dad talked the army into giving him two days leave to get off the train in Wyoming so that he could marry my Mom. When Dad got off of the train in Wyoming not just my Mom was there to meet him, his Mom was there too. Grandma Sproule refused to let them get married as it was Friday the 13th. She made them wait until Saturday the 14th and then went with them to the little cabin Dad had reserved that was in the mountains. According to Mom they had to hike out into the woods to get some time alone and as they were walking they came to a wet swampy area and Dad tried to carry her across only to drop her in the mud. She didn't have fond memories of the occasion.

Dad had to get back on the train and get on the Liberty ship in Seattle. The ship did not sail immediately as the convoy was not complete yet. My Dad had a good conduct medal from the army. Dad said that it was for all of the things that they didn't catch him doing. What they didn't catch him doing in Seattle was jumping ship, hitching a ride to Hayden Lake in Idaho where my Mom was working taking care of Dr. Roulette's children at the cabin he owned on the Lake. Mom had been working for the Roulettes in Laramie, Wyoming where Mom was attending the University of Wyoming. She earned her room and board by cleaning house and taking care of the children. Dr. Roulette hired her for the summer to care for the children at the cabin in Idaho. The end result was a delayed honeymoon, then Dad managed to get back on board the ship without getting caught. The convoy was complete and left the next day.

My sister Marie was born while Dad was still overseas. I was born in 1948 after Dad returned to Wyoming.

The early days in Wyoming include a lot of memories of my Dad. He remained best friends with my Uncle Bud. Bud was married to his wife Jean and they had kids similar in age to the kids in our family. In particular, my cousin Richard was about six months older than I was. It gave him an advantage over me in that he could always convince me that he was older and therefore knew more. I usually did whatever he suggested as his wild side was a good match for mine. Bud and Jean and the kids would often come over to our place after church on Sunday.

Remember we did not have electricity or running water. That meant no refrigeration. We did have an old oak ice box that was on the porch. Ice cost money and it would take a lot of ice to keep the ice box in use full time so it was only used for short term situations. Dad worked in the winter cutting ice from the river and helping to store it in a big warehouse full of ice insulated with saw dust. It was usually Uncle Bud who would buy ice cream and then ice to keep it frozen long enough to have it for dessert after chicken dinner.

My part was to go get two chickens out of the hen house. I didn't like that part. I hated going in the chicken house and trying to catch the birds. They flew around and feathers flew in the air and the dust was so bad I couldn't breathe. I eventually learned to be stealthy and pretend that I was only getting the eggs. I could slip my hand into the nest and grab the chicken's legs before it flew. I still had to hold on and not let go when my Dad chopped the head off. The wings would flap and beat on my arms and blood would spurt from the open neck but I would be in trouble if I let go. I did once but then you have to catch a chicken running around with its head cut off. There is a reason for the saying. The next step was to scald the chickens in boiling water and pluck the feathers. It is not something I would choose to do now. I wouldn't eat chicken for a long time before I gave up beef and pork. I actually convinced the manager of the food service that I worked in my senior year of college that it was inappropriate to assume that everyone ate chicken and got him to offer an alternative when chicken was on the menu.

Once the chickens were plucked my job was done for a while and I was free to wander around with Richard and find some way to get into trouble. That was never our intent but was frequently the result of our being together. Once after a rain storm had soaked the ground for the last time for a while. The ground dried out in big cracks that split the soil into near bricks. The dirt was about two inches thick and dried hard. Richard and I worked very diligently piling the pieces up into the walls of a fort. We had a lot of fun but Dad was not happy when he saw what we had done to his level field.

Our neighbor to the east was a farmer named Hans Blond. He raised Hereford bulls. The fence between the pasture where the bulls were and our back yard was a high board fence. We were left to our own with time on our hands. We were told to stay in the back yard and not go wandering around. There were a few missing knotholes in the board fence where we could look at the bulls in the pasture next door. Boys will be boys and it didn't take us too long to figure out how to climb up the fence and sit at the top so we could shoot at the bulls with our slingshots. Hans was an old man and he and my Dad did not always get along. I could have been part of the reason. The other part was that Dad resented Hans getting his social security after only paying the minimum into the system. He got in as soon as farmers were eligible and retired as soon as he could to begin drawing payments. What rubbed my Dad was that he wasn't retired he just kept on raising bulls and making money but he put it all in his wife's name.

Perhaps the best story to illustrate the problem of the wild child and his Dad is the story of the picnic in the Rocky Mountains. If I remember the circumstances at all, Uncle Bud was working on a road job where he was the foreman. The job was somewhere up high near the pass over the Rockies by Dubois, Wyoming. Since Bud was working Dad took us up there to meet the Dierks family for a picnic in the woods. I am not sure where we actually were but it doesn't matter. There was a nice cold creek flowing near the spot we were at and Uncle Bud had brought a whole case of soda pop with a bunch of different flavors. There was strawberry and grape and orange and root beer. A case of pop in those days came in a wooden crate of tall glass bottles.

The way to cool the soda pop was to put it in the creek. Dad and Bud found a nice spot and put the case of pop down into the creek. The whole dang bunch of cousins and aunts and uncles then took off on a hike except for Richard and I. We were stuck like flies to the outhouse. We had soda pop on the mind.

Now what is hard to appreciate is just how rare a thing a bottle of soda pop was let alone a whole case with all of the different flavors. I had probably only had two or three bottles of pop in my short life. Richard of course was more familiar with all of the different flavors and while it was his idea, I have to say I didn't resist very hard when he suggested we help ourselves to a bottle. After all with all of the other cousins we might not get the flavor we want if we wait until the pop is handed out.

Well, one pop led to another. What I never did know was just where everyone else went for such a long time and why they didn't figure out that Richard and I were missing. Let us just say that by the time they all came back the pop was almost gone and to make matters worse Richard had decided to smash the empty bottles in the creek to hide the evidence. So back then the bottle was almost a third of the price of pop. The deposit was there so you would bring the bottle back. We were not met by happy cousins. Everyone was upset. Uncle Bud proclaimed that he was going use his belt and beat Richard till he couldn't see straight. Here is the rub, Uncle Bud insisted that my Dad do the same to me. My Dad was totally against using a belt. He could hurt you bad enough just using his hand and he had experienced the belt as a child and never would do that to anyone. Not even me at this time when I probably deserved it. Dad told Bud that he would not use the belt on me and that he would handle it his own way.

Dad's way involved work. Usually the harder the better. I think it was about this time that he decided it was time to get electricity and running water into the house. The house was a three room building that Dad had got somewhere and moved onto Grandma Sproule's. It had just been set on the ground on a cement footing. There was no room under the house at all. I was small enough so my job was to use Dad's army shovel, the folding entrenching tool, and dig a tunnel from the front porch under the house then tee off one way to the kitchen and the other way to the bathroom that we were going to have when Dad finished the addition which also included two bedrooms. It took me a while. I was a tunnel rat and filled buckets that Dad would pick up at the end of the tunnel.

When we finished the plumbing it was time for electricity. The only way to get wires around the house was for me to crawl between the floor joists pulling the wire as I went. The house had been there for three or four years. There were spiders and snakes, mice and bugs, and cat shit to crawl through on the ground but the hardest part was they had used long nails when they nailed the flooring to the sheathing and these nails stuck down far enough that if I raised my head, a nail would poke me. I wasn't given a choice. It needed done and I did it.

It seems now that Dad figured out that I had a restlessness that only work could cure. I always had something that I was supposed to be doing. He kept projects in front of me and I had assignments to do things while he was out working in the bee yards or on what extra work he managed to line up for himself.

Learning to Drive

Let's just start telling stories about learning to drive. My earliest memories are of sitting on my Dad's lap as he drove the pickup around the farm. As soon as I could he would let me steer while he worked the gas and brakes. I was a quick learner so I was soon trying out the shift lever on the car while us kids were left in the parking lot. Not so good as once I was able to get the car into neutral but we were on a bit of a slope and the car moved a ways before I managed to get it stopped and back in gear. Little by little I learned. And yes, Dad noticed and chewed me out a little.

I got my first job in a gas station when I was seven years old. It was part time and temporary but I had fun. We had just moved to South Dakota and we were living in a cabin at a motel. The motel also had a Texaco gas station in the front. The gas station was normally operated by Ray the son of the people who owned the motel, however, he had broken his leg, He could not go out to the island and fill the cars, but he could sit in a chair and run the cash register. I worked the pump and told him how much. This was in the fifties so the hardest part was finding the gas fill spout. The cap was often hidden under the license plate or behind the left tail light.

One thing that I remember clearly is the large yellow rock

that was used as a doorstop for the front door of the gas station. It was a triangular lump about the size of a basketball. Mr. Woodson, the owner liked to impress the tourists by bringing out his Geiger counter and putting it close to the rock. When he did the instrument chirped like a cricket. It scared the tourists and me. He just laughed and said, "Don't worry its harmless."

I got a bicycle for Christmas when I was eight so I could get a paper route. Dad also had me working in the bees. I started refilling the supers after the combs had been sent through the extractor. There were five baskets in the extractor and there were five spare baskets. As the extractor was spinning Dad and his hired helper would cut the caps from the combs and place the combs in the spare baskets. It took thirteen combs to fill one basket. When all five baskets were filled the extractor was shut down and the baskets were removed and the combs dumped out on a work bench for me to fill the supers. Each super held eight combs so it took 8 supers plus one to fill the extractor. The process of extracting was a continuous race until you were finished for the day. On a good day of extracting we would process around 200 supers.

When the combs were full you had to start the extractor out slow and then speed it up in steps until it was at full speed. The steps were achieved by moving a drive wheel in closer to the center of the circular plate that was on the top of the extractor shaft. There were four steps and it became my job to shift the speed as well as put away the combs. Dad just kept adding to the tasks as I figured them out.

I had been going out to the bee yards since I was a little kid when I just sat in the truck and waited. Dad soon figured out that I was good help after he got me a hat and veil and gloves. I did whatever needed done. Not always cheerfully and sometimes I wanted a break so I could play with my friends. So Dad decided to make it more fun. One day when I was nine he told me to get behind the wheel and drive the truck. We were on Peterson's ranch about thirty miles from anywhere on a dirt road, that really only the Petersons drove on. It was a section road which meant it was on the section line between two sections of land which are one mile square. This road went straight east for several miles and then turned south and went one mile and the turned left and went back to going east.

The first time I drove I had a little trouble shifting the gears and working the clutch so I didn't get going too fast and eventually Dad took over and drove the thirty miles home. The next time we were out at the Petersons, Dad let me try again. This time I was so proud of myself I managed to shift all of the way to high gear and I was just rolling along. The bee truck was a Ford two ton flatbed and at this time we were just checking the bees as it was too early to take off any honey, so there was no load on the truck.

I arrived at the corner and started around, then the rear wheels hit the loose gravel that was piled up around the outside of the corner and we slid around in a circle taking down a bunch of barbed wire fence next to the road ending up in the field. Dad had tried to grab the steering wheel and turn into the skid but he wasn't able to stop the slide. When the truck stopped Dad said, "I thought you were going too fast." Then we got out and started fixing the fence. When we were done Dad had me drive down to the next corner so I could do it right. The Peterson's daughter was my fifth grade teacher in her first year of teaching. I never saw her on the farm and only knew her as Miss Peterson.

When we went on trips to the White River area of South Dakota which was about one hundred and fifty miles from Hot Springs where we were, Dad would get up at 3:00 o'clock in the morning and head out. I would wake up as soon as I heard him moving around and get dressed to be ready to go. After I was able to handle the truck ok, Dad would drive out of town a couple of miles and then pull over to the side of the road. "Do you think you can handle it?" he would ask. I always said yes, then he would slide over in the seat and I would jump out and run around and get in the driver's seat. Shortly after I got the truck up to speed and headed down highway 18, Dad would be asleep. I would drive about 125 miles and then he would wake up and tell me which bee yard to go to first. The trips east to the bees on the White River were always an adventure.

We often went on Highway 16 instead of 18 depending on which bees Dad wanted to go first. To get on Highway 16 we first had to go north to Rapid City on state road 79. When I was first learning to drive my Dad loved having me drive through Rapid City although I was 10 years old. On the south side of Rapid City was a stop light. What made this intersection annoying was the railroad crossing that was parallel to the intersecting street. The railroad had a high berm above the rest of the road so that it had a steep incline which was where I would invariably get stuck when the light changed. Someone would always stop right behind the truck so you couldn't let it roll back. I had a terrible time getting the clutch engaged without killing the engine. Dad bailed me out the first couple of times by holding the emergency brake so I could keep my foot on the gas after that I was on my own. After one time of killing the engine and wasting two lights while people sounded their horns, I figured it out.

Dad wasn't a person who explained things and he hardly ever got mad if you screwed up trying. I only heard him swear twice. Once was when I was driving coming home from one of the close runs so the truck wasn't fully loaded but it had load on it. I had to back the truck into the driveway so we could unload the supers into the garage. We had a big mirror on both sides of the truck so I should have been able to see but Dad was leaning over and looking in the mirror on his side so I couldn't see what was on that side. What was on that side was Dad's brand new 1959 Oldsmobile 88.

I couldn't say to Dad what he would have said to me, "Line your ears up so I can see through them." Since I couldn't see I thought he would say, "Stop" if I needed to.

Dad said, "You're getting closer."

I figured if he wanted me to stop he would say, "Stop." I kept backing up slowly.

Dad said, "You're getting closer."

I figured if he wanted me to stop he would say, "Stop." I kept backing up slowly.

Dad said, "You're getting closer."

I figured if he wanted me to stop he would say, "Stop." I kept backing up slowly.

Dad said, "Why the Hell didn't you stop?"

I stopped and got out to look. I had put a scratch about nine inches long just into the white paint on the hood of the car. It would be there to remind us of our inability to communicate until Dad got rid of the car years later.

Working the Bees

A little background information for clarity will help. Dad had bees in two areas of South Dakota where there were enough blossoms through the summer to sustain the honey flow. Along the Cheyenne River in the area around Hot Springs where we lived there was an irrigation project that had alfalfa fields. In the irrigation project there were lots of ditch banks and road sides covered with white and yellow sweet clover which the bees love and it also makes the best honey.

The other area was along the White River east of the Badlands where there were hay fields in the bottom land and wheat on the hills. The area was owned by large land owners, ranchers whose ties to the land went back to the beginning of the settlement of the area. There was also a lot of wild sweet clover in this area as well making it ideal for the bees. The two areas were separated by about 150 miles so Dad had his plan to make it all work.

When the railroad was built across South Dakota they laid out towns every ten miles. Stamford was one of those towns. Most of the towns didn't last. Stamford lasted longer than most. There was still a grain elevator next to the railroad track, a gas station next to Highway 16, which had the post office and general store in the back, living quarters for the owner and his wife was a small house next door. There was an old house that still stood up on the hill that Dad rented for a few dollars. It became our home away from home.

There was one decrepit old bed in the bedroom which nicely was the only room where the roof didn't leak somewhere. There was an old stove in the kitchen that with a bottle of propane and some cleaning worked. Dad had the electricity turned on in the summer so there were lights and I got the old water pump to work. It was an electric pump with a small pressure tank that pumped from an old cistern. When I opened the lid the cistern was very low so I convinced Dad to have a truck of water hauled in to fill it up. That made it possible to prime the pump and get it going. A water heater made it possible to shower and clean up. We drank the water and it was always cool being several feet below the surface and we never got sick.

When we were there the one summer the population doubled. The woman had twins. We would get gas there and Dad would get groceries and sometimes a six pack of beer that we would split. We went in there one evening to get beer after working all day in the sun and in the backroom among the tires, sacks of dog food, and cases of oil there was a poker game going on. Two of the players were ranchers who Dad had bees on their land. They spoke to Dad and invited him to join the game. Dad looked at the piles of money on the table and said he couldn't even afford to ante.

Zack Word, one of the ranchers where we had bees, pushed a handful of money over to Dad and told him to play till he lost this. He told Dad he needed to take a break. Dad opened a beer and handed me one. He sat down and I found a bucket to sit on where I could watch. I knew enough not to say one word. Around the table was the owner of the store, Zack and Don Word whose ranches were on the south side of the White River, and John Korchow whose ranch was on the north side of the river across from the Word brothers and Chick Abhorczek who was an outlaw and my Dad the beekeeper.

Dad played to stay in the game, because he wanted to hear the stories as much as I did. I had heard the name but I never thought I would meet a real old west outlaw. He looked old and gray with long hair and a beard. He was wearing a bowie knife that you could see and a gun that was hidden until his coat fell open as he coughed and rasped with an old smoker's effort to clear his lungs. He still gave off the feeling that he could kill you if he wanted. The Word brothers were trying to learn more about these two Italian guys in suits who were out in middle of South Dakota asking questions about Chick. I thought that he might be hiding in one of their out buildings. They owned over twenty square miles between them in one piece. There were a lot of old sheds and barns on the property. After much prodding, he finally admitted that he had to leave Las Vegas in a hurry. The two guys were trying to collect $10,000 that he had taken from some casino. He didn't think they would last for long out in the heat with their suits.

Dad didn't last much longer in the game and we had to work the next day. The game would go all night and later that week Dad and I saw the Italians in a truck stop café. They were already headed west to Vegas.

Dealing with Problems

One of the best illustrations of dealing with problems is a trip we took in 1962. Our truck was in the shop having the engine rebuilt and we needed to check on the bees in the spring so the mechanic who was working on the truck loaned Dad one of his pickups. It was an old Ford but it ran so away we went. We went up to Rapid City and headed east but we weren't on Highway 16. Interstate 90 had just been opened from Rapid City to almost Wall, South Dakota. It was brand new there was no one on the 4 lanes of interstate but us. Wouldn't you know, nothing lasts if it's a good thing and blam, the left rear tire blows out. With some foresight Dad pulls into the median between the four lanes. There is no traffic in either direction so we look for the jack, no jack, we look for the lug wrench, no lug wrench.

There is a spare tire. Dad looks around and finds a good sized rock which he wedges under the differential. He tells me to get my hive tool and start digging.

I answer, "Ok, but we don't have a wrench."

Dad's answer was, "I'll get a wrench."

We are parked in the middle of Interstate 90 and so far there has not been a car or truck in either direction. Finally, off to the East we see a puff of diesel smoke as some truck driver just shifted gears coming up the hill. It is over two miles away as the truck crests the hill. My Dad calmly stepped into the right lane of traffic and held up both hands and started waving. The truck slows and stops in front of my Dad. Dad steps over to the driver's side of the truck and says, "We need to borrow your lug wrench for a couple of minutes."

The truck driver gets out and looks but can only find an eight inch crescent wrench. Dad grabs the wrench and steps over to the pickup truck and takes the lug nuts off and I hand him the spare tire. Dad replaces the lug nuts and hands the driver his wrench.

The driver immediately heads down the road and we get in the truck and drive off leaving the hole that I had dug in the median. During the time that this went on there was no other traffic on Interstate 90. I would see the hole in the median for a while but it eventually got grown over by weeds and grass.

Moving Bees

One year Dad decided to move one yard of bees from the White River area back to the Cheyenne River area. That fall as we were finishing up taking off honey we made one trip just to move the bees. The bee yard was up on a hill above where the hay fields were and the hill sides were covered in clover but the winter winds across the hill top caused too much winter loss in hives.

We got there in the afternoon and began the process of picking up all of the various stuff that had accumulated in the years of the bees being in that location. There were a few dead hives and other junk we needed to pick up because we were not coming back after we moved the bees. The hives had already had all of the extra supers taken off when we finished with the honey. They were all two full depth supers and weighed about 160 -180 pounds.

The bees would be flying about until it got dark so the

entrance was left open so they could get back to the hive. I noticed that a lid had blown off one of the dead hives and was lying on the ground behind where my Dad was standing. I went over and started to pick it up but as I raised the front edge with my right hand I quickly became aware of a curled up rattlesnake shaking its tail. I froze with my arm maybe a foot from the snake. The other end of the lid was beside my Dad's feet. I said "Dad" and Dad immediately jumped about twenty feet straight down the hill. He later claimed that he knew it was a snake by the fear in my voice. When the snake heard my Dad jump, it turned its head and I jumped back keeping the lid between me and the snake.

We always carried a shovel and Dad got his revenge on the snake. We did not want it to crawl under a hive we would be picking up in the dark. Dad and I went around and tipped up the hives and checked just to be sure there was not a second snake.

When we finished with the prep work we drove out to a local café and ate. We had to wait for it to get dark before we could pick up the hives. When it started getting dark we drove back to the bee yard. I got out and started plugging the entrances so the bees couldn't get out but Dad stopped me and kidded me about being a little kid again. I said ok but he would have to carry the front end on all the hives and we started loading the hives on the truck. When the hives were all loaded and tied down we drove back to the highway.

Dad was driving and as we were going to have to wait until dawn to unload in order to be able to see where we were setting them down, we decided to sleep first and then drive when there was less traffic in the early morning. Along the highway through the middle of South Dakota were 150 Minuteman missiles that were just recently completed. Dad pulled off of the highway onto the driveway to one of the missile sites and parked in front of the fence that surrounded it and in no time he was asleep. We slept two or three hours and then woke up to drive to the Cheyenne River where we were going to put the bees.

The truck would not start. The battery was dead. At this time of day there is no traffic on the highway.

Dad says, "I'll get a jump."

He walks over to the fence and gives it a really good shake. A short time later a blue four door Airforce pickup drives up with an officer and five guys with guns. They get out and ask Dad what is going on.

"I need a jump", Dad says.

The officer replies, "We can't give you a jump."

His army time in the war lead Dad to say, "Then you can explain to your commander that you have a yard of bees at this site because when daylight comes they are going to start flying and I'll have to set them off."

"Do you have any jumper cables?"

We did and got our jump out of there.

Unfortunately, it was not the end of our difficulties for the night.

By the time that we got to the brand new stretch of I-90 the lights on the truck were starting to dim and we realized that the generator was not charging the battery. In order to keep the engine running it was necessary to turn off the headlights. They were pulling the voltage down too low. There was no other traffic out that night. We saw only a few rigs heading east. The moon was almost full and the fresh concrete almost glowed so it was not hard to see where you were going.

Amazingly enough someone had built a brand new truck stop next to the brand new interstate just before we got to Rapid City. I pulled in and pulled up to the station. It was sparkling clean, white and red with two big service bays with high glass doors that you could get any rig into. I had to stay in the truck keeping it revved up so it would stay running. Whoever owned this place planned ahead. It was already stocked with a parts department that included a generator that worked on our truck. There was only one kid not much older than I was working the night shift and he didn't want to work on the truck but Dad talked him into letting us use the garage and tools while he sat in the office and waited for someone else to appear out of the night. Dad opened the high bay door and I drove in. Inside was brighter than day with the lights that they had in there. It didn't take us long to swap the generator but I could tell Dad was wishing that we had plugged the entrances on the hives. The bright light woke some of the bees up and the place was full of bees when we drove out.

W made it to the location that Dad had picked out for the new bee yard and unloaded the hives. It was already getting light as we finished and went home.

Bad Luck in the New Truck

Things had been working fairly well with the bees until Dad wrecked the truck. On a rare occasion of doing something that was not work, my mother convinced my Dad to send my younger sister and I to church camp for a week up in the Black Hills. I was not with my Dad when the accident happened and didn't know it had happened. The church camp ended on Friday night with a program that the kids put on for their parents to show off all they had learned and then everybody packed up and left. My sister and I looked around we had no parents there to pick us up. We waited until eventually no one was left but the caretaker of the camp and he wanted to lock the gate and go home. We are standing outside of the gate with our bags and the caretaker is locking the gate. He is going to leave us standing there. I am twelve and my sister is nine. We are worried. About that time a car drives up and Ray Woodson gets out. My first paying job was pumping gas with him.

Ray tells us the story of what happened. Mom was with Dad in the Hospital in Rapid City. Dad had been moving a load of bees to the White River area and as he went on the highway that past Rapid City he crossed a railroad track that was at a sharp angle to the roadbed of the highway. When the truck hit the railroad crossing the load of bees shifted on the truck and caused the truck to turn over and my Dad was thrown out. His hip hit on one rail of the track and his right arm and shoulder on the other. Ray was riding with him to help unload the bees when they got to the White River but he was not hurt. He had been asleep when the accident happened and ended up on the floor of the truck. The bees were scattered across the highway and the Highway Patrol had to hire beekeepers in Rapid City to come out and gather up the bees so they could open the road.

Dad was in the hospital in Rapid City for weeks. He was so broken up that they put him in traction for his right arm and leg. The pieces were let to grow back together. The year was lost in rehab and Dad had to have another beekeeper take care of his hives that summer. We didn't get any honey that year.

One year later and Dad and I are on our first run to take off honey down on the White River. We have a new 1962 Chevy truck and I did most of the work building the sixteen foot wooden flatbed on the frame of the two ton truck. We have a good harvest for three days and have probably nine ton of honey in the supers which are stacked almost all of the way to the back of the truck and are eight high. It is the first time the truck has been really loaded. Dad is driving and while he is going up a long hill soon after we got on Highway 16, the engine blows and the truck dies right at the top of the hill.

Dad coasts on down the hill as far as he can and rolls to a stop on the side of the road. There are no trees for miles. It is 110 degrees in the shade and there is no shade. It does not take Dad long to get a ride. He tells me that I should take care of the truck but it is probably going to be a while because he needs to find a wrecker that can pull the truck loaded with honey. He is gone and I am waiting. By the time the afternoon sun is coming in the windshield of the truck, it is so hot that I can't sit in the cab with the windows wide open.

I get out and sit on the ground under the flatbed of the truck.

There is shade but before Dad gets back with the wrecker, the heat has started melting the combs in the top of the stacks and the honey has run down and is dripping through the cracks between the boards of the flatbed. I struggle to find a place to sit that is not sticky.

The wrecker Dad found towed us into Wall, South Dakota. The wrecker dropped us near a garage about a block from Wall Drug which is the home of free ice water according to all of the road signs.

This should have been a warranty repair but there is no dealer until you get to Rapid City so Dad is borrowing tools from the old man that has the garage next to where the truck is parked. We get the engine apart and find one piston burned down past the rings. Everything else seems to be fine. Dad calls and orders a piston from Rapid City which they will put on the next bus. We have time to wait. Dad gets a cheap room and we get some supper.

The next day while waiting for the bus I wandered around in Wall Drug and looked at all of the wonders of automaton bands that they have. I probably scared the tourists by the looks I got. When the bus comes in it does not take us long to put the engine back together and get on the road. I was not party to the discussion that took place between the Chevy dealer and my Dad when we got back home.

Working at the Refinery

The Hot Springs Refinery in Hot Springs, South Dakota was owned by Ted Bonde. He was in his sixties and had a son Ted

Bonde Jr. His son operated a branch office in Edgemont. The refinery was old and decrepit and then it caught on fire.

Dad started working there a few years before the fire but even then they didn't refine much. I think Ted Bonde was the last of the one man operators. He owned four oil wells which in total only produced a few thousand gallons a week. He owned several gas stations and a truck stop. He also had delivery service for heating oil and propane and he had a service man to repair furnaces and water heaters. The refinery never operated again after the fire. Ted had a tanker truck haul the crude to which ever refinery gave him the best price that day and he had another tanker truck to haul refined products. He would buy from the refinery that gave him the best price each time he needed a load of gasoline or heating oil.

Dad started working at the refinery shortly after we moved to South Dakota from Wyoming. Dad drove the propane delivery truck. This was an ideal situation for my Dad because there was not much call for bulk propane in the summer. The people that only used propane for cooking and not for heating usually used the 100 pound cylinder of propane. Al Schafer who did the furnace and other repairs delivered the 100 pound cylinders. The thing is Dad would take me with him in the propane truck just like he did in the bee truck. I started riding around with my Dad whenever I could. It was almost always interesting. The unsettled areas of South Dakota were still unsettled when I was a kid. There were cattle rustlers, horse thieves and poachers. They just happened to be your neighbors or people you saw at work.

We were going out on the edge of civilization to deliver propane to the ranchers on Cooney Table. Cooney Table was a large high mesa flat on top without a tree that lay between the Black Hills and the Badlands. The top was divided up into wheat fields and hay fields. The wind blew across the top almost continuously and it got cold in the winter so the people who lived out there had their buildings and homes below the top in one of the draws or gullies that led down the side of the mesa. Since it was a long drive out there we stopped with the propane truck at all of the residences and topped off the five hundred or one thousand gallon tank that most of them had in their yard. Everyone who was home would invite you in to visit. They would offer refreshments as an enticement. On this trip we stopped at the house of this farming couple who were in their eighties. They had us come in and sit down. The most amazing thing in the living room was the magazines.

There were magazines stacked in neat piles that were organized around the two chairs that they sat in. They subscribed to several publications and had saved every issue. The oldest was at the bottom of the stacks. The stacks went almost to the ceiling and almost filled the room. There were passage ways to walk between the rows of stacks. There were two chairs for visitors placed in the corner of the piles so that you could face the chairs that the couple sat in. We sat and talked about the weather and the coming winter. I picked up some of the magazines and carefully put them back exactly as they were when I finished looking at them. I really wanted to get to the bottom of the stacks to see how old they were. They had every issue of every magazine that they subscribed to. I have wondered what ever happened to those people and who did what with the magazines.

There was another place that we would go to that Dad told me before we got there that the old guy was going to ask us to stay and eat. "I don't care how hungry you are you just ate." He said. The first time we went there, the old man invited us in and immediately insisted that we stay for lunch. He walked over to the table and chased the chickens off the table to the floor. There were several plates on the table with scraps of food that the chicken had been eating. As he is telling us the soup is ready he picks up the plates and scrapes the food off on to the floor for the chickens. Then he puts the plates back on the table and tells us to sit down. "I just ate." I said.

JOHN OF GOD

─────────────── ✿ ───────────────

Wʜᴀᴛ ɪᴛ ᴛᴀᴋᴇs ᴛᴏ ʙᴇ healed.
Spiritual Healing with John of God.
My trip to Brazil in October 2013.

A Gift Given

It is always hard to know where to start telling a story. This is a story
of miracles and begins with suffering, unrelieved misery and pain.
Included was a broken heart that occasionally hesitated to beat.
The story is a story about gifts and the joy of giving and receiving.

No one knows the reason why about one third of the people
who have had chicken pox later on develop the form of the virus
that is called shingles. About one third of the people who get
shingles will develop a neuropathy that does not go away and
remains active continuously. I was one of the unlucky ones and
after my shingles had appeared and disappeared as a red virulent
rash they remained as sensitive spots and never left entirely. There

were bad days and days that weren't so bad but the shingles never let up. The first shingles appeared in 2003 and it took me a while to figure out what these weird pains and feelings were. When I did I asked my friends who were also in the three year program of the Foundation for Shamanic Studies to do a healing. When the request went out, the shingles vanished off my back and were gone for years. The shingles reappeared in 2007 and began about three years that the shingles would appear in the spring and last until the fall. Sometime in 2010 the shingles arrived and never left. I had several episodes were I could barely walk. Unfortunately I was trying to play in the band during some of the worst times.

I was trying lots of various things to try and alleviate the pain and misery but the only thing that really helped was acupuncture. I was told it would take four treatments which it did and then after that a treatment would last about four to five weeks and cost eighty dollars. My acupuncturist explained that nerves are digital signals, they are either on or off. The shingles causes them to be locked on. Her treatments would set the nerves back to off.

What isn't talked about in the advertisements that you see on television is that the pain and misery are accompanied by depression and fatigue. There are times when you don't want to move for days and it is hard to explain when there is nothing wrong with you by outside appearances. People wonder why you are not out working in the garden. It is hard to communicate the feelings of helplessness as you spend day after day in pain.

I remained as active as I could and as I needed to be. I taught at Gonzaga during the spring semester and as the shingles are stress related and seemed to reoccur during the spring I wondered about the relationship. In 2012 on Father's Day, I had a heart attack while I was home alone. It was the use of Reiki and the help of spirit that got me through because this was before I had any medical coverage.

The end result of this heart adventure was that I survived but had times of unstable or irregular heartbeat. I can honestly say that I came to a point when I no longer thought that it would get any better. I just needed to adapt and adjust and accept this new way of life. One of the weird things about humanity is the ability to accept and adjust to increasingly dire conditions. We are like a lobster in a pot of heating water. We adjust and adapt and keep on doing the best that we can. I kept on keeping on as best I could.

One day I came home and my wife Virginia told me that my friend Maurah had called and talked to her about giving me a gift and that I was supposed to talk to Maurah but that I could not say no. I was supposed to say yes. That got my curiosity working so I called Maurah and listened as she explained her gift.

Maurah had met someone who had been down to Brazil and saw John of God. The person's description of the healings taking place and the miracles that were happening captured Maurah's interest. She wanted to go so she asked her spiritual helpers for advice. They told her that she should go but that she had to take me with her as I needed the healing.

Maurah had already talked to Virginia and got her permission to take me. I had already promised Virginia I wouldn't say no so I agreed to go to Brazil. I was of course immediately filled with fear and doubts. It is not an easy thing to be given a great gift of healing. What if I was not healed because I didn't do something right.

Preparing to Leave

My desire to be healed and to not waste this opportunity led me to research John of God and what they did at the Casa Dom Ignacio. In my reading I became aware of the idea of blessed water. The drinking water that was sold at the Casa's snack bar was said to blessed and to have some magical properties. I became intrigued by the idea and since spirit is in charge of our life and I wanted some of this water, spirit arranged to have some given to me. A person who had been down to see John of God had brought some back with them and had contacted me about doing some shamanic work for her. In trade she gave me some blessed water which I shared with Maurah. So we began drinking the blessed water before we left for Brazil.

I researched John of God to learn all that I could about how he did the healing. What I learned was that John of God did not do the healing. He allowed spirits to use his body to perform the healings. The person of John of God would be in a complete trance and have no memory of what his body did. I learned that about thirty different spirits could work through John of God and they would decide which one was best suited for each person's healing.

Among the rules that I read about for receiving healing from John of God was one that required that while you were in the Abadiania area you were not supposed to use any other forms of healing or spiritual work. I understood the reason for this. The healing spirits wanted you to be aware of what was done down there by them. I use Reiki as a part of my daily life but before I went to Brazil it was essential for me to keep up a daily practice of doing Reiki on myself to counteract the effects of the shingles and to keep working on my heart. I was concerned about all of these rules and how I would be able to deal with being down in Brazil. I am a worry wart about wanting to do things the right way when it comes to working with spirit, however I knew I needed my daily Reiki to keep on an even keel.

I was drinking the blessed water that I had been given from the Casa and I knew that the spirits from Abadiania came with the water so during one of my journeys to see my helping spirits I was able to connect with some of the spirits of the Casa. The discussion led to a negotiated agreement on how we were going to handle the transition. I would use Reiki up to the time I got off of the plane in Brasilia, when the spirits of the Casa would take over and would provide the needed care. I was also told to learn the rosary and to use the rosary as needed instead of calling on the Reiki as I usually did when I was in pain.

I got a cheap student model rosary at the Value Village and asked my son's wife for help in learning the rosary as she was Catholic. She got her mom who taught catechism to give me a lesson. I also printed instructions off of the internet and a copy of the rosary in Portuguese. I started learning about the mysteries, some of which I had never heard of before and I began learning about Mother Mary. Which was all new to me since I was from a Lutheran background.

Among the other benefits of the blessed water was a need to clean up my act before I left for Brazil. Literally, I found it necessary to clean my office and desk. I had to go through my computer and delete and clean up and I had to have every detail of clothes and what I was taking completely ready more than a week ahead of time.

I was prepared to leave but Maurah was concerned that

some of our connection times between flights were a little short if we were delayed. I printed out the itinerary and placed the Reiki symbols all over it and asked for Reiki to take care of the arrangements for our flight.

Leaving Spokane

Arriving in Brazil

It was early Sunday morning on the 13th of October 2013 when we left Spokane, Washington to go to Brazil. Our connections were though Salt Lake and then Atlanta. We arrived 15 minutes early and had no problems with our connections, everything went as smooth as possible. Maurah had tried to get seats next to the emergency exit whenever she could in order to give me more leg room. To my surprise when we arrived in Brasilia the exit on the plane that they opened to meet the jet way was the one I was sitting next to. I was the first person off of the plane which put me first through immigration and customs. I went down the stairs to the luggage carrousel and my suitcase was the first one to come down the chute. I laughed as I thanked spirit and Reiki for the wonderful arrangements that they made for our benefit.

It was Monday morning with the sun just coming up as we landed in Brasilia. We met the people who were the guides for our group and then we waited as the rest of our group gathered. When the van arrived to transport us the rest of the way, it was a tight fit to get everyone and their luggage in. I was told to sit up front with the driver because I was tall and could use the room. That was fine with me but as we got headed down the highway, the driver used the power window control and rolled down the window on my side. The air blowing in across my body was setting off my shingles so I rolled it back up, the driver back down, I compromised with it open a few inches which kept the air from hitting my skin.

I settled back and watched the plain roll by with numerous curiosities to see. The red brown termite mounds rising up three to four feet that were scattered here and there gave explanation for why the fence posts and power poles were made of concrete.

This part of Brazil is not a jungle but a vast mesa that stretches for over a thousand miles in all directions. It is about 3400 foot in elevation and is deeply eroded with rivers and small streams. We passed cattle ranches and farms but there was a lot of just open space. We slowed down to pass through a couple of small towns and settlements and then came to Abadiania and turned off the highway onto the road to the Casa.

We arrived at our posada, got our rooms and had lunch. This was the first of our meals that were served cafeteria style. You just walked in and helped yourself and sat down with your group. The meals were wholesome and delicious as fresh fruit, vegetables, and local supplies were used. I saw a small Toyota pickup being unloaded into the kitchen by the family that had grown the vegetables that filled it.

During lunch our guides Steve and Debra outlined the schedule for our time there. The schedule of John of God for doing the healing ceremonies is Wednesday, Thursday, and Friday. Steve explained that there were things to do to prepare before Wednesday. One of the things to do was to go to the waterfall. I had heard about the waterfall but was not sure what the actual story was. I had heard that healings took place there so it was on my list of want to dos and here we were going to go there the first thing.

The First Healing

We changed into our bathing suits and put white clothes over the top. Rules for the waterfall require men and women go in separate groups. I saw a few people walk but we took a taxi. The road is dirt and winds down below the Casa about a mile until you come to a parking area with a roofed shelter for waiting for your taxi to come back which some how they magically do. The driver drops you off and drives away because who knows how long this is going take. From the parking area there is gate that leads to a paved trail that leads down to the waterfall.

On the left side of the gate was a sign in four languages that said to ask for a blessing and say a prayer of thanks. I have to admit that at that moment my prayer was a roughly expressed "I just want to give the shingles to the waterfall!" There is a paved path that leads down the hillside until you come to a gate with some benches poured in concrete on the side of the hill. The process is to wait until the group ahead of you finishes and then your group can go down. When our turn came our group of men went through the gate and on down the path until you come to another bench where you can take off your outer clothes and then walk over to the water fall in your bathing suit. I was in the middle of the group so I ended up standing on the little bridge that crossed the creek that flowed away from the waterfall. I stood there on the bridge wearing nothing but a bathing suit with cool moist air flowing all around me and I remember thinking "That's weird I don't feel a thing."

My turn came to go under the waterfall. You have to be careful and hang onto the rail to keep from slipping on the rocks. Then you duck your head into the flow. It hits surprisingly hard for such a small stream. I still felt only the water. There was no pain from the shingles. There has not been any shingles since and I plan on keeping it that way.

After you walk back up the trail and into the parking lot, the next miracle is that, moments later your taxi driver pulls up to give the return ride back to your posada. I ended up going to the waterfall two more times while I was there, but I didn't have any experience that matched the first.

It was a great way to start the two weeks in Brazil. The next day was an introduction to the grounds of the Casa and an orientation that explained the process that we would experience the next day on Wednesday, the first day of the healing ceremonies for us. The orientation was given by a man named Arturo, who as he spoke, paced back and forth in front of the watching people. Periodically as he walked, he would say out loud. "I am walking here. Do you see that I am walking here?" He would then continue on with the orientation. Finally he said, "Do you know why I am saying I'm walking here? I was totally paralyzed when I came here. They carried me in on a stretcher."

I found out that he bought the posada that I was staying at so that he could be of service. He considered that he was providing a part of the healing that took place there. He had the women who worked at the posada bring you your meals when you were in isolation after an operation with John of God.

We also had an opportunity to experience a crystal light treatment. I was amazed at the experience that I had just lying under some blinking colored lights. I was able to clear out some issues that dated to my early childhood. The crystal lights also work with the spirits of the Casa so the process is spirit aided.

In the gift shop at the Casa I got some things for friends and I bought a rosary that was made of stones to use instead of the cheap one that I got at Value Village in Spokane. I began to use the rosary each night as I was going to sleep. It had some emeralds and seemed to be tuned to me. I began to wear it around my neck on a continuous basis.

Maurah and I ready to see John of God

First Visit to John of God

Wednesday came and we got up and had breakfast early and made our way to the Casa. We got there early enough to get seats but that meant that we had about an hour to wait before the start. The time was spent in watching the people fill the building until no one could find a place to sit or stand. We are all dressed in white. There is a well honed process that is conducted by volunteers, who as near as I could learn were all healed of various serious ailments.

The people who volunteer to sit in the current rooms line up in the center of the room until at 7:30 the door opens for them to go into the current room and begin the meditation. The process of sitting in meditation for several hours is a daunting task to most people but there are those that come day after day, week after week, month after month, some come that often until they are healed, some come that often because they were healed. The meditation provides the energy that makes all of the miracles possible by providing anesthesia for all of the operations that are taking place.

The orientation had explained that everything about the healing ceremony was guided by spirit so no person actually had a plan a follow. Each session could be completely different in the order in which they did things. At each session there is a time when they have people line up to see John of God according to whether they get in the first time line, the second time line, the operation line or the revision line. On that Wednesday morning, when I got into the line for first timers, they had already done one of the other lines so the crowd was thinned somewhat from the wall to wall people that had started the day. I was not expecting that everyone would be so cooperative about getting into the line. The guide for our group wanted us spaced out in the line so that there was time to help each one through the meeting with John of God. As everything is in Portuguese it is necessary to have the guide there to interpret what John of God says. We were placed into the line as needed and no one thought that was unusual. They just let us in where necessary.

Sometimes the line moves fairly quickly as John of God spends only a few brief instants with each person. He looks at them, says what he needs to, and writes a scribble on a piece of paper for a prescription if they need herbs. Then he moves to the next person. I watched as the line moved forward until I was in the door of the current room. Now I could see what they were doing. There were people sitting in rows of church pew like benches along the wall on the left side. They had their eyes closed or were wearing blindfolds and sitting in meditation. The line of people moved through the first current room and into the second. Here the line turned to the left and went between rows of pews. At first all you can see is the people in front of you.

As you get to the front of the room, there are giant crystals standing next to the wall and portraits of the helping spirits on the walls. When the person ahead of me steps up to the seated John of God, I got my first glimpse of him. Then it is my turn, He looked at me, said something that my guide said later meant operation this afternoon. Then he waved his hand in front of my chest almost as if to shoo me away, I immediately gasped and began staggering away. In shock and pain, hardly able to breathe I followed the line out of the room. As we passed by the people in the front of the current room, one in particular caught my attention. It was Mother Mary in all of her fine clothes and jewels. She was breathtakingly beautiful and I wanted to fall at her knees and kiss her skirt. I didn't. I continued on but the sight of her gave me the ability to breathe but my chest still ached and I was panting rapidly.

One of the miracles that happens every day that they do the healing ceremony is the soup. Everybody is given a bowl of soup and some bread as they exit out of the Casa. Our group of people and our guides met me as I came out and they helped me to get to the soup. As I ate the soup the pain passed and my breathing slowed to normal. I was asked what happened. I could only say, "He worked on my heart." I knew from my reading before we left that if there was something that you really needed he would do it immediately. My heart beat was steady and it has not skipped a beat since.

Our group went to lunch and then regrouped for the afternoon session. I knew from my reading that it is possible and ok to ask for more than one thing when going for the operation. During lunch, Steve our guide explained that it was his experience that you could ask for as many as nine things. My plan changed, I had only been going to ask for three things but now the possibility opened up and I included my eyesight and prostrate among the others I had listed. When I was preparing to go to Brazil, I learned that you need to have an expectation of being healed in order to be healed. My various physical ailments had gone on for so long that I no longer had any image of myself that I could find that was me in great health. I finally found a picture that was taken of me when I was probably in the second grade. It was before I had glasses and I looked happy and healthy. I copied that picture and took it with me as my image of what I wanted to be like.

Going for an Operation

I listed the things that I wanted healed on the piece of paper with the picture of me and folded it up and put it in the pocket of my shirt. We went back to the Casa and began the process of waiting for the calling of the lines to begin. When they called the line for Operations, I got up and walked to the end of the line. I began to notice that people just walked up and got into the line where ever they wanted to be. I was still at the end of the line some time later without having moved. At one point I felt that I needed to look at my list and I got it out of my pocket and went over it in my mind. I calmed myself and said to myself, "it is all being taken care of."

I was standing calmly waiting and a feeling of peace and joy came over me. I felt a light touch of breath on my cheek and I smelled the scent of roses. I said to the people in front of me "Do you smell that?" They just looked at me as if they didn't understand English. I realized I had been kissed by Mary. As the end of the line got closer to the door at the front, they stopped the line and I was the only person left outside of the current room. I realized that John of God had come out onto the small raised platform in the front of the room.

In the morning he had also done some healing up front but I couldn't see clearly because of all of the people in front of me. Now I was standing right in front of him as he worked. It happens so quickly that it is hard to see even when you are in front. It is easy to see that John of God is in a trance. His head hangs to one side and he is not actually looking at what he is doing. He waved his hand in front of the person and they relax into a state of trance and then he scrapes an eye or cuts a small cut into the flesh or sticks a forceps up the person's nose and twists it. I watched all three. As soon as John of God finishes the person drops into a wheel chair and they are taken to the infirmary to recover.

Later on at a different time, I talked to one person who had the forceps up the nose and they said that they didn't feel a thing. But they did have some bleeding from their nose later.

When he completed the demonstration, John of God left and I went through the door to the current room. I figured out the process as I stood there waiting. The room they call the operation room is similar to the current rooms in that it has rows of pews. They fill the pews full of people that are meditating on being healed as they sit. When the room is full, they pause for a brief moment, say a few words and then everyone files out. The process is repeated as needed until you get to the last person in line which this time was me. As I walked into the room John of God was standing by the door and he reached over and patted me on the shoulder as I walked by.

As I was the last into the room, I no sooner sat down to begin to meditate on my healing and they said it was time to go. I stumbled out to find Steve the guide waiting for me. I felt confused because I didn't think that I was in the operating room long enough for anything to have happened but I later realized that they had been working on me while I was in line. Steve took me to a taxi because you are not supposed to exert yourself at all after being operated on.

When the taxi gets you back to the posada a twenty-four hour period begins when you are supposed to lie down and stay down. Believe me, by the time I got to the room I felt like I had been operated on and had no trouble staying down. I slept most of the time with dreams interspersed with waking visions of spirits in my room walking around me and looking down at me from various places on the wall. One spirit in particular caught my attention and I felt like he was the one in charge of my healing. The only times I got up were to go to the bathroom and to answer the door when the maid brought my meals.

The next day, I was able to come out for the evening meal and rejoin the group. There were others that had also been in isolation and we compared our experiences. There are restrictions that last for various amounts of time if you have an operation. You begin taking your herbs and following the regime and since there is no reason to get in the lines again, it is possible to volunteer to sit in the first current room.

Sitting in the Current

Friday morning I got up with some of the others and ate early to get to the Casa early and stand in the current line so we could get a seat in the first room. I took a cushion to sit on and some mints and a water bottle. Of course I was wearing white and I had a blindfold for my eyes. Once you go in and sit down you are told to keep your eyes closed and if you need to go to the bathroom to raise your hand. The monitor will come and help you get to your feet. Once you are standing up you can open your eyes and walk out past the line of people waiting to see John of God. They want you to come back in and sit again to help maintain the current. However, if you can't sit and maintain the flow they would respect your wish not to come back rather than have you upset the balance.

During my first session I sat for quite a while but eventually had trouble with pain in my butt bones and joints. I began trying to learn about the current that I was sitting in. The first thing I did was ask to be shown the current. I was shown that it is very much like a river of energy that is flowing through the room. The depth varied as the people in the room varied in their conscious level. I learned that the current washed away a lot of the energetic attachments that people may have on or with them. Everyone in line is either sick, broken, or helping their sick children carrying them through the line. There is a lot of stuff that is washed off that is carried in the current. That is why you don't open your eyes, you don't want to absorb any of the stuff. Once you are standing above the flow it is safe to open your eyes.

Sometimes the monitor will give you a hint as to what is happening in the line. Sometimes they find it necessary after four and five hours to remind people why they are there and give them a little encouragement by reading some verse or bible passage. After the last person passes and everyone is clear of the operating room and John of God has finished, the monitors tell you it's ok to stop and open your eyes. Everyone is given a small cup of blessed water to drink as they leave and then you head over to get some soup.

The schedule is a session in the morning and a session in the afternoon every Wednesday, Thursday, and Friday. It has been going on this way for many years. A lot of the time, John of God will travel and do healing ceremonies in another location on Sunday, Monday, and Tuesday. He keeps an amazing schedule and attends to his businesses as well.

I enjoyed sitting in the current room as frequently as I could and then on the weekend I took part in some of the activities at the Casa. Including a session where everyone recited the Rosary together. It was in Portuguese and even though I had a copy I had a hard time following just where we were sometimes but it went around and around with different people of the locals leading different parts of the ceremony.

Mother Mary Comes to Me

Every night as I slept I would wake up around one or two in the morning. I would see spirits in my room and then I would do the Rosary until I could go to sleep again. During the night after saying the Rosary with the people in the Casa, I was visited by visions of Mother Mary. Not one but a different one appeared for every bead on the Rosary. I was shown that Mother Mary is a Divine Feminine spirit that is universal in human culture. A Buddhist friend told me that they have 144 incarnations remembered of the Divine Feminine.

One of the things that we did was to get together in a group and talk about what was necessary for healing to take place. Steve led us to see how other people can choose completely different experiences than what we consider to be normal. We discussed fasting and living on light among other things. The idea was to get you to see the possibilities that your mind could create. At one of the sessions where we were going to watch a video about John of God, I forgot the restriction on doing anything physical and moved a chair where I could be more comfortable. Immediately I knew that I had made a serious mistake. The pain reminded me continuously and I ended up going back to my room and basically doing another day of isolation and staying down. I spent the time talking to the spirits expressing my apologies and begging for them to take mercy on me, they did. I had not thought about the consequences of the simple act of pushing a chair across the floor.

During the time that we had free, it was always good to walk around the gardens of the Casa and sit and meditate. During one of my meditations I was told that I should have asked my friend Ken's wife if it was ok to ask for healing for her. She was on a list for a heart transplant and her blood type was the rarest possible. She was being kept alive with a mechanical assist pump but her heart was declining. I went to where I could make a phone call and called their house and amazingly she answered. After I explained where I was and what I wanted to do she said yes.

I wrote out the request and placed it in one of the triangles that the Casa has placed for people to put their requests in. As I was holding my head in the triangle and phrasing my request, I heard a clear, "We will find her a heart." Skip to a quick aside in the future. When I got home, Ken told me she had been moved up to number one on the list. It was a week later that she got her heart. She still does well recently flying to her school reunion.

The next step was to go back in front of John of God in the revision line. The purpose is to see if you need any more treatment but you can also take in pictures of people that you brought with you from home. I took in pictures of Virginia and the woman who had given me the blessed water. When I handed them to John of God he wrote out prescriptions for each of them and then looked at me. He said something the guide said later meant "You are done, goodbye, have a nice trip." He waved his hand at me as if to say see yah and that was that.

Healing is Finished

I was done. The healings received included the shingles, my heart, and my eyes from macular degeneration. My memory, my prostrate and my asthma were all improved helping me to feel great. What remained of our time passed quickly. I enjoyed walking around and taking pictures of all of the different colors of flowering trees that were in bloom. I picked out some small gifts to take to family and friends. I had gathered some things that I enjoyed. There was an old man selling cashews in front of his wife's clothing store. They were fresh roasted and good. There was younger man that walked the street with a bag of these tiny little peanuts roasted in the shells. They had an incredible flavor about six times as much as you could expect for something so small. I also got two potatoes that had an unusually sweet flavor. There were also some chocolate bars at the gift shop of the Casa that were made without milk or sugar and they were incredibly good. The sweetener was a native plant called yancun. I got several to take with me.

Visiting the Native People

I came to a small shop of crafts that were made by a family of natives from the area. I was immediately captivated by the workmanship and colors. Everything was made of shells and bones and feathers and stones and seeds all tied and laced and braided into some very beautiful ornaments, earrings and headbands and rattles. As I picked through a display of ear dangles all made from the most intricately tied feathers, thinking to get some for my wife, my spirit helper said, "Put those back, those are an endangered species. You'll never get them through customs."

That was my first thought about customs so I decided to listen and I put them back and picked out a necklace made of bright red seeds that was tied in a repeating pattern. The woman who made the necklace showed me the pods the seeds came from that looked like a type of locust tree. It was one of the few things that didn't have a least some feathers on it so I bought it.

Leaving Brazil

I went back and finished packing for the return trip. The trip from Brazil was uneventful but you fly for a long ways without seeing any lights until you get to what I recognized as Venezuela. Then you finally land in Atlanta. When you are on the plane they give you a custom declaration form. When I saw what was on it

I had a quick discussion with my spirit helpers. I told them that they didn't tell me about anything but the feathers so it was their fault and they had to take care of customs.

I marked down that I didn't have any plants or agricultural items and no foodstuffs. I had to wait until the bags showed up and then when I had my stuff I stood looking at which custom line was the shortest. As I stood there a customs agent walked up, opened a new booth and waved for me to come over. I walked up and handed my form to the agent. He took the form without looking at it, put it in the drawer and waved me to go on through without a question. I went through and out but had to wait for Maurah to get all of her stuff past the gate, which she did.

One interesting thing that happened on the way out of Atlanta as we went through security, I had to go through the body scanner. I was wearing the rosary around my neck outside of my shirt. I glanced over at the readout screen of the scanner and my whole chest was a glow of light surrounding the cross of the rosary. The security people did not say one thing and waved me through. I have continued to use the rosary and say the Hail Mary whenever I need help. It has not let me down.

On arriving home, I found it very hard to get used to all the Americans. They were everywhere I went. The smiling faces and beautiful people of Abadiania will be in my memory for ever. It is now over two years without a shingle or missed heartbeat. I know it will stay that way. I thank spirit often and continuously for the gifts they have brought to me.

What is happening in Abadiania now November 2022?

Recently, I was asked about the Casa and what happened to

John of God. John of God was found guilty on numerous counts and was sentenced to jail but he has been serving time under house arrest. People still come to Abadiania and go to the Casa for the healing ceremonies. The Healing Spirits are still there and as I understand it the process is much the same as it was but without John of God. The buses still arrive with about one thousand people on the days of ceremony. The healings still take place because the spirits are still there.

SHAMANIC EXPERIENCES WORKING TO HELP SUFFERING BEINGS

THIS ESSAY IS A TALE of my life focused on my experiences with working with the spirits of the dead and my experiences with near death, death, and journeying about death. I was fortunate and had the opportunity to study with Michael Harner and the Foundation for Shamanic Studies which he started. I would like to thank Michael for all of the ways that he helped me, in spite of me trying his patience at times. I would not have had any of these adventures if it wasn't for Michael Harner and the Foundation for Shamanic Studies. My life is a continual gift of Spirit for which I am grateful. I owe Spirit thanks for all of the people who came to Unity and to my classes for the Foundation for Shamanic Studies because they created the opportunities for Sharing and Caring in Spirit.

Michael's method of teaching was to introduce an idea and

then give you an opportunity to have an experience to learn about that idea. He would let you figure out the meaning of your experience. I believe that my whole life was a set of experiences which led me to my current understanding of the process of death and our societal lack of understanding of that process.

I will tell about some of those experiences and some of the people whose death affected me. These experiences occurred over a life time and were written down at different times so there is some variation in the sequencing of some things that took years. This retelling has been combined from some earlier versions written for other purposes with some new added work to help clarify what some of the events were like.

For clarity, when I refer to Spirit with a capital S, I mean the all encompassing wonder that expresses itself in all that is and continually creates the flow of all life. In this writing, spirit helpers, teachers and allies are my personal guardian angels that help me every day all day long.

Early Life Experiences

I was never an ordinary child. I was allergic to my mother's and all other types of milk when I was born. I was asthmatic and stopped breathing every time my mother tried to feed me. It was a struggle to find something to feed a baby who could not tolerate any type of milk. In 1948 there was soya powder which was ground up dried soy beans. This was mixed with malt to make it more palatable. The feeding problems meant that I never really bonded with my Mom. As I grew up, I spent a lot of time with my Dad because my

Mom didn't want me around. I was wandering in the outdoors in the fields or down by the river. I had a job to keep me busy, which was keeping the sheep out of the road in the afternoon when they liked to lie in the dust in the shade of the big cottonwood trees. I also had to haul water from the well to the house. Mom didn't care as long as I wasn't around her. I learned to exist in my own mind comfortably talking to my friends that I now know were spirit helpers. The one that I knew best had taught me how to breathe when I was a tiny baby struggling with asthma.

My Dad worked at truck driving and warehouse jobs as well as being a bee keeper. I spent a lot of time riding around with him. On one occasion when I was three I went with Dad while he worked at a warehouse. I could not be where he was so he told me to stay in the truck. It was a weekend so there wasn't anyone else around. This warehouse had a large bay where semis backed their trailers into this long dock. It was in the winter and the trucks that had last been in the warehouse had a lot of snow and ice that had melted and fallen off of the trucks. The melt water accumulated with the drips of oil and grease that were on the floor. When I got out of the cab and started walking around I became fascinated by all of the pretty colors that rippled in waves as I stomped my feet in the water lying on the floor of the warehouse. Unknown to me was the fact that there was a large sump with a drain that was supposed to take all of the water away, not to mention the fact that the drain was plugged and that earlier, someone had tried to clear the drain, failed, went home and left the grate off the sump pit.

I walked on stomping one foot and watching the rippling golds, purples, blues and greens as they flashed across the floor, then I would step forward and stomp the other foot and watch again as the ripples washed away. Then as I stomped my right foot, I went down into the pit of slimy water, as I hit the bottom and before I could panic, I felt a hand grab my coat collar and pull me out of the pit. As I cleared my eyes and looked around there was no one anywhere near me. As I looked back towards the truck where I had come from there was only my footprints in the oily water. It had happened so fast that my coat and clothes were hardly wet. I went and set quietly in the truck until my Dad finished working.

As I don't know how many times spirit had to help me to stay alive as a tiny baby. This was the first time that I know of that a direct intervention of spirit was responsible for my continuing existence. It would not be the last. Around the same time or a little later, I remember my Dad's uncle, Luther, dying of a heart attack. Mom and Dad had left us kids in the car outside of the hospital, while they went in to see him. When they came out, they talked about how quickly he had died. He had been out to visit us not too long before he passed. I really don't remember much involving the funeral. What I do remember is the talk was all about how his young wife had already left town taking all of Luther's money and Sinclair Oil stock. This was the first time in my life that any one I knew died.

My life has been a series of adventures where as John Lennon said: "Life is what happens while you are making other plans." My childhood was one where I learned early on to work to make some money. It was necessary if I wanted anything for me. I bought one of the first transistor radios with money from my paper route. I would listen for hours to KOMA in Oklahoma City while I read at night.

One complication of asthma is that while you are struggling to breathe, your body has some defense mechanisms that it employs to help you to breathe. One of the things is the secretion of adrenaline. As a result asthmatics can be restless, have a hard time sleeping, tending to thinness and low weight. I have slept less than four hours a night for most of my life and at six foot two inches in height, I weighed one hundred and forty two pounds when I graduated from college. I read a lot as a child because I could not sleep. I also spent every moment that I could, out of doors in nature walking long distances just to be out in the forest. I had hidden forts and secret places that I went to. The walking helped to burn up energy so I could sleep.

Walking long distances at a hard fast pace became a meditation technique that my spirit friends taught me as a way to deal with the stress that I had as a child who wouldn't fit in, wouldn't shut up, wouldn't sit down, wouldn't give in to bullies, wouldn't respect authority and damn sure wasn't going to do what I was told. The process of hard walking allows the mind to be free so if you give it a question at the beginning of the walk, you walk until the answer appears in your mind.

About the same time that they taught me the walking meditation, my spirit helpers showed me a special place that I could go when I needed their help. At this special place there was a rock cliff that curved out over the top of you so you were covered if it rained. Between the precipice and the river were a bunch of maple trees that grew above the height of the cliff. The leaves of the trees were so thick that the light that came through was green. There was enough room under the cliff to sit on a rock bench that had fallen from above and let the green light heal you as you discussed your problems with Spirit. This place was a refuge that I sought out when I had no other resource to help me deal with my anger and depression caused by my alienation from and fear of most of the people that I had to deal with.

My parents were Lutherans and an active part of the church. My Mom was the Organist for the choir and my Dad was the Treasurer and a Deacon. I was paid $30 a month to mow the lawns and maintain the flower beds. In the winter I had to shovel the snow on a city block's worth of sidewalks before church after I finished my paper route. For several years I was the altar boy and assisted the minister with the service as well as lighting the candles at the beginning of the service. I became aware of the presence of God as I walked in front of the altar lighting the candles and I felt like this was our time together. The magic was also felt while I was talking to people who needed help. Several times I felt that I was given the words to say to help someone who was questioning their faith and asking for guidance. I enjoyed teaching Sunday school to the younger children because I felt that connection to spirit as I talked to them.

My Dad started teaching me to drive the truck and help him with the bees when I was nine years old. During the time that I was working for him he would pay me $50 a week. Each week he wrote me a check, had me sign it, and then took it back and deposited it in the bank. That way he could deduct my wages from the taxes. I didn't care. I was driving a two ton flatbed truck down the highway with a load of honey when I was ten. When I was thirteen, I was working so well that my dad didn't hire any help that summer or thereafter. I was never on a baseball team as I was always working in the summer.

My Grandma Sproule was often my caretaker when I was little. She stuck up for me and would tell me stories of life on the frontier when she was little. She had used her homestead right when she was twelve to claim a piece of South Dakota sage brush land to live with her grandmother in a sod shanty after having been abandoned by her parents somewhere in Nebraska. Also at the age of twelve, she obtained a patent for improvement of the ox yoke. When I was a small boy she lived in a wooden shack that was ten feet by twenty feet. It had a table on one end, a big wood cook stove on the back wall in the middle, and a bed on the other end with a dresser. There was usually a double barreled shotgun in the corner by the bed. I always thought that I could trust my Grandma but one day as we sat playing cards, I caught her cheating at Canasta.

She was not very big but she was tough as nails. In 1922 when my Dad was two and his brother John was four, they caught small pox. The town ran them off at gunpoint and Grandma spent the winter in a sheep wagon up in the Rockies with two small boys. When they were still alive in the spring, they were allowed to return. During the Depression as I understand it, she made beer and sold it in town to feed her two kids. I have the pistol that she carried while delivering the beer.

Early in 1964, my Grandma Sproule died. She had had heart problems for a long time and always took some little white pill when she was having trouble. We got a call when she was hospitalized and drove from South Dakota to Wyoming to see her. With all of us in the room, she insisted that she was fine and also insisted that we leave her alone and go home so we could go to school and Mom and Dad could go to work. We drove back to South Dakota, I say we because my Dad and I did all of the driving, on Sunday getting home in time to get ready for school the following day.

On Monday before my Dad left for work, the hospital called to tell him his Mom had passed. She had waited for all of us to leave. She didn't want to die with all of us watching. I was at a loss as this was the first person I was close to who died. We went back to Wyoming and saw my uncle John at the funeral who informed my Dad that John got the bank account and Dad got the remnant of the farm that had not been sold off to support Grandma over the years. It was just the land around the house. I got Grandma's car. It was a 1953 Chevrolet. The first thing I did was to take off the fender skirts and sun visor that hung over the windshield. I did not drive it for long unfortunately.

I was nearly killed when I was sixteen as a speeding driver hit my car directly on the driver's door. I felt my head hit the side window in the door three times. Bang! Bang! Bang! It felt like my head was split in half by an ax and I had to push the two halves together with my hands. The impact caused a serious concussion. I ended up going into convulsions that lasted for several hours. The world turned into the Sunday cartoons with wild colors and visions I could not understand. I am sure it was spirit friends distracting me from the pain that continued with each new convulsion.

After Dad was finally able to get in touch with the doctor

in town, the latter called the pharmacist, who went downtown, opened the pharmacy, and gave my father some drugs to bring home to stop the convulsions. When I saw the size of what my Dad had in his hand, I said "I can't swallow that." He said, "That is not where it goes." It took two before the convulsions slowed and then finally stopped. I had raging headaches even after I finally went back to school a week later. Car wrecks were not my friend for several years, but they kept showing up any way trying to be.

In 1968 I was riding with a friend who had been drinking more than I thought when I got into a car with him. He was speeding down a narrow county highway and refused to slow down when I told him that there was a serious corner coming up. I thought about trying to put my seat belt on but it was too late. We entered a thirty mile an hour corner at one hundred and ten and failed to make it all the way around, then smashed through three guard posts and flew across the canyon into the side of the hill. His wine bottle got smashed between my face and the windshield and clip that held the sun visors cut across my scalp, thus peeling it back. I was bleeding profusely from cuts across my face, neck, and left arm and my skull was exposed. I found my broken glasses and we climbed the embankment up to the road.

We were 14 miles from town on a road that only a few farmers lived on and they had been asleep for hours. I had no hope of getting a ride at one in the morning. However, when we climbed out onto the pavement, a car drove up immediately. The driver wasn't someone I knew and he didn't say who he was. He insisted on driving us straight to the hospital. I could see a pool of blood around my boots on the floor of the car but he wasn't concerned when I offered to get his car cleaned and neither would he give me his number. We got out when we got to the hospital and he drove away as I walked to the door. My feet squished inside my boots as I walked, leaving bloody footprints that scared my Mom when she and Dad arrived. This was a small town where everyone knows everybody and their nose is in their neighbor's business. No one drove me to the hospital that night who could be accounted for in the area. He vanished as soon as he drove away. I have always had the feeling that it was Jesus Christ, himself, but he wouldn't say.

It was after this accident that I was able to look at my depression and realize what I had been doing. I had been living and driving very recklessly for several years. It had been my way to commit suicide. As a Lutheran I had been taught that suicide was a certain path to Hell with no possibility of salvation. I wasn't sure that there wasn't a Hell at that time so to hedge my bet I was trying to kill myself by accident. Now that I know for sure that there is no Hell, other than the one, humans have created in our society I no longer have a desire for suicide. The curiosity of what my body is going to pull next keeps me entertained. The realization that I had at the time, was that Spirit had gone to a lot of trouble to keep me alive on more than one occasion and my curiosity then was why. Why and for what purpose had I been kept alive?

When I went back to college, I truly looked like Frankenstein's monster. Since my social life wasn't going anywhere I focused on graduating in Mechanical Engineering as soon as possible so I could make some money. The low point was getting through spring break as the University almost completely shut down. The food service I worked at was closed, leaving no job and no place to eat. I had $1.43 that I finally spent on a foot long chili cheese dog after I walked to the drive in at the edge of town. The rest of the time I spent trying to get something out of the vending machines in the basements across campus.

I lost interest in the Lutheran church when the minister preached that it was our God given duty to go to Viet Nam to fight the godless communists. I began reading spiritual books from all paths. The search was to find the meaning and reason for me to choose to go on with life. I read a lot of Hindu, Buddhist, Zen, and Taoist texts. I did not find a path but I learned to work on techniques for telepathy, meditation and changing consciousness with dance and sound.

Working for a Living

I graduated with my degree in Mechanical Engineering in May of 1970 and went to work for Westinghouse Electric as a service engineer installing and repairing generators and motors. I got to work on the largest equipment in the world but I paid a price with my health. I lost a lot of my hearing because of the noise level being off the scale in coal fired steam turbine plants. I am also sensitive to every chemical that gives off fumes because of the resins and solvents I was exposed to.

It was while I was working for Westinghouse that I started having results with finding solutions to problems by asking the unconscious mind to find solutions for me while I slept. I would formulate a clear statement of the problem and a statement of what the solution needed to do to solve the problem as I went to sleep.

I would wake up usually around two or three AM with a dream in my mind that gave the solution. Sometimes with complete engineering drawings if needed to convey the information. Some of the solutions were patented by Westinghouse. I did not tell Westinghouse how I arrived at the solutions. I also found that I could feel the way a generator or motor was working and sense if something was out of whack. I would sit inside of the large machines while they were running and listen to them and feel their vibrations. I was able to diagnose a couple of very serious problems this way and prevent damage to the machines. I became noted for my ability to solve problems and was given more difficult problems as a reward.

I was working at Grand Coulee Dam installing the generators in the Third Powerhouse and I had to crawl through the generator running at full load to inspect an overheating problem where the power left the generator. I was within inches of the leads carrying 38000 amps at 18000 volts. When I realized that I was going to have to do this more than once, I decided to try and boost my ability with telepathy by tapping into the field of energy around this power. I was successful but as I get older and weird things happen with my body I wonder now what else I influenced. Affecting me at the time were the solvents and resins that were used in the insulation process on the generators. I became sick even using complete gear and a respirator. This was before the employee right to know act was passed so Westinghouse just said the resins were not a problem.

When I was practicing telepathy, the person who I connected to with the most power and frequency was my Mom. Some aspect of our continuous conflict helped to boost the communication between the two of us. It provided the framework for us to finally heal our relationship. We didn't have to argue because we always knew what the other person was feeling.

One of my last jobs for Westinghouse was supervising the rewind of a generator at Kerr Dam in Polson, Montana. Part of the job for the engineer is to perform high voltage tests at the completion of each day to make sure that the day's work was not damaged in the process of assembly. One night after completing the tests, I was shocked by over 40,000 volts DC as I reached in to ground out the winding that had been tested. I was blown across the generator bore and landed on the other side. When I realized I wasn't dead, I closed the job for the night and went straight to the Wolf's Den Bar in Polson and drank six shots of tequila as fast as the bar tender could pour them before I began to calm down. The DC voltage seemed to fill me with a weird energy that needed to be drained out. Every cell in my body was at a charged state and I finally went to my motel and stood in the shower for a long time. I was eventually able to sleep.

At the next job at Boundary Dam, I spent several days doing loop tests on the generator frame where the noise level was over 135 Db. It felt like you were being punched in the stomach from the sound waves. My abdominal muscles were actually sore after spending the several hours that each test required. The powerhouse of Boundary Dam is carved out of solid rock and the hollow space was just the right dimension for a standing wave to form in the room. I learned to position myself in the nodes where the effects were less intense. I left Westinghouse at the end of 1979.

The next year and a half were a continuous experiment in trying to find a way for me to be happy. I was tired of living in motels and bars, airplanes and powerhouses. I wanted a family and a place to settle down. I chose Spokane because it was the nicest friendliest place that I had traveled through. I had spent a lot of time in Spokane while I was working at Coulee Dam, Lower Granite Dam, Boundary Dam, and Kerr Dam in Polson Montana. I had met a lot of people, most of them musicians. The time was spent growing a garden and trying to find a way to make a living. I started Fat Chance Records and produced one really good album. I built fences and other construction projects, painted a house and interviewed for a job as a drug dealer, which I turned down. I was working as a gardener, when I met the woman who would become my wife, who already had a son so I got an instant family and then I got a job with the City of Spokane at Upriver Dam.

Growing Magic Mushrooms

In addition to planting fruit trees and a large vegetable garden a friend gave me some starts for growing psilocybin mushrooms. He and I each had several frames of mushrooms that we were waiting to start sprouting. As they began to fruit, we began to sample and test them. We were very orderly and weighed out how much we were eating each time. Thinking that we could control the dose and the effects, we started with a small amount and added a little more each time. After one time with an uncontrolled setting where we were interrupted, we decided to go to a small local lake where we would not be around people. We ate our proscribed amount for that test and drove out to the lake. We took some fishing gear so that if some people did go by they would just see fishermen. We had fished this lake several times and knew a good spot to go. There was a small point that stuck out into the lake that had a small sandy beach that we could sit on while we were fishing. As we sat there, we noticed some hellgrammites crawling out of the water on some of the weeds growing at the edge of the lake. As we watched, the mushrooms activated and we were in an altered state when the hellgrammites dried out in the sun, their back split open, and the Dobson flies flew off to find a mate. This vision captured our attention and we wanted to repeat it.

So we did our best to duplicate the experience by using the same dose and timing and we went back to the lake to the same spot on the beach in the sun. This time as the mushrooms kicked in we became the hellgrammites as we fell back onto the beach and lay there in the sun as our chests opened and our spirits drifted up into the sky where we remained looking down at our bodies on the beach. I was met by one spirit and my friend by another.

The spirit who approached me said to me. "You think that your pretty smart don't you?"

I replied, "Yes."

"You are not smart enough to grow your own finger nails."

I had to admit that he was right. He had some other comments on my general unworthiness and then challenged me to come back when I could get there on my own. My friend and I were sent back down with the additional challenge to figure out how to get back into our bodies. It was not easy. As soon as you thought that you were back in you would pop right out again. Pure fear kept me in my body as I drove to town while my friend was gone most of the time and I kept shaking him to pull him back in. I drove to a friend's house that I knew was moving that day. We got there when it was time to move the big heavy stuff and that is what finally kept us in our bodies. Carrying all of the heavy furniture forced us to stay in until the mushrooms finally wore off. It was the last of our mushroom experiments and I began wondering about the getting there on my own challenge.

Grandma Dierks

During this time there was one event that happened that was significant from a spiritual sense. My Grandmother on my Mom's side passed away and I was asked to be one of the pall bearers. My Dad, my youngest sister Becky, and I went to Wyoming for the funeral. We stayed at my Uncle Bud's place and I was sleeping outside in his camper. I was close to my Grandma, she had taught me to knit and the last quilt that she made was for me. I had never been a pall bearer and I was worried about carrying my Grandma to her grave.

That night as I was sleeping, my Grandma came to me and showed me her death. She had worked for many years cooking in a hospital and had watched several friends wither and die in the hospital after they had a stroke. When Grandma had a stroke she insisted on going home and she started making quilts for her thirty five grandchildren. She did not like hospitals and didn't want to be in one. Three years later she was having a lot of abdominal pain and my Mom insisted that she go to a doctor to find out what was happening. The Doctor put her in the hospital to do a bunch of tests to find out what was happening. What she showed me was that during the night she had to go to the bathroom. She got up out of her bed and walked toward the bathroom. I watched as her spirit stepped out of her body and walked up and away as her body fell to the floor and lay lifeless. She was out of the hospital and she didn't have to do any more tests.

The next day I was able to carry the casket without any problem as I knew she wasn't in it, only her shell. The casket actually felt light but I also had five cousins who helped to carry it. The hearse was of course at the front of the line followed by a car carrying the pall bearers. The grave yard was on a hill a ways out of town. We stood and waited for everyone to arrive as the line of cars stretched all of the way back to town. This is the first time that I am aware of when I had communications with the dead.

Living and Dying

Virginia and I got married and bought a small house in town not too far from her parents. It helped to have built in baby sitters. Things went well as we enjoyed gardening and boating with her parents on Coeur D'Alene Lake where they kept the boat at Rockford Bay. When our next son was born, the first time I held him he told me his name was Terrence and we were linked telepathically from then on. He was a bright happy child who was inherently good. Not like his Dad who was always the black sheep of the family.

I was busy at work supervising the construction of a new powerhouse holding two hydroelectric generators. It was familiar work for me and I enjoyed the challenges because I was involved in every aspect of the construction not just the generators. A fun aspect was I learned a little Japanese from the engineers from Fuji who supervised the construction of the turbines and generators. When we completed the construction and had the powerhouse operating, City Hall wanted a big dedication so all of the politicians could make speeches and claim credit for the work. As a City facility there wasn't supposed to be any alcohol on the site, but the Japanese said according to their customs the generators would have bad luck if they were not blessed with Saki and everyone who was there had to participate. They brought gallons of Saki and everyone toasted the generators.

It was a big day for me but also my wife and I were expecting another child and she was going in for her final checkup as the baby was due any day. When all of the guests had departed, I locked my office and went home expecting to see my wife. She was not there and as I waited, my imagination worked over time. I could only wait. Finally the phone rang, it was someone from Sacred Heart Hospital saying that they wanted me to come in but I shouldn't hurry, she had been in a car accident.

When I got to the hospital it was a disaster. She had been run into and hit right in the driver's door. The baby was lost as it took the impact. Virginia was in the ICU and they had given her forty-eight pints of blood keeping her alive. The next day she was full of tubes but awake. She kept asking about the baby and wanted to hold the baby. The hardest thing in my life was to go down to the hospital morgue and get the baby. I carried this perfectly formed, red haired, blue eyed little girl in the hospital elevator and into the ICU for Virginia to hold. She could hardly move to try and hold the baby and all we could do was cry. Eventually, I had to take the baby back down and make the arrangements.

Virginia would end up with hepatitis C after all the transfusions but not AIDs. This was before they had a test to check blood for AIDs and Spokane's first AIDs patient was dying in the ICU right across from Virginia. She eventually came home and we went about changing our life as all attempts at having another child failed because her womb had been damaged beyond the possibility of carrying a child.

We moved out in the country where Virginia could have a pottery studio and horses. We have a big garden and fruit trees. We are five miles straight west of the top of Mt. Spokane. We have acreage that is mostly forested and some that is pasture land. On the hill to the south is a view of the surrounding farms and the mountains to the east. On the top of this hill we released our daughter's ashes. We had named her Nova as befitted her short time here. Over time the hill top became a prayer wheel and a gathering place for those who wanted to connect to the natural world and is now called The Wheel.

Our life went on as Virginia built a successful pottery business and a career as an artist. I worked through the various problems with the city water operation, FERC Dam regulations, Safe Drinking Water act requirements for additional water testing, and helped start the Spokane Aquifer Joint Board by originating the character of the Spokane Aqua Duck.

I had a friend who contracted cancer at the age of 46 and lost the fight at 47 years old. What was remarkable about Harry was his attitude. The tumors had taken over his body and he was unable to swallow any food so he basically starved to death. He was in a lot of pain and used very little of the drugs that Hospice had provided. One day as we were talking we looked at each other and at the same time, he said "I am dying." as I said "You're dying." He and I got past the inevitability of his death to where we could talk about the things that were going on objectively. I asked about why he didn't use the morphine and his answer was, "I am only going to die once and I want to be there when it happens."

He had everything planned out including giving me one of his sets of golf clubs. He was a Viet Nam vet but did not want a military funeral. He had a simple pine box picked out. About two weeks before he died, his Dad and his Stepmom came and stayed with him. His Dad who was a Navy vet had him shipped back to his home in Alabama for a fancy box and a military funeral. Harry was the first person that I sat and visited with during the time they were dying. I know that Harry was glad to see me each time I went and I know that I learned a lot about the process. It is not all that easy to die. Your body wants to live even when it has been taken over by some foreign agent that took control and eliminated the vital functions one by one.

As the years went by I began to notice a pattern that repeated at the same time of the year. Around the middle of July emotions ran high and everything was in turmoil. Virginia and I would find ourselves yelling at each other over some little thing. After peaking around the 19th or 20th the emotional level would go back to a calmer ordinary turmoil of pottery shows and getting the hay in. This pattern would repeat year after year regardless of what else we were doing.

I was under a lot of stress in my job. I was on call 24 hours a day, seven days a week for all of the twenty years I worked for the city. It was hard to take any time off to go anywhere. We were doing week end art shows selling Virginia's Pottery and I was Scoutmaster for Troop 247 for several years. We were adding to our gardens and orchard and also dealt with horses, chickens, ducks and geese, a pot-bellied pig and a goat named Stinker. Some of the cats and dogs lived close to twenty years but a lot of kittens and puppies, ducks, geese, and rabbits didn't. I finally said no more rabbits because I couldn't stand it when they died.

Beginning the Study of Shamanism

At some point Virginia convinced me to go listen to a shaman talk. We went on a Friday evening to the house of someone Virginia knew, who was sponsoring this visiting person who was named Phil Morgan and he did spiritual healing. In his talk he described Soul Retrieval and the method that he used. I was curious enough to sign up for a session for Virginia and I the following day. When we went there, Phil explained again how he listened to a cd playing a monotonous drum beat that helped him to change consciousness and then he was able to journey into the spirit world to get information and do spiritual healing for the person he was working on.

It sounded so simple. He sat behind me and put on his headphones and a blindfold, then put his hands on my shoulders. I sat and quietly waited. After half an hour, he removed the headphones and described his vision. I was amazed at the accuracy with which he related the accident when I was sixteen and had the concussion. I welcomed back the soul part and a power animal that he had brought back as well. I was filled with questions as to how he had done what he did. He had studied with Michael Harner and recommended that I do the same.

I did as he suggested, I bought Michael Harner's book "The Way of the Shaman" and ordered the drumming cd from the Foundation and I signed up to take the basic workshop in the fall of 1999. I wasn't sure that I should even go to the basic workshop. I wasn't having much luck in the process of journeying to the cd. I went. I struggled. The others in the course seemed to be so far ahead of me. I wondered what I was doing there. I don't see much visually I told Sandra Harner at one of the breaks. She said that is all right some of the most powerful shaman are not visual. Focus your attention on all of your senses and listen to the drum. My only success was when I did the Upper World journey to meet a teacher, the spirit from eighteen years before who challenged me to come back when I could get there on my own was waiting and said, "It took you long enough." It turned out that he was my old friend who had taught me to breathe when I was a tiny new born and was my original guardian angel.

I struggled and then we learned about power animal retrievals.

My turn came to practice the retrieval. I wanted so much to succeed. I begged the spirits not to let down the person I was trying to help. I tried to see. I thought I saw a chicken walking on the ground but I wasn't sure. Then a couple of shadows seemed to be crows flying. I saw couple more going in a different direction just dark outlines that felt like crows. I realized that the first thing that I thought I saw had been a crow and not a chicken. If I saw one more for the four you are supposed to have to be sure I would have it. Then right in front of me was a crow. I reached out. I could feel the feathers in my fingers and the wings beating on my arms as I pulled it to my chest. I blew the crow into the person I was working with. I was filled with a joy that overwhelmed my senses. I had done it. I succeeded in doing something extraordinary. My understanding of the material world changed. I could not get the feeling of holding the crow to leave. I have no doubt there was something there. Then too soon the weekend was over and I returned to ordinary life.

I tried telling people about this. Most of them, even my friends, could not understand the reality of the experience. My wife has always encouraged me in this area and she continued to support me as I began having more success with my daily journeying to the drumming cd.

I was still having trouble at work with the upper management and was increasingly depressed. I didn't even think about shamanism for a while. As time went on I became more desperate and more stressed as the job had me treating people in a way that I didn't like. I could not get a grip on what was happening no matter how hard I tried. My wife suggested that I needed to take another workshop and get back on track. I signed up to take the seminar on Divination on Whidbey Island in the spring of 2001.

My parents lived on Whidbey Island. I could stay with them and attend the sessions in the daytime. My Dad was doing better after having bone cancer and colon cancer. The doctors had found that the colon cancer had spread to the liver in a location that was inoperable when they were operating to remove the section of his colon that was blocked by the cancer. Dad had decided that he wanted to be able to take care of my Mom and was gaining strength. There was not a chemotherapy treatment that would help the liver so he was taking vitamins and eating healthy to build himself up. It was good to spend the time with them.

The Divination workshop was in a beautiful setting and was a small group of dissimilar appearing people but we shared an interest in the practice of shamanism. Once again I was back in a setting with a group of people embarked on a course that most of the normal American society would dismiss. It felt like home to me. However, I still had problems with some of the exercises. I could not connect with the crystal at all, yet the casting of stones came clear as a bell. Divination is something I had done before because I had studied the reading of Tarot cards, but this was so much simpler and not confused by the expectations that people have of Tarot. I was really enjoying myself.

We did an exercise that was a journey to find our hearts desire. We were to journey to see a vision and then draw the vision as a picture. I drew this scene of a hillside with a path going up over the hill. It had a tree on one side and a hawk flying above. When I saw the drawing I knew that my heart desired a new path. I wondered what that new path could be as I drove back home.

Less than a month went by. I was at work and hurrying from one meeting to the next driving my city owned vehicle and made a U-turn right in front of a one-ton Chevy van that I hadn't even seen. I was knocked from the path I was on. After months of discussion and counseling that I went through at the City's request I decided to take my retirement after twenty years and find something to do that my heart could agree with.

I journeyed to meet my spiritual teacher, I asked for help, I asked for direction. I was not willing to give up on the beauty of life just to have a job that paid almost enough but required me to treat people in a manner that I didn't agree with. My wife thought I should sign up for the Two Week Program. I wasn't sure if I was good enough at journeying to be able to complete two weeks of intense work. I journeyed again and asked for a sign. I insisted that I wanted to see a sign that clearly told me what to do. I wanted to see if I really belonged in the program. I got a vision of a rustic old outhouse behind some cabins. The roof of the outhouse had a solar water heater that was connected to a shower that was at the back of the outhouse. It was all open. On the side of the outhouse was a series of pegs that you could hang your clothes on before stepping around the corner to the shower. Above the pegs was a sign. I read the sign. It said, "When you remove your clothes, you remove your fears. You're among friends and spirits here." I decided to apply for the Two Week Program.

I was accepted and immediately started worrying about how I would do and doubting my abilities. I kept up my journeying but did not get any more crystal clear visions. The bone cancer that had begun my Dad's decline started coming back. The liver cancer had continued to slowly grow and Dad had to choose what to do. He could take the chemo for the bone cancer, which would help alleviate the pain but would not help the liver cancer and might make it worse. He chose to try the chemo. I went over to stay with them in November. Dad was declining more rapidly. I stayed through December, came home for Christmas, went back and stayed through January when my sister from Texas came up. I was hoping that everything would work out so that I could still attend the program in February. In January the decision was made not to have any more chemo because it was not helping. The time spent caring for my Dad was heartbreaking but fulfilling. I would not have wanted to miss it but I wish no one else had to watch cancer destroy someone they loved. My Mom was struggling because she wanted the best for my Dad but could not yet let him go.

Learning about Death on many Levels

In February, as I was driving down to the Two-week Program I saw a coyote that followed along the hillside as I drove past and an eagle flew along for a while as I was driving along the Columbia River. I got to the retreat center south of Portland where the program was to be held. The cabins were small but not rustic and they had indoor plumbing. No shower at the back of the outhouse. Oh well, I was definitely among friends and spirits as I learned at the first session that Sunday night. We began by journeying to find out what our partner needs. I was not sure of myself and lacked confidence but my partner felt that what I had sensed had meaning for her.

The next day I began by calling my Mom. Dad was not doing well. She began trying to get the family together. My brother in Roseburg, Oregon was having trouble getting off from work. I told her I would come back up if necessary but I wanted to complete the program if I could. I had breakfast and talked to the other participants and then the sessions began.

We did a journey to the lower world to find someone from the past native culture and ask them how we could help their descendants. I met a shaman with a fancy headdress that showed me his Bear and told me we were brothers. I was told that I should treat his descendants as brothers and to not judge or criticize them. I was to open my heart and to be thankful for the opportunities they gave me. I thought I understood what he meant. I have been critical of native peoples in the past. I vowed to change.

That night Michael Harner taught us a power dance. There was a particular type of drumming and a set procedure to follow if you wanted to dance. Only one person was to dance at a time and you were to wait until your spirit helper taught you a song. You were then supposed to teach the song to the drummers who then followed you around as you danced and sang. I watched as a couple of people took their turn and got up. They did great and had beautiful songs and dances. My body wanted to get up. I keep telling it to sit down. You don't have a song. I felt these growls growing inside of me. Another person danced and then there was a pause, as no one got right up. The drummers circled and as they beat the drums each beat seemed to pass right through me stirring me to get up. You don't have a song I told myself again. The drums were like explosions and as they came close to me, I stood up with a growl that came deep from within me. I had never felt like this. The drummers couldn't hear my rattle so someone gave me a larger one and we began to go around the circle. I was not me but a large bear that was annoyed by these villagers who were beating drums trying to drive me from their village. I growled and roared and tried to turn on the drummers but they beat the drums and drove me around the circle. Around we went until I collapsed with exhaustion. It took a while to catch my breath and my throat would be sore for days. I was exhilarated and confused. What had happened to me? I didn't know it then but the Bear had become a part of me. The native shaman that I had seen in my journey that morning was right. We were brothers in the Bear.

This occurrence changed me and I was empowered by the memory of the Bear for the rest of the two weeks and probably the rest of my life. We also did a healing drum ceremony that evening that was led by Alicia Gates. She asked me to help by being one of the drummers. I was glad to help and was grateful for the opportunity to be close to her and watch what she did as she blew power into the drum. It would not be the last time that she amazed me with the strength and power of her spirit helpers.

The sessions were scheduled with ample time for eating and sleeping but not much else. Several people besides I were early risers and got up and walked in the surrounding area. I called Mom each day before breakfast to see how things were going with

Dad. I had been able to keep him eating but now things have progressed to where my sisters are just able to get him to drink a few liquids. He was failing rapidly and was beginning to have difficulty breathing as the liver cancer was taking up so much space in his chest. I reassured Mom that things are as they are meant to be. I told her that when you saw Dad in the spirit he was still the big strong man that he always was and that this process was just to set his spirit free. She was beginning to see the necessity of letting him go but she was not yet ready still.

I realize that I should have focused on taking better notes because a lot of what we did has become blurred in the intervening time. We began each session with instructions and I have good notes on some parts of that. I didn't keep a time line or log of what we did when. I know that I was oriented in two directions and not always thinking clearly. We did exercises on extractions and soul retrieval. Michael's method was to give you instructions and then you journeyed to your spirit helper for the actual technique of what to use and how to use it for the soul retrieval. When I journeyed for instructions I got a clear message to trust the bear. I was able to bring back a soul part for the person that I was working with and she brought back two soul parts and an eagle for me.

The first had to do with a boy afraid of drowning. When my partner mentioned a loud sucking sound I was pulled back in time to when I was in the deep end of a large hot spring swimming pool. There was a large drain grate that the water rushed through at the deep end of the pool. Older boys were trying to push me down against the grate where I would have been trapped by the flow. I clearly remember summoning all the power I could and hitting the one boy on the jaw. He let go and I was able to escape to the surface. I even remembered his name and saw the look on his face as I hit him. What I hadn't realized was that from that day on I never swam in water over my head and I never ever swam under water again. I went from loving swimming to only getting in the water to go water skiing when I had a life jacket on. I tested out whether I can swim in water over my head and swam under water one summer up at Priest Lake. It felt good to realize that I could.

The other part I didn't recognize and didn't get any sense of what it had to do with. Later on I journeyed during one of the afternoon sessions and came to realize that the vision of a small boy and man at the edge of a cornfield that was relayed to me as the second part of the soul retrieval was my Dad and I burying my dead kitten Snowball. My uncle as punishment to me, for telling about the abuse that he had been doing, had killed my kitten. I had spent most of my life thinking that my Dad had not believed me and had not stuck up for me and now I knew that he had. The abuse to me had been relatively minor but it was a good feeling to clear this up now.

Then Friday during the evening session I got a message to call my Mom. She said the Hospice nurse who was there that day thought Dad would be going into a coma soon and if anyone wanted to talk to him now was the time. I talked to Michael and decided to miss the Saturday session. I got up early Saturday morning and drove north to Whidbey Island. As I drove up to the house a bald eagle circled overhead. I had been seeing eagles frequently lately. When I went into the house the hospital style bed had been installed in the living room. Dad did not like it and was not finding a comfortable way to sit up. He was not able to talk much and was drifting into sleep most of the time. He slept that night in his own bed. As I helped him into the bed he told me thanks for taking care of him and I told him thanks for being such a good Dad. The next day he hadn't gotten out of bed by the time I left. I had to wake him up to take some of his medications and I told him goodbye.

I returned in time for the Sunday evening session. Everyone was very supportive which I appreciated but the most comfort was just being back with the group and participating in something extraordinary. The lesson that I missed on Saturday was on a healing technique where you journeyed to the upper world to request a method to heal your partner. When Amanda explained it to me I realized that I had done exactly that before the seminar even began. My wife had a swollen jaw that the dentist said wasn't a dental problem and her doctor said she didn't need antibiotics but she was still in pain. As we went to bed that night I journeyed and asked my teacher for help. In my journey he took a blue dagger of light and stabbed her in the jaw. In the morning the swelling and pain were gone. I marveled to myself about how the lesson that I missed had been given to me ahead of time on a journey that I did spontaneously to help my wife. I was able to step back in and work with the group not having missed a thing.

Then we did a journey to seek a dismemberment type of experience. The idea of the journey is to seek an experience where you are dismembered in some way and then wait to see what happens or how you are put back together. I started out just like I was walking through the woods on a pleasant afternoon. I came to a high castle set upon a hill. As I walked up to the castle to see who was there, the inhabitants attacked me. They were a rough bunch of ogre like people. I was seized and cut up and roasted like beef. The offal was thrown out the window and the dogs ate the bones. Birds picked at the remains and an alligator ate the parts that landed in the moat.

I was gone until a garden angel or deva appeared. Then I noticed how good it felt as I was absorbing the sunshine and just being there in the earth. I realized that I was the growing plants along the side of the moat and it felt so good. I stretched out to feel the sunshine and continued to grow and then I heard voices. The people had returned. I heard someone say, "I'll have some salad." Then I was cut up and devoured again. After a while the deva appeared again and the next thing that I knew I was back in my body and returned to the ordinary reality. I was killed and eaten twice, once as meat and once as vegetables. The lesson I got was to not make too big of a thing of being a vegetarian. If you eat, something is being eaten. The Shamanic experience of dismemberment is so much more but I can't explain all that Michael told us. I know I was amazed at the stories that others were telling of their experience. Each of them had received a lesson or healing appropriate for them guided by Spirit.

The next day we did a journey to the time immediately after death to learn the destiny of the human soul. It seemed to take me a while to get going but after a while I saw beings that were coming to welcome me. Then there were other types of beings there. One was a being of bright light like a star being. After a while I had visions of various scenes from my life. Some were very mundane and ordinary. I thought I was supposed to see what happened after my death and then I realized that this was a recounting or remembering of what my life had been. I had a vision of a being that looked like the pictures of Christ, very glowing and welcoming. I was wandering sort of confused and dazed not knowing what was happening and then I saw my Dad. He was sitting over at the side on a low garden wall. As I started over toward him the call back drum sounded. I didn't want to leave but had to follow the drumbeat back.

I could hardly wait for the session to end. I went out to call home and I had to wait to use the phone. Why didn't I call that morning like I had been doing? I don't know. I finally got through and asked Mom how things were going? She said it has been a rough night and I'll let you talk to Becky, she has been with your Dad most of the night. My youngest sister came on the line and related how Dad had struggled most of the night and had finally gotten to sleep. When he woke up before noon that day my sister said that what he said to her was "It's very beautiful there but I am not quite ready to go." I was stunned and then I told my sister that I had seen my Dad there. My brother arrived late that evening and he was able to talk to my Dad and help care for him. Dad was slipping fast and could not get out of the hospital bed the next day and only said a few words.

I continued to call home frequently as I wanted to help Mom and my siblings understand as much as I could tell them about what I was learning about the spiritual side. My family is and I was raised as fairly strict Lutherans. My sister Jocelyn has been a deaconess in the church and is completing her studies to be an ordained minister now that the church has opened to accepting women in that role. I didn't want to cause any conflict in the family at this time but I wanted to help them accept what I was learning in my journeys. Death is not final and is just opening the door to a world of experience that we can't even imagine in this physical realm.

We had done a journey to explore the other side and I had gone to levels above where I had been before. Our instructions were to pay attention and learn our way around so that we would be familiar with the realm. I however, had gotten lost wandering in amazement and wonder so that when the call back drum signaled I had no idea where I was or how to get back. I appealed to the spirits there and they turned me into a pitcher of golden sand and poured me down through the levels until I came out back in my body. Again as people related the story of their journey I was enthralled with the wide range of experiences and the immensity of what they described. It was possible to speak to my family and reassure them that the faith they had in the next world was true and that it was indeed very beautiful there.

During the first week of the session Michael had shown us a dream dance that was historically called the Ghost Dance and was taught to the plains tribes by Wovoka. The group used the dream dance to ask for a ritual to teach us to live in compassion. Each member of the group received a different part of the ritual. I received the message that we needed the eagle's vision from above to see that all is one and to know the interconnectedness of all life. During the ritual we should ask for the vision of the eagle.

It was our assignment as a group to put the information that we all received together into a ceremony that we would perform on Thursday the last afternoon session of the seminar. We worked on this during the times we were not involved with the actual training sessions. There were forty-six people with different visions that somehow had to be united. It took more than a little discussion but we kept working at it.

The training continued with more discussion about the things that can happen to human souls that die a violent or sudden death. These spirits can be caught not even acknowledging that they are dead and not knowing which way to go. I found some of the information that Michael relayed to be unsettling. The numbers of these spirits trapped as suffering beings particularly bothered me. The journeys to the time after death were made to acquaint us with the territory so that we could help these suffering beings that were trapped in time not knowing that they were dead. The discussions about depossession caused me a little unrest. I wasn't comfortable with the thought of a high number of spirits that could be attached to the people around you.

Later during the training I would be completely amazed as I witnessed the removal of spirits from volunteers among the participants. Michael and his assistants did these demonstrations. There was no doubt in my mind what was real as you heard the spirits describe their state of awareness and suffering. I watched in fascination as members of the group took turns being the practitioner and removed spirits from their fellow students. I did not feel that I was sufficiently aware to be able to do this and only took part as an assistant.

The day came for the enactment of our dream dance ceremony. We had a rehearsal in the morning and everything was confused and we struggled to get the sequence and timing worked out. There were a couple of personality conflicts as people wanted to be sure that their vision was expressed the way that they had seen it during the dream dance. I was not confident that all would go well but the time came and everyone gathered outside the room. Our preparations had been made. The time was now. We all entered in silence and the program began. Each phase followed in order as prayers were made and blessings were offered. The dance sequence worked with precision and it all flowed as it was meant to be for over an hour. When the formal ceremony ended we all stood in awe of what had happened. Then someone said it is time to dance and the drums and rattles began. Everyone was filled with a huge amount of energy and some danced their spirit helpers as never before. The power filled the room and echoed through each of us as we danced and danced with joy.

The last day of the program began with people trying to take pictures to preserve something that we all knew was coming to an end. A very special time had been shared by all of the participants and we all sensed that nothing would ever be the same again. I was not in any hurry to leave. I knew what was waiting for me on Whidbey Island. That morning we did a final journey to help our partner and then said our goodbyes after lunch. I got in my car and headed north.

When I arrived at my parents, an eagle was perched in the tree below the house and my Dad was in the hospital bed and comatose. I talked with my sisters and brother about what had gone on the last couple of days. Dad had gone through a period of high fever and had been sweating profusely. That was now over but he had lost a tremendous amount of weight during the week, as he had not had anything but a minimal amount of fluids.

The cancer was consuming him. His face was gaunt and his cheekbones stood out. He was not in pain and most of the time he rested quietly and only stirred occasionally. I don't remember what we had for dinner but after dinner we all sat around and talked. Each of us told some story about Dad that related something special that he had done with us that the rest of the family didn't know about. Mom told us how Dad had been carrying her across a creek while they were on their honeymoon and had ended up dropping her in the mud when he slipped. It was a very special time for the family. As it came time to go to bed, I played my guitar and sang "All My Trials" for my Dad. I could hardly get the words out, as I knew all of his trials would soon be over.

We all went to bed but I don't think that any of us slept well. I got up twice in the night to check to see if Dad was still breathing. In the morning we had breakfast and sat around talking. We had all talked to Dad at some point and had told him that it was all right for him to go and we had promised him that we would take care of Mom. As we sat there talking and wondering what would happen, Dad took one last breath and gave out a large sigh. He was gone. We gathered around him and held hands and said goodbye. Mom, my three sisters, my brother, and I held each other and prayed. After a while I called the minister from the church and he came over and sat with us for more prayers. We let the Hospice nurse know that she didn't need to visit that day and then called the funeral home. While we were waiting for them to arrive, Becky, Steve, and I washed Dad and put him in clean pajamas. When they arrived and backed down the drive, I went out to meet them. The local flock of ravens were all around the house, sitting on the roof and lawn and trees in the yard. They stayed until the van pulled away taking Dad. Then the flock followed the van down the highway.

We made arrangements and I left the next day to bring my wife and sons back for the funeral. When I was at home I journeyed to see my Dad and saw that he was happy and he told me that he could help with my spiritual healing work if I did it in the name of Jesus Christ. We went back to Whidbey for the funeral and then came home. After we were home I had time to share some of the things that I had learned with my wife. We had lost a daughter when my wife was in a car wreck while she was eight months pregnant.

Thinking about that and the suffering beings that we had learned about bothered me. I could not rest thinking of this baby suffering for the last seventeen years. I realized the turmoil in our life that reoccurred annually had been around the time of her death. The turmoil was her reminding us that she was still there. I journeyed and found Nova and asked my Dad to come and get her. In my journey I placed her in his arms and he walked away carrying her. I think of my Dad often and I have journeyed to see him several times only to be told that he isn't available, or he is busy learning his new tasks. I know that it wouldn't be heaven for my Dad if he didn't have something to do. As time went on we realized that the turmoil no longer came to remind us that there was unfinished business. It had been taken care of.

I have done several healings for family and friends and I find that the Bear is ready and willing to be there to help. I have learned to tell people to expect that the bear will come out when I am doing these extractions as otherwise they are surprised with all the growling and grunting. I know that I have a lot to learn so I registered for the Three Year Program and I am looking forward to the experiences that will bring. In the mean time I am learning to use the wood lathe that was my Dad's and I think of him each time I use his tools.

I had been using some of the time that I was staying with my parents to study for the Professional Engineers License exam and I took the test not long after my Dad passed. When I learned that I had passed the exam, I went about beginning my Engineering practice. Trying to find my first clients was job number one.

I took care of my Mom for a while after my Dad died. She went through the process of deciding what to do and where to go as I cleaned out the house and got it ready to sell. Even though they were all still practicing Lutherans, I had told my family about my study of Shamanism. One day my Mom said to me, "I am not afraid to die you know. I already died once years ago so I am not afraid to die." She reminded me about dying while being given anesthesia for a medical procedure when we were kids. She had been gone for a while and was difficult to revive. She said she liked it there. Then she asked me to help her to pass on. I told her I would think about it. I consulted with my friends in the spirit world and they said that it was too soon as Mom still had things to work out with my sisters. I took loads of stuff to the dump while my sister and Mom checked out various care facilities. They picked out one where Mom kept a fair amount of her furniture and had a little kitchen. I went back to living more normal after Mom was settled into the care facility and returned to the farm north of Spokane. Virginia had been doing everything without me that it took to keep the place going. It had not been an easy time for her. As time went on and Mom's dementia worsened, she moved into a series of greater care, less space, more costly adult family homes.

Michael Harner described the Three Year Program as a series of initiations. The first session began right where the Two Week Program had left off. There was a schedule to each week that was similar. Breakfast, morning journeys, lunch and some free time then afternoon journeys. Dinner was followed by evening sessions that went until ten. It was hard work but we enjoyed it. We journeyed so much on so many different things that we joked that we could do a journey in three drum beats, because we were never quite back to ordinary reality. Michael was always curious and would try things that seemed odd but he explained that he wanted the classes to be so that anyone could do them. He knew it was in the human spirit for everyone to have access to spiritual help and he wanted to remove any barriers that stopped people from journeying if he could.

At some point I began a practice of journeying to the drumming CD for one half hour. I got up in the morning and did this every day. At first I just journeyed and asked spirit to show me something. I had a power animal that was a horse to take me on travels to see things like the Aztec ruins. One day as we started on our journey the horse looked back at me and said, "There is more to riding a horse than sitting on the back." Spirit was teaching me a valuable lesson. You need to have a reason or purpose and then your journeying will have meaning. Journeying is not intended to be used like turning on the TV to keep a three year old entertained and out of your hair.

I also began hosting a drum circle at the Unity Center which was twice a month on Monday from seven until nine PM. It gave us time to do three journeys and talk about the results. It was open to whoever chose to show up without any requirements and a donation was taken to help Unity for the use of the space. Over the years many people came. Some came for a specific purpose and Spirit would have led them there. They would attend a few sessions until they had the experience that they needed and then they would stop coming. Others became regulars and some went on to take classes from the Foundation with a couple going all the way through the Three Year Program.

I did not have an agenda at that time or a program of journeys to work through. In fact I had no idea what I should do to lead a drumming circle. When I started I used my daily morning journey to ask what we should do each evening that we met. Spirit always had a plan and it was fun watching over time as Spirit would anticipate who was coming and set an appropriate course for the evening. It was always fun and many times it was exciting.

First Building Clearing

Shortly after beginning the drum circle at the Unity Center, I had someone come to the group, who after a couple of meetings, asked if I could help her. It turned out that she worked for a real estate company in the office. The company she worked for had bought a different building and had recently moved all of the office staff into the new space. Her office was in the lower level in the records department. She described all kinds of weird feelings as she was trying to work and always felt cold drafts around her. When she told me where the building was, I knew the place. For years it had been a funeral home. I had gone to the funeral home years before to pick up the ashes of the baby girl that we had lost. The lower level had an area where shelves were filled with boxes of unclaimed ashes. I had been in the lower level to pick up the small box that held our daughter's ashes. It was scary thinking of all those people, and no one cared to pick up their ashes. It was so sad.

I began journeying into the spiritual version of the building. It was easy because I had been there. It took several trips to work out removing all of the spirits who had accumulated into the space. I began in the lower level and worked my way through the entire building. I took journey after journey and moving as many spirits as I could each time. Finally, I was done in the building, so I went outside and there were spirits wandering around and waiting on the corner for the bus. We took care of all of them and then I was able to tell Mary that the place was safe to work in.

An Angry Spirit

On one of the Monday night sessions at Unity, a woman named Katherine came. She was clearly agitated and emotional as she explained that her Mother had recently died. Her mother had been nasty with her children to the point that she was the only one who went to the hospital and she had been with her Mother when she died. Katherine was sensitive enough to know that a spirit had attached to her as she sat there with her Mother's body. She soon understood why her Mother had been so irritable.

Katherine knew she needed help so she went on line, found the Foundation for Shamanic Studies and found the listing for the drum circle at Unity. She had come hoping someone would help her. I reassured her that I would help her. I knew that the best way to remove the spirit was when she was asleep and I could journey to talk to the spirit. When you talk directly to the spirit without the person being awake, they have no memory of the process and they wake up as themselves. I told her to rest easy that night after she gave me the location where she would be staying. I journeyed late at night to the location and quickly talked the spirit into leaving. It had had enough and wanted out of here, which was why it was so angry.

We were meeting twice a month at Unity and two weeks later she was there again. She came this time to thank me. She was not interested in learning about shamanism but she was happy that I was able to help. She did not return and went on with her life.

THE SPIRIT OF HUMANITY

The Spirit of Humanity

After one of mass killings in Colorado, the drum circle at Unity had questions about why these types of things happen. We discussed the idea that we know everything is part of creation and is therefore divine, so how do these shootings work for the divine. We were led to journey to the Spirit of Humanity for the answer. The answer is that the Spirit of Humanity is a growing consciousness that includes the thoughts, feelings, and emotions of all of the humans who have lived. Through much of our history humans have lived brutal lives of suffering due to wars, slavery, and imprisonment.

Little by little things have started to improve. We have a long way to go. Each human has the choice of what they contribute to humanity. Your life is your contribution. If you want humanity to be compassionate then you have to be like the Dalai Lama and always act compassionately. It is also necessary to speak compassionately and feel compassion in your thoughts about others.

We learned that when one of these shooting events happens, people see it on the news and they react with strong emotions which impact the accumulated feelings of the Spirit of Humanity. The Spirit of Humanity moves as we move and grows as we grow. We have an enormous emotional backlog of hate and fear that needs healing in order to change the balance within the Spirit of Humanity. We could start to live as if we were an intelligent species but we would first have to learn that everything is conscious and nothing can be owned. When we become a mature species and start to act responsibly, the rest of the Universe may lose their fear of us and allow us to sit at the adult table.

We had several group meetings at Unity about the Spirit of Humanity. In one meeting we had a wide range of people from different backgrounds and ages. There were about thirty people there. Many of whom had no experience with journeying prior to this meeting. The people of the drum circle were excited about their interaction with the Spirit of Humanity and invited the whole church to come for this meeting.

I explained that it is possible to learn directly from the Spirit of Humanity and you can learn what any other human learned by asking them directly. If you want to learn from a teacher or artist or scientist, you can ask the Spirit of Humanity for someone who fits your needs and meet their spirit. To illustrate my point, I asked everyone to think of something that they wanted to know that some previous human would have known but that they would not know. Each person picked their own question to ask the Spirit of Humanity. I told them to listen to my drumming and ask to meet the Spirit of Humanity. I only drummed for five minutes. Everyone had success. Even the children got their question answered.

When I relayed the results of these journeys to Michael, he sent me a reply that he knew of no previous references to a spirit that consisted of all of humanity. I don't know if he journeyed to the spirit or not, he did not say. He felt that I was the first to discuss this possibility.

Jonathan's Tuvan Drum Healing

In that first session of the Three Year Program was a demonstration of Tuvan Drumming by Paul Uccusic. Paul was the head of the European section of the Foundation for Shamanic Studies and had been on the Foundation's first trip into the Republic of Tuva following the fall of the Soviet Union. The Tuvans wanted to bring back Shamanism and had invited the Foundation to visit. Paul was shown the method while he was there. As I watched Paul's demonstration, I could feel the excitement from my spirit helpers. They couldn't wait to try the process. It became one of my things. Every time I could I would drum on as many people as would let me. One of the drum healings was particularly interesting. I will insert a report that I wrote to the Foundation at the time.

I wrote this about a Tuvan Drumming that I did that was unusual and I thought it would be of interest to the Foundation. I continue to use Tuvan Drumming as a first step to show people what I do. They always get a good feeling and I have done some very strong healings for people. This time was really a surprise to me.

At our usual first Sunday night of the month Toltec meeting, I realized that Jonathan was in a troubled place. I offered to do a Tuvan drum healing on him. I had my drum with me and he thought it would be a good idea. I had previously done other healings for members of the Toltec group. I started in without a lot of preparation. I was just doing another simple Tuvan drumming so it would be fun and no big deal. I began with some light drumming around him and asked the Great Bear for help and guidance. I was doing a general drumming all around him when I became aware of something on his right shoulder. I have done extraction type of things while doing Tuvan drumming before and at first I thought that this would be something similar. I continued to drum in the area around the back of his right shoulder with a steady heavy drum beat. I continued to feel a presence there and walked around him doing some general drumming to loosen the hold of what was there.

I got back to his right shoulder and began drumming with a heavy pulsing rhythmic beat. I sensed some form of low level intelligence and said in my mind, "You need to leave. You don't belong there." There was no sense of personality but a deep feeling of dark foreboding. I continued to drum and will the thing to leave as it was not responding in any way. As I drummed, I was suddenly shaken by a violent flurry of motion that was totally uncoordinated and accompanied by fierce snarling. I knew it was a spirit now that it had jumped onto me. I got control of myself and stood a few feet from Jonathan and began a journey type drumming for me. I called in more of my spirit helpers and asked that they help to take this thing where it belonged.

When I knew that it was gone, I went back and finished drumming around Jonathan. The drumming now seemed like an ordinary Tuvan drumming. The effect on Jonathan was very profound and he was very quiet. I asked for spirit guidance and was told to smudge around him which I did. I then smudged all around the room and asked that the influence of the spirit be gone. I gave Jonathan a glass of water that I had empowered and had him drink it down. I asked him to envision it as a golden light that was filling him with power.

When Jonathan returned to conversational, I talked to him about scheduling a soul retrieval. I learned some of the things that he was going through in his life and tried to help him deal with some of the issues but it was clear he needed more help. I strongly recommended that he call me. On the way home, Virginia asked me about what was going on. She thought that I was getting carried away by my bear act again. When I told her what was going on, she understood the seriousness of the situation.

The next day during my normal practice journey, I asked about the being that I had encountered. I was told that it was old, as old as the earth. It was so old that the way things were when it was created no longer existed. It had no understanding or volition as we understand spirit and was in one way, the oldest trapped suffering being. I had done what I could but I was warned that I should be more aware and conscious as I entered into any shamanic practice. I was shown that it is never wise to consider anything to do with spirit as ordinary.

Jonathan called the following day and scheduled a time to come out to my place on the following Sunday for a soul retrieval. He asked more about what had happened and I explained what I could tell him about what I had learned. I did not want him to dwell on what happened but on what he needed to change in his life. When I talked to Jonathan I learned that he had spent time in the ruins in Mexico at night and had never felt right since. That was probably where the entity had become attached to him.

Jonathan came out and I did a soul retrieval for him. One part was caused by the demands that his father, a harsh taskmaster, had put on Jonathan as a young boy. He felt as if what he did was never good enough. These same feelings contribute to his behavior today.

I talked to Jonathan again and he came out to the Wheel at the equinox. We talked about the things that were bothering him and he offered up an airline bottle of whiskey to the fire to symbolize his breaking away from alcohol. The interesting thing that I saw was that the bottle was in the fire and when it melted a stream of burning alcohol shot right at Jonathan and hit him on the right foot. The booze tried to get him one more time. I will see Jonathan again but the last time I talked with him he was doing much better with his family and work.

Helping after a Suicide

During the time that I was the Scoutmaster for Troop 247, my friend Bud was the committee chairman and he took care of a lot of the paper work and kept track of the finances. His youngest son was about the same age as Terry and was named Willy. We had a lot of adventures together building our own kayaks and going on fifty mile hikes. Bud's oldest son Ryan was in the Navy and was doing well as a machinist mate repairing whatever was broke down. The ship that he was stationed on was a tender and was designed to service the other ships of the Navy. After he had spent a tour in the Mideast, he was stationed in Bremerton and had gotten married.

The heartbreak of every parent is to lose a child and one day Bud told me that Ryan had committed suicide. Rumors blamed his wife with getting him involved with drugs but anyone who knew Ryan knew that wasn't possible. Bud and his wife had come to one of the Drumming sessions that we had at Unity Center and Bud had had an interesting time and had met a helping spirit. The family was Catholic and discouraged further participation so they didn't come back to Unity. Bud asked if I could help Ryan.

I began to journey to talk with Ryan. At first he was angry and upset still wanting to strike out at everyone. Eventually he was able to talk with me and I learned some of what had happened. When he was in the Mideast, Ryan's ship was sent to the aid of the USS Cole which had been bombed in a terrorist attack. A large hole was blown through the side of the ship. Inside the ship seventeen sailors died. Ryan was working trying to keep the ship afloat so he was right in the area of the explosion. Some of the spirits of the sailors who were killed attached themselves to Ryan. It was the turmoil that they caused Ryan that caused him to commit suicide.

Once I had separated the spirits of the sailors from Ryan and helped them to move on, Ryan began to get better and I was able to talk to him. The next step was to explain to the parents what had happened to cause Ryan's death. I also asked them to forgive him and to let him know that it was ok. I told them that this was important to help him move on.

The next time I journeyed to see Ryan he was a vision of the bright young man I had known. I asked how he was and he was happy to move on and ready to go. I then asked if he had something to tell his parents and he made a waving gesture with his hand and said, "Thanks, Mom." I knew that I had to relay the message exactly the way that he had given it to me. When I talked to the parents I did just that after I explained that Ryan had moved on. The effect was amazing. I had not known that was something that Ryan had done since he was a little kid. His parents had no doubt that he was ok. They were able to move on with their lives and appreciate the kids and grandkids they had.

Corey and the Burlington Hotel

This was written for a friend of mine. She was a member of an artist cooperative that had rented an empty old hotel near Oakland. They were going to have studios on the upper floors and use the lobby and first floor as a gallery. When they tried to move in, all of these artists being sensitives were too weirded out to be in the building for very long. I was approached to see if I could help. The project moved forward after I sent Corey this note.

Corey,

I think that I should write this out for you. I journeyed to the Burlington Hotel and in the place that I saw the building was brick in the front and another larger lighter colored block on the sides. I went into the building and asked if there was any spirits there who would like to move on. I drew a crowd of interested spirits. I was amazed at the number. Something led me to ask if they had friends and relatives in the neighborhood who would also like to go. A larger crowd assembled. I started to lead them away from there when Bear reminded me that a lot of these people wanted to go to the Lower World. For some reason I am not sure of, Shamus, my teacher, suggested that he take the ones who wanted to go to the Upper World and Bear would take the rest to the Lower World. I was left standing there on the second floor.

A sense of doom or foreboding filled me with dread. I knew I was not alone. I never actually saw a form but I felt this presence that was dark and suffering. I asked, "Why didn't you go with the others?" The response was that the being felt that it was too evil to move on. It felt that it was not going to be accepted anywhere because of its evil doings. I didn't ask what it had done but I found that I needed to be able to approach it as an empath. I felt this strange feeling come over me. I had memories of myself as a child trying to help others who were picked on. In particular I remembered Raymond Ecoffy who in the third grade was a Lakota boy that everybody picked on. He never was accepted and eventually left school and never returned. I remembered trying to be his friend and the pain that he felt caused him to strike out and push me away. I was unable to help him. Somehow all of this helped the being to see that I was really sincere in wishing to help him and we began a discussion about evil. I was able to use a lot of the stuff that I have learned about the other side to help him see that evil is only in this world and that he could be helped in the other world.

A deep feeling of sadness then filled me as I realized that he was truly sorrowful about his life. I could not get the being to leave this feeling until I shifted again to a feeling of joy that I brought from the other side to give the being hope. When I showed him the joy he was willing to go with me. Afterwards I asked and was told that the space was clear. I was deeply moved by what I had to do to help this being. I remembered things that I had forgotten about myself as a child. I have confirmed again that there is no evil, there is only us calling people evil. I was given this lesson about looking at the ugliness of people as a measure of the hurt and pain that they have suffered. This is truly a lesson I needed. This was a powerful healing for the spirits and me.

The artists were able to set up their studios after the space was cleared.

Description of My Service Project

During the Fall 2003 session of the Three Year Program we did a journey that was relatively simple but has had far reaching impacts on my life. I felt that I hadn't gone to the correct place during the middle world journey in which we were instructed to go as far as you can. In the discussion after the journey it was apparent that many people had taken the instructions differently than I had and had an incredible journey as the result. There were several people who mentioned a common encounter with a large number of trapped gray beings who were spirits that weren't able to move on past the barrier of the middle world.

I came home and did the journey over for myself. This time I didn't wander in the hills of California and end up in a bar drinking beer, I went to the far reaches of the Middle World. There I also encountered the vast number of trapped beings who are there stuck not able to get through the barrier of the Middle World. I was not able to walk away and I was unsure what to do. Something struck me about this situation as being unfair. Not that I have learned to expect fairness as a criterion in this world. However, it was the idea that most of the trapped spirits were there due to circumstances beyond their control that made me angry. In my life I have known the hopeless feeling of being abused on a daily basis without any ability to change the circumstances. I know what it feels like to be a trapped suffering being. I have experienced that in another shamanic journey series that showed me another side of death.

In the second year of the three year program we did more exploration into being dead. In fact shamanism is a study of being comfortable being dead so that you can work with the dead without fear. We did a series of journeys exploring our own death. I had several scenes that gave me an appreciation for the torment of being a trapped spirit or suffering being as Michael liked to call the spirits who were not able to move on. In one of the journeys to my death, I watched my friends talking about me and I heard one say, "Did you hear about Leon? He died in a shaman experiment down in California." It was a difficult journey and I was led to change my daily practice journey into always working to help the trapped spirits.

My personal experiences called to me to have pity on these beings and I decided to act. I decided to use my energy body as a bridge to allow the passage of the spirits from the Middle World to the Upper World. I began a series of experiments with the help of my allies from the Upper and Lower Worlds. I normally did a journey in the morning in which I would do healing journeys for the requests that I had received. If I didn't have any healing requests I would normally just journey on something that I was curious about. Now when I finished the healing part of the journey I would have my spirit allies help me move suffering beings from the Middle World where all of the trapped beings are to the Upper World reception area.

Shamanic practice involves an awareness of more than one level and I worked to be able to continue this practice as efficiently as possible. If a person who is working to free a large number of trapped beings takes the time to know each one personally, two things happen, you become overwhelmed emotionally and you don't get very many spirits moved. I experienced this as I began. In order to be more effective I realized that all of the beings who were at the membrane of the Middle World were ready and willing to move on. They did not have confusion about their state nor did they have attachments that connected them to their life in the Middle World. I came to the conclusion that they only needed someone to hold the door open.

The spirits are accumulated in an area around the North Pole. They are there because it is possible to become energized from the cosmic energy that causes the Northern Lights. If they become energized enough they can get through the barriers and get into the Upper or Lower World. In one of my basic "Way of the Shaman" classes, one of the students who was a total beginner at journeying, started relating a bizarre description on his first Upper World journey that sounded familiar to me. I asked what he had used to go to the Upper World. He told how he had been to Alaska and had seen the Northern Lights and had decided to use them to go up.

He had unknowingly gone into the area of the gray spirits

which I recognized when he described how they behaved. I explained to the class what he had encountered and asked him to try a different way up. He did have success on the next journey to the Upper World using a column of smoke. I asked Michael later if I should tell people not to use the Northern Lights and he said no. I should follow what the Foundation suggested and this was an opportunity that Spirit took to give a lesson.

When I was trying to set this up and get everything flowing, I received some opposition from some realms of the spirit world. Not everyone approved of what I was doing. It became necessary to make a declaration and invoke my divine right of creation that was my right as a conscious being. There is an inertia or lack of creativity that does not welcome change and keeps what is happening from moving forward in continuity.

The City employees had a saying that they used each time after the elections stirred the possibility of change. "Things will go on a being the way they been a being." I was given this name for the process as I was writing this today. The phenomenon is the result of the Consciousness of Convenience. The patterns of behavior are constructed with little actual thought about the results. When asked, people will say, "We always do it that way," or "It was that way when I got here." A modern example is the way the state name is handled on all the forms that you fill out on a computer. Calling up a list of names to choose from is more effort and more time consuming than just typing the name or the two letter abbreviation but no one changes it when they create a new form. It was that way when I got here.

The Middle World is cursed by these unconscious creations

of thousands of generations of humans who shed the blame by saying God did this. All aspects of the Middle World that are not benevolent are the responsibility of humans, including the structure of the possibilities of life after death.

I had my spirit allies set the feet of my energy body in the membrane of the Middle World above the area of the trapped beings and I extended my right arm around my head which thrust through the membrane of the Upper World. This allowed the spirits to flow up between my feet and through me going out the top of my head and walking away into the reception area of the Upper World.

I learned as I did this that it took an amount of concentration that wasn't total. I was able to work through various modifications of my methodology until I had streamlined the process and could continue the process for a half hour of the journey cd that I listened to. As I continued on my way, I found that one day of working to release spirits to the Lower World would balance with three to the Upper World. What that means is that there were a lot less spirits in the gray cloud that wanted to go to the Lower World. As I worked each day I could feel the tension decrease as the spirits realized some hope when they sensed that others were moving on. On days when I worked to the Lower World, I only worked to the Lower World so the spirits that wanted to go down had to flow through those that didn't. The result was always fewer spirits were moved to the Lower World on a day than to the Upper World.

What I actually did was to position my physical body in the position that allowed me to use my right arm to hold the opening in the barrier to the Upper World. My body was in a wool blanket and tightly covered even in the summer. My left hand was positioned on my chest to monitor my consciousness. I said that it did not take all of my awareness to maintain the flow of spirits once it was started but my left hand was given the job to let the rest of the body know if the flow was interrupted so that it could be corrected. The left hand would signal by twitching two fingers letting me know that I had to reset the flow. I put on my headphones and bound a bandana around my head for an eye covering. Everything that I used was filled with power from participating in so many Shamanic adventures. The blanket was used to cover me when I did the Bound Shaman exercise and the covering on my pillow was a Tzoot head covering that had been worn by a Shaman from Guatemala. It was gift to me for healing work that I had done for a woman who had gotten it from the Shaman.

Once I had the flow established I could allow my attention to move forward along the flow so I could see where each spirit went or I could ask a question and let my attention follow the answer. This way I could allow my curiosity to find the answers to the questions that were troubling me. If I went too far or became too interested in what I found in my wandering, my consciousness would shift and my two fingers would twitch alerting me of the need to reset the flow. I would return and be more careful if I wandered that path again.

Each and every time that I began this practice I experienced something new and exciting because I used the opportunity to ask questions about things that I didn't understand. Some of the questions that I asked are "What is the nature of suffering beings?" And, "Why are there suffering beings?" The whole idea that just because someone was killed in sudden manner caused them to become stuck in the middle world and trapped in the circumstances of their death bothered me. It seemed that it represented a certain lack of foresight on the part of God.

There were a few times that Spirit came to me and requested assistance as I was beginning my morning journey. The first time this happened, a massive earthquake in Afghanistan resulted in a landslide that killed several thousand people. I was basically acting as a pickup for the lost and wandering spirits. A lot of them not recognizing that they were dead were moving around looking for their children or their parents. I was picking them up and sending them on up to the next station where they were sorted into who went where. As I was doing this, I met another gatherer who was a feeder on souls who had haunted this area for over five thousand years. As we met, I knew I had power over him, and I gave him the choice to free himself from the burden of all the souls he was carrying, after draining them of their energy, and I would reward him by letting him come along. He chose wisely and I was able to free an enormous number of souls and one soul thief.

A later earthquake in Pakistan got me called again. This time the helping spirits placed me in the rubble of a collapsed school building. It was tight quarters with little light and not much air. My job was to get the souls of the children, who had died, out of there as they were not making it easy on the children who were still alive. It was a tricky situation but I was able to read later in the paper about these children who were rescued after being dug out of the rubble after three days of being buried.

I said earlier that I was angry at the forces that held the suffering beings trapped and I meant I don't think this is the way things were meant to be. In my inquiries to spirit I learned a great deal about the influence of the human on the nature of the world of spirit. I established no rules or criterion for acceptance for the spirits that I helped. They were there and I was there so the process occurred. I was able to observe where people went and compare it to what they were expecting and I found that they always matched. I also found that no matter what the person expected that was what they received as a reception.

From where I was in my shamanic consciousness I could see each spirit move to their appointed door because that was the only door that they saw. For some it was a long tunnel to the light but not everyone saw things that way. I saw the long tunnel with door after door going a long ways. Those spirits who went to the Lower World almost all saw a river that they had to cross. What was waiting on the other side was completely different in many ways. Over time I realized that if the mind of man had envisioned some variation on the theme of the after world it existed.

After I had the flow established, I spent day after day choosing to go back into the past to witness the beginning of human society. I watched the discovery of fire happen numerous times in many places. Most of the time it was the result of a lightening caused fire, the people warmed themselves around a burning tree stump and learned to keep it going. Once people had fire, people would gather around it. Once people started gathering into a group they began to recognize one another and began to understand the relationships that brought them to the fire.

These first steps of human society did not all succeed. I watched and I learned as again and again groups formed and died away. There was nothing that bound them together until sometimes there was a strong leader who lived a long time and he or she was able to keep a group together because of their knowledge and abilities. The strong leader who lived for a long time, cared about the people around the fire because she or he knew who they were and recognized their grandchildren. When this aged elder passed away, their spirit chose to stay to help their descendants. It was the strong love and compassion of the elder that provided the power for the spirit to stay and watch over their descendants.

This period of development occupied about the first forty thousand years of human existence. Prior to the spirits of the elders choosing to stay, all spirits just returned to the unknown for rebirth. This deviation led to the formation of the Spirit of Humanity and our spiritual relations. The spirits who chose to stay learned to communicate with some of their descendants though visions and dreams enabling them to provide effective help in finding food and guiding their descendants in learning better ways of living. In time, some of the people learned to contact their ascended elders with drumming and dancing and the use of plants and mushrooms that are psychedelic. This began the development of spiritual practices to learn from a helping spirit and or from the spirits of nature.

Ancestral spirits helping their descendants is how it began. In those places where inherited authority was allowed to overrule direct experience, Spirituality was replaced by religion. Men who had power but lacked a direct connection to Spirit created the concepts of sin and guilt and the need for repentance to reinforce the power structure that men created. The threat of hell and damnation reaped many dollars for many churches. It is also the promise of nirvana and enlightenment and Scientology's E meter to test to see if you are clear that continue to sow confusion. There is no limit to what church leaders will spout all in the name of God and no limit to how much money they want to help you find your way.

This brought me to the realization that all of this is the product of our human creativity. What everyone thinks of as the creation of God is in fact the creation of man. Our true nature is that we are God. Our true problem is that we don't recognize it and don't practice using our abilities with wisdom. One of the reasons that this is so is because we are locked into the human understanding and description of the world.

As I did this work some of my own spirit helpers wanted me to stop. I was damaging my body doing what I was. My right shoulder was nearly useless after years of being wedged into the opening. We negotiated a change in the set up. My spirit helpers would help so that the spirits were not actually passing through my body. Unfortunately, I still had to use my legs and arm to hold the openings so it was still physically an effort to keep the opening going for a half an hour. I asked for no more days of nothing but babies. We continued this way for a couple more years and then one day which was near my birthday, I was told as I started my journey that I would not be allowed to do this anymore. I was told that my ten years of effort had been enough to create a permanent opening to the Upper and Lower World. My spirit helpers had worked to make it possible for me to take a break and I ended my daily practice of journeying.

Virginia's Dad's Passing

This report is what happened with my journeying to assist my father-in-law, Del Carter. He was ninety years old and had suffered the effects of Alzheimer's and dementia for a number of years. He had progressed to the point of not being able to do anything for himself and no longer recognized any of his family.

His family had tried to keep him at home but he had progressed to the point that they could no longer care for him. Then he fell and had to go into a nursing home. He resented his family for putting him there and he was angry that he couldn't go home. He could hardly speak and I had to connect with his mind and talk to him telepathically to get him into the wheel chair at the nursing home so we could get him out of the car.

I began a series of journeys so that I could talk with him more easily.

Thursday Sept 9

I began fairly quickly connect to Del's spirit but he was argumentative and angry. I tried many ways to talk to him but he argued about every detail. He didn't want to go down so I suggested he go through a hole in the clouds overhead. After much discussion about the details he finally agreed to take a peek through the hole but not go through. After looking through the hole in the clouds, he started a discussion about Mormons and how they took care of their elders and ancestors.

Friday Sept 10

Once again I connected quickly. He was not as angry much calmer and talked for a long time about how he felt about everyone was wanting him to go. I told him that everyone didn't want him to go and that they had been holding him here until their business with him was through then they would let him go. He can choose to go when he wants. He finally went through the hole with me and I asked him who he wanted to see. His mother Della came and then he realized that he was whole and was not limited by the effects of age. He started recalling adventures on Couer d'Alene Lake. That was a good time.

Sept 14

Del did not want to go anywhere. Instead he asked all about what is happening with the house and dog and bird. He went back to when he fell and why he had to go to the hospital. He had to hash over all of the things that went on and why he didn't like them, however he seems to be settling in at Park Place. He likes the friendly people and he thinks that they are not mean like his family.

Sept 27

In today's journey I got Del to go look through the hole in the clouds to see his brother Keith who had died when he was a child. Del had always missed him.

Sept 28

I journeyed to see Del. He has determined that it is ok to die but he still has fear of the figure known as the grim reaper. I talked to him about Kali. Kali is a different vision of death that is seen as a blessing when she comes.

Virginia went to see him at the nursing home and he was very withdrawn and has not been eating.

Sept 29

We got a phone call about 5:30 am that Del had passed on.

Virginia's Hospice Work

While Virginia and her brothers were taking care of their Dad, Virginia signed on to be a Hospice volunteer. She would spend time with people and do what needed to be done, whether it was washing dishes or cleaning or taking care of the person. On the first long term client that Virginia was assigned, she got me involved to try and help Nancy. She was a smoker and dying of lung cancer, but she was on Hospice for a long time. When I met her she explained that she didn't have any knowledge at all about the afterlife. She told me she had not been a good Mom. She drank and smoked and cursed and beat her kids. She was married and divorced twice and had kids in and out of wedlock. She did have some sincere regrets about not being a better Mom because none of her kids even wanted to come and see her.

When I talked to her she really had no idea about life after death. She had no religious training and no expectations because she didn't know anything. I had never really known anyone who had no upbringing. When I journeyed to see what I could do to help her, it was suggested that I talk to her about some of the material in the Tibetan Book of the Dead. The portion that my spirit helpers wanted me to talk about was when the dead soul learns that it gets to choose its next life. When I talked to Nancy, I explained the idea and gave her the background information of where the idea came from. I told her that she could choose what she wanted to do in her next life. She said she would think about it.

The next time I saw her, she told me that she had it figured out. She had not been a good Mom in this life but in her next life she was going to dedicate her life to children who needed help. After she made this decision, some of her children started to come to see her and before she died all of them managed to show up. Virginia and I went to the funeral and they were all there. It was an interesting family.

Virginia went on to volunteer for many years and had several people who lived for a long time while on Hospice. I did not meet them all but I think that it is interesting that Virginia was helping people before they died and I was helping people after they died.

The Loss of my Brother-in Law, Jim

Go the light is a simple spiritual directive. But it has one huge drawback. It doesn't work if you are not able to see the light. What do we need to do to teach or enable others to see the light? Is it even possible to help someone grow spiritually? At what point do we accept that others can only learn what they are ready for and nothing that we do can influence them?

All of these questions and so few answers. We need to be our brother's keeper but not his jailer. We need to free ourselves from the judgments that we place on others. If we presume that someone needs help then we are judging them and placing the limits of our understanding on them.

I throw out all of these thoughts without any answers. On Monday, my brother-in-law committed suicide. He has been struggling with alcoholism and lost the battle. He was not one to ask for help even if he understood what I do with shamanic healing. I have journeyed for his healing by asking his spirit or higher self if there was something I could do. I was told at that time that he was on his path and I would not be able to change what was happening.

At one point, a couple of years back, I wanted to help someone I knew who was dying and was striking out in anger and doing threatening things to his family. I journeyed to ask my teacher what I could do. In this case, I was told I could talk to the spirit that was attached to him. Tom had been in the Army in WWII and somewhere in his travels through Europe, the spirit of a dead German soldier had become attached to him. As Tom had approached death the spirit was in a panic and it was the spirit's fear that was causing Tom to act out so violently, which was totally not his normal behavior. The attached spirit was willing to move on, when given the chance, and Tom was able to then have a peaceful time with his family for the last several of weeks of his life.

After that success, I realized that I could talk to the spirits that were attached to other people that I knew. I went around for a while removing spirits from every one that I know. The end result was nothing. The only benefit was to the spirits that I helped to move on. The people who were still living quickly became attached to another spirit and made no move toward healing. Healing requires effort on the part of the person who is healed. They must want to be healed and they need to work at integrating the healing that they receive. I had included my brother-in-law in these depossessions.

After I learned of my brother-in-law's death, I journeyed to check in with his spirit. I have done this for others who have died and I wanted to be able to help him in his transition. At that time I helped two attached spirits to move on but there was a crowd of about twenty other suffering beings who did not desire to move on. They felt that their chances of finding another alcoholic to prey on, were so good they weren't willing to leave. Imagine the difficulty of quitting when he was surrounded by stuck spirits going, "Take a drink. Take a drink. Take a drink."

I also did a soul retrieval for him with the help of my teacher. This is only the beginning of the healing that he needs before he will be able to move from where he is. I have told my sister that I would work for her healing and she said ok but I can only offer and wait until the time is right for her.

More questions. Do I feel I should have done more to help my brother-in-law? Am I guilty of not always being a compassionate being? Am I too in need of healing that I am not fully participating in? Do I have my own addictions and attachments that bind me within the thoughts of my fellow men and women? And of course, the answer to all of these questions is yes.

I am not dead so I am still experiencing and learning. I know that we are all connected by the wonder of our thoughts and feelings. How this all works, I am not sure but I know that we create ourselves and each other by the things that occupy our mind. Perhaps, the best healing that we can do for someone is to think well of them and to know that they are on the path that they have chosen for their experience and to support them as best we can in having that experience.

These thoughts are not quite two cents worth but they will have to do until I can give you change.

Arnold and Emily

I don't remember when I first met Emily and Arnold but it had to be around the time that Virginia and I got married. They were a couple that devoted their lives to each other. Head over heels in love and everybody knew it. They both had good jobs and they enjoyed working on social causes and dancing to live music. The last time we saw Arnold alive was at a Friday night art opening of one of Virginia's pottery shows. There was a good crowd there so Arnold and Emily were there visiting and hanging out. That weekend Arnold went fishing with a friend who had a small sail boat on a small local lake. While they were fishing a gust of wind caught the sail and swung the boom around knocking Arnold out of the boat.

He never came up. He had not been wearing a life jacket and

he became entangled in the weeds. When his friend got the boat turned around he could not see any sign, Arnold was just gone. He was not located by the search and rescue people. After two days, Emily asked if I could help. When I journeyed to the lake I did not find Arnold. My spirit helpers told me that I needed to go to the lake with my drum and do a healing for Arnold so I did. I sat on the hill side on the south of the lake and drummed and chanted and called to Arnold to show where he was. A seagull was flying by, circled around and landed on the lake near the middle but on the north side. A steady breeze was blowing across the lake with small waves moving to the east. What caught my attention was the seagull. It remained stationary in the same spot as the waves moved past it. I realized that it was over the location of Arnold. I shifted my drumming and journeyed down into the water to talk to Arnold. He was so embarrassed that he didn't want to be found. My son, Chris had talked to him at the art gallery and had told him to wear his life vest when Arnold told him he was going fishing but he hadn't. I explained that he needed to think of his family and Emily and let himself be found so they could go on.

The search and rescue crew returned the next day and soon found Arnold's body. Emily never recovered and in a short period of time she came down with cancer and in spite of much healing effort she passed away. I knew that it was not the cancer that killed her but a broken heart.

I had one other person who drowned that totally refused to come up because of the regret for the stupid thing that he had done to cause his drowning and he chose to have me take him to the Lower World so he could remain where he was. His body was never recovered. His fiancé has not gotten over his passing and lives without a good relationship in her life.

The Last Lesson

For many years my friend Rick's Dad was the owner of a pawn shop. He was always doing something behind the scene to help others and over the years he would give me things. He would ask me to help with some small thing at the shop such as removing boxes of junk and I would find that the boxes were full of tools. He knew that I welded animals and bugs and flowers as garden art and many of the broken old tools ended up in the animals. But not everything in the boxes was junk as one day I discovered a silver belt buckle with turquoise inlays. One day he asked me to bring my truck and cutting torch, so I parked out back of the store and went in to see what he needed. He wanted the bicycle racks removed as the shop was not making any money for all the space they were taking. It took some doing but I ended up with a pickup load of angle iron and steel tubing.

Over the years I learned that Bob was helping a lot of people besides me. Friends have related how they would need something but couldn't afford it and they would find it later sitting on the top of their car in the parking lot. He started recycling aluminum cans and had his friends among the downtown businesses saving their cans as well. He would gather the cans, sell them, and give the money to the food bank. Most of the things that he did people didn't know about. I learned later that he lived a life of service as his job which in Hebrew is called avodah.

He would always have a joke to pass along when you saw him. Bob joined Rick and I, for golf sometimes and he would be joking and telling you about life as you went along. One Father's Day he holed a shot from about one hundred and fifty yards. It was the highlight of our golfing days. When he got cancer, everyone was sad but Bob, he remained the same affable person who was more concerned with others than he was with himself. Unfortunately, he did not recover and eventually he was on his last days in Sacred Heart Hospital. I went in to see him one more time.

When I got into the room, he was glad to see me and almost immediately told me a joke and then began the story which was my last lesson from him. He related that some functionary of the hospital had come into the room and told him that he would have to be moved into a nursing home as Medicare would no longer cover the cost. He told the person to have the financial manager come see him. When the manager came in, Bob told him that he was dying and did not want to be moved, and he wanted to negotiate the room rent. Bob reached an agreement and was not moved. After he told me the story, he told me that was my final lesson. "It is all negotiable." He passed a day later.

My Mom's Passing

I would visit Mom when I could and I once tried a technique that Michael Harner had suggested could work if the person was ready to move on. Mom just started laughing so I knew it was still too soon. It was getting where it was hard to have any type of conversation with Mom. Sometimes she would sit and look through a pile of mail on the table next to her chair. She would look at each item, stare at it for a while, and eventually would reach over and put it in a pile on her tray on the right side. When she reached the bottom of the pile on the left she would start looking at the pile on the right and place the items back to the table on the left one by one and endlessly repeat the process.

I began taking my guitar and just sitting and playing for her, mostly melodic instrumental pieces which she seemed to enjoy. Eventually she did not seem to notice or care. Some person had given her a koosh ball which had a light in it that blinked for a while after you shook the ball. Mom would sit and shake the ball, watch the blinking light, and then shake it again. And again. And again. I had a very hard time watching the Mom, who had been the president of the school board, starred as the Mom in the play "Cheaper by the Dozen" with the local theater group, and had overseen the restoration of a historic hotel, in this condition.

I decided to try a new tactic. If you showed Mom a picture of Dad she would say, "Who's that man?" She didn't know but she was interested. It had been some time since I had visited with Dad in the spirit world so I talked with Dad and suggested that he start hanging out around Mom and just keep asking, "Come on Dear, let's go for a walk."

As a bit of background, My Mom and Dad got married on the fourteenth of July in 1945. Dad had finished his Army Training in Texas and was being shipped out of Seattle to go to the Philippines. Dad had talked the Army into giving him two days leave to get off of the train in Wyoming to marry my Mom. He had it all arranged including a cabin in the woods for a honeymoon. When he got to Wyoming and got off of the train not only my Mom was there but his Mom was there and she refused to let them get married because it was Friday the thirteenth. She made them wait until the fourteenth to get married. Then she went with them to the cabin. It did not go well.

I did not make a note of the date when I talked to Dad but it was a little while maybe a few weeks, when early one morning I got a call from my sister, Mom had been fine when they had checked her earlier but at six am when they checked she had passed. When my sister was telling me about this she related that earlier that week Mom had found Dad's wedding ring and had put it on. She had also become more cheerful and communicative. Then I had the realization it was Friday the thirteenth and Mom had gone to be with Dad and Grandma could not say a thing about it. It made Mom's passing a more joyful occasion for the family.

Sheila and the Montessori School

I have a friend who is a school teacher in a Montessori School. The school moved to a new building that had previously been a church for two very different religions. The most recent was a Subud church and before that it was a Protestant church. When Sheila called me, she related that these normally well behaved children were bouncing off the walls by afternoon. She asked if I could look into the building to see what was going on. When I went there in the spirit world I was told by my spirit helpers that I would have to actually go to the building. Since the kids were flipping out every day I arranged to meet Sheila there on the next Saturday.

The Subud Church practiced a meditation that was called the Latihan. The men and women met in two different parts of the church. The men met upstairs in the main seating area of the church and the women gathered downstairs. In their meditation they practiced opening to receive. They were not specific in what they were asking to receive so all types of energies and thought forms came to entertain them. When Sheila and I went there we took drums and rattles and two types of sage and some palo santo sticks to burn. She is a good Catholic and understood the purpose of the sage. Using the bitter silver sage first and then white sage as I walked and drummed and chanted our way through every part of the building. Sheila followed behind burning the palo santo to put positive healing energy to fill the spaces we had cleared. We found one area upstairs and one area downstairs where all of these useless energies had concentrated. Each area was carefully cleared and smudged.

It was when we reached the choir loft in the upper rear level of the church that I encountered something different. This was the reason that I had to come here. A soul part of someone who had been abused and molested in the choir loft was still there. The soul part was stuck in their fear and pain so I calmed the soul part and told them I would help. I consulted with the Bear and was informed that the person was still alive in this world. Since I had no way of contacting that person, the Bear took the soul part for me to the person who was living in Vallejo, California.

When we finished the clearing and closed up the building, I told Sheila to let me know if the children still acted up, she thanked me and I have not heard from her in this regard since. She taught many more years in the building. I will suggest to anyone who is meditating to receive to be very specific about what it is you are trying to attract.

Spirits Found in Nature

When I am walking or driving out in the world there have been times when I realized that a stuck spirit was trying to get my attention. One of these, a place that I drove by a few times a month, kept trying to get my attention until I finally journeyed to the location in the Middle World. What I found was a truck driver who had lost control of a loaded cement truck while coming down a steep hill. He missed the turn at the bottom and ended up in a small creek. Unfortunately, he was pinned in the wreckage and drowned in the creek. Although the truck had been removed from the creek and he was given a proper burial, his spirit was still stuck in the creek where he drowned.

I was unsuccessful on my first attempt to convince the spirit to move on. The driver wanted his name cleared. The newspaper had blamed him for going too fast when in fact it was a mechanical failure that let the truck free wheel out of gear down the hill. On my second journey to meet with him I explained that it was in the past and the paper would never print an apology to him. He still would not agree to move on. He wanted his day in the court of public opinion. On the third journey I just gave him a choice to go now or be there forever. When I told him I was not coming back he accepted my offer for help. I am sure that he will find healing where I took him in the Upper World.

On a trip in Idaho, Virginia and I found a curiously unfinished tunnel that went through a hill so we stopped and walked into it. In one area I could see that a rock burst had collapsed a large section of the tunnel wall, as I stood there I felt a cold draft surrounding me. When I got home the next day I journeyed back to the tunnel and met the miner who was killed in the rock burst. He had given up any hope of a change in his existence and was joyfully grateful for the opportunity to move on. The tunnel was being built for a railroad that was never finished as they went broke. This caused me to remember the rock burst in Boundary Dam in one of the passage way tunnels where a miner had been killed that I saw when I was working there. I journeyed there and helped the miner and a worker who had drowned at the Dam when he fell in.

Most spirits that are stuck in the event of their death are ready and willing to accept help. Some however, have attachments to some aspect of the material world and are not willing to let go of what is holding them captive. These are usually the smokers, alcoholics, and drug addicts but not always. I found one spirit dragging a cast iron cook stove through eternity. He had hauled it up a mountain to his cabin where his mine was and he didn't want to leave it behind. He was killed when an avalanche removed his cabin from the hillside.

The other attachment type is the one that causes the most problems for the world. That is the need for revenge. In the Mideast is the heaviest concentration of violence begetting violence. I can't imagine coming to the conclusion that the right thing to do is to blow myself up trying to make the world a better place. Can you imagine being surrounded by spirits going, "Blow yourself up. Blow yourself up."? I journeyed for the Mideast many times while doing the service project asking for information about how the world could heal this problem. I was shown again and again that it has to start with the Israelis. They need to realize that they have become what they hated and despised. Then they need to atone for the harm they have visited on the Arabs.

More Dying

It was Father's Day in 2012, I was home alone working on cleaning house, while Virginia had run into town to the store. We were expecting Terry to come out to the house later. I don't remember how it started but the process of leaving the earthly vale was well started when I tried to check my blood pressure. It was 60 over 40 and I was sitting in my chair in the living room. As I drifted into altered consciousness, I sensed we were in a negotiation for what remained of my life with the spiritual hierarchy. They recognized that I needed help. I was not coping well with the shingles reoccurrence that was in the fourth year of neuropathy without pause. They agreed to help me and give me another chance. In the end I would be alive but my life was to be in service to Spirit in return.

The board of review agreed to accept that my physical limitations were responsible for my failure to complete my tasks promptly. They said that they would get me some help. When I gained consciousness, I was very shaky and my blood pressure was a little low, when I checked, not quite back to my usual 120 over 70. I was left with a periodic abnormal heart beat. I had been talked into signing up for Medicare Plan C and this was my first year of being covered. Although my Doctor ordered tests to determine what was happening United Health rejected all of the tests.

Spirit had something else in mind. One of the persons who had started learning at the Unity drum circle was in the middle of taking the Three Year Program of the Foundation and in discussion with one of the other participants she learned about John of God in Brazil. Maurah decided that she wanted to go to Brazil and did a journey to ask her spirit helpers if it was appropriate. They told her that she should go, but she needed to take me. Thus began an adventure that was completed in October of 2013 when the two of us spent two weeks being healed by Spirit in Brazil.

My shingles went away the day we arrived and when I saw John of God, he waved his hand and fixed my heart. I have had heart tests since and I have almost no possibility of a heart attack. When we came back Maurah and I started a Healing Center and I began teaching some of the advanced classes for the Foundation in addition to the basic class, "The Way of the Shaman", that I had been teaching.

In this case spirit not only saved my life on Father's Day but arranged an unbelievable experience that restored my physical body and spirit. I have a picture of me in the Spokane airport on the way out and another picture of me in the airport in Brasilia as we are leaving. It is amazing when you see the difference.

A Close Call with Death

My son Chris was here visiting and he reminded me that I should tell at least one story of bringing some one back from the brink of death. He was referring to himself. He was working on the Oregon coast and had been to visit his daughter in Vancouver, Washington when he was struck down with acute pancreatitis. He was in the hospital in Vancouver when we got the call from the ER. I immediately started sending Reiki and contacted my spirit helpers. I was told we needed to go there right away. Virginia and I threw some things in the car, asked the neighbors to feed the horses and the cats and the dog, and drove straight across the state to the hospital in Vancouver. We were met in the ICU by the Doctor who had been working on Chris. He told us he was not sure that Chris was going to make it out of the coma. He basically said that they had done all that they could and then he walked away.

Virginia and I went into the cubicle where Chris lay not moving. The room was full of monitors beeping and the IV machines were pumping him full of drugs. I knew what needed to be done as I had done it before in a different hospital. I had Virginia stand in the doorway so no one could come in and interrupt what I was doing. Listening to a drum beat in my mind, I began to dance and change into the Bear. When I had shifted consciousness I began using the Bear's claws to pull up the healing power of the earth through the levels of the hospital. When I had gathered a ball together in my claws, it was heavy enough that I could just pick it over the bed rail and drop it into Chris's abdomen. As soon as I did, Chris opened his eyes and said,

"Thanks, I could feel that, Dad." He drifted back to sleep as the monitors began reporting more normal patterns of heart beat and his temperature began dropping. It was a long hard recovery with a relapse back into the hospital but he survived and learned that he has his own debt to Spirit.

The Not Normal Year

In 2020 after the Covid crisis stabilized, I decided to go ahead with replacing my right knee that had been bothering me for sixty years. My plan was to have the surgery in the morning and walk out to go home in the afternoon. It all went well except that one of the prescribed medications that I was taking was Celebrex. I did not know that I was allergic to Celebrex until my heart started stopping. One night after waking up soaked in sweat three times, I was too scared to go back to sleep. I realized that I had no pulse when I felt myself once again getting really hot.

One of my best experiences in Brazil was learning the Rosary and having experiences when Mother Mary would visit me. I started saying the Rosary and on the third course, I felt my pulse start back up. This started about four in the morning and continued until I was able to wake my wife about seven am. Every few minutes my heart would stop and I would start the Rosary. Again and again my heart stopped and Mother Mary started it back up, until I lost count of how many times. Some have asked me why I didn't call 911. I can only say that when you are in the middle of trying to keep your heart working and about half of the time you have no pulse, my only thought was "Holy Mary, Mother of God, Pray for me now and at the hour of my death but please don't make it today."

When I was able to contact my Doctors office they told me to go to the ER. I ended up spending a day in the hospital doing tests to find out what had happened. After I stopped taking the Celebrex and it had time to work its way out of my body, I stopped having the heart stoppages but the Doctors were worried that I had damaged my heart. After all of the tests the result was no permanent damage to my heart. I still have some other side effects of the Celebrex, however. I am so grateful to Mother Mary and I know that is unusual for a good Lutheran but I haven't been a good anything for most of my life.

New Adventure

Here I am working away on recounting my experiences while working to help the spirits of the dead and I get I message from one of my granddaughters. She needs help. Her Dad had told her to get in touch with me after listening to her description of what was going on in her life. During my first consultations with my spirit helpers, I was told to ask her to send me a picture that was current. When she e-mailed the picture, I could see the spirit looking out of her eyes. In another discussion with my friends in the spirit world they explained that this spirit was going to be difficult because it didn't want to leave because it was having fun being a beautiful young girl.

My spirit helpers told me of practices that the natives had used in the past to keep the person isolated after a spirit was removed.

A spirit that was attracted to someone would not want to leave the person alone and would follow them if they could. One practice included burying the person for three days so that the spirit could not find them. The removed spirit would wither away if they did not find someone to cling to in three days. I knew that this would not work in this case and I planned to meet the spirit with compassion and convince it to leave but I wouldn't let it wander. I would take it where it needed to be.

I talked to my granddaughter on the phone and explained that I was going to bring her a Power Animal and we set a time that I would visit while she was asleep. As I prepared to do my journey, I gathered my necessary smudge, water, and fire. My special rattle asked to be included and the leg bone of a bear that is only used when directed by the Great Mother Bear asked to come along. I appreciated the reminders that I had a lot of spirit on call if needed. I put on my vest and settled in to listen to the drumming cd.

I intended to do a Middle World journey across the state to where my granddaughter was sleeping so that I could do the healing work that was necessary. I also wanted to bring her a power animal to help her through the recovery. I got to the location and found the interfering spirit and began a discussion. It was not interested in leaving but I appealed to the spirit and asked it to have compassion for my granddaughter and I would return the favor by helping it to go where it could truly be happy. The power of the Bear showed the spirit that there was another way and it relented and agreed to let me take it where it wanted to go, which was the Upper World.

After checking to see that there was no other influences that needed to be dealt with, I began finding a power animal for Trista. I found a Blue Heron and blew it in as she lay sleeping and then returned across the state to home.

As I thought about what had taken place, I realized that I had been given a reminder that what I was really supposed to be writing about was the need to see everything through the eyes of compassion. We are all just suffering beings in one way or another. When we recognize that we are not separate and only just fragments of the Unity of creation, we can learn to have compassion for all and begin to heal each other.

At the time that I began my service project my spirit helpers gave me an estimate of eight billion stuck souls as a back log of suffering beings that were accumulated through the millenniums waiting for relief. I began originally with no hope of making a difference. I just knew I had to do something if there was ever going to be a chance for peace on earth. I knew that resolving the spiritual unrest was a key to mankind being able to move forward. I pushed forward with my plan on my own when I did not find a lot of people who were willing to work with the dead and dying. I did have one person who after learning about stuck spirits at the drum circle at The Unity Center decided to change her life. She stopped coming to the drum circle and got training to work at Hospice attending to people at the end of their life. Her idea was to make sure that they did not become stuck spirits and suffering beings.

I never thought I could turn the tide but here are some numbers that surprised me when my spirit helpers told me to calculate them. I did not write down the exact start and stop dates so this is an estimate for illustration. I did the service project for ten years which is 3652 days. Since I worked one day to the Lower World for every three days that I worked to the Upper World, the Lower World total days was 913 and the Upper World total was 2739 days. When the spirits were flowing well one went through on each drum beat that I was listening to, but there was always some lag time getting started and some interruptions. So instead of the six thousand possible in a half hour, Spirit told me I averaged 4000 souls a day to the Upper World and 2750 souls a day to the Lower World. The total to the Upper World for the ten years is 10,956,000 and the total to the Lower World is 2,510,750. For a total of 13,466,750 souls that are no longer stuck.

When I ended it was because I had been replaced by a permanent opening that functions the same way that I had. If you show up you can go through. It operates with three days and one day in the same pattern of Upper and Lower Worlds that I used. The difference is the opening is twenty four hours, seven days a week. It has not yet been ten years since the open door was created but at ten years of elapsed time with 192,000 per day to the Upper World and 132,000 a day to the Lower World, the totals will be 525,888,000 to the Upper World and 120,516,000 to the Lower World and a total of 646,404,000 souls that are freed.

This is why Spirit wanted me to write this out, about 150,000 people died every day in 2017, the last year that I found a number. It is probably higher now with the Covid. If a lot of the current deaths end up being stuck spirits, it will slow the progress but progress is being made. If we worked at eliminating violent deaths, it would be possible to clear the earth of stuck and suffering beings in less than a hundred years. If we allow the violence to keep increasing the open door will just maintain the status quo. It is up to us to grow into responsible intelligent beings so that we can limit the number of stuck spirits being created.

What I Have Learned

Death comes in many ways and the result is not the same depending on how the death occurred. Sudden death due to violent causes can leave the spirit stuck in the circumstances of their death. These spirits need help to escape their circumstances. The process of helping stuck spirits is relatively easy and is something that anyone could learn to do. Stuck spirits can cause emotional and physical difficulties to people that they become attached to. Many of the world's problems in areas such as the Mideast can be attributed to the influence of the numerous stuck spirits wanting revenge.

People who die with a strong belief system will find that their beliefs will lead them directly to where they want to go. People who die suddenly from heart attacks or cerebral aneurism can be in this category. These are deaths that lack the violence that can cause a stuck spirit. When a person takes a long time dying their spirit helpers have time to educate them by taking them across for a visit before they actually pass. Shamans can also help during this time if desired.

Some people will wait to die until all of the family has gathered around them and said their goodbyes, while others will wait until the person who is sitting with them leaves for a moment to get coffee or go to the bathroom and pass while they are alone. Death is an individual experience or is shared by hundreds when a disaster strikes. We can plan our passing and prepare for it but death may not cooperate and intervene suddenly. A strong relationship to Spirit regardless of the description and names that are used can protect you from death and help you through the process.

Addictions and desires can interfere with a peaceful passing. Some people have tasks that they feel they need to complete, while others live like there is no tomorrow and sometimes they don't have a tomorrow but their name is on the Darwin Award list.

I believe that the difference in the number of stuck spirits that want to go to the Upper World compared to the Lower World is due to the cultural difference of the groups of people. Where people live in a shamanic culture not as many become stuck spirits, but also the shamans work to help the people who have passed so that they are not stuck for long if they did die a violent death. I learned this when I was helping to move spirits after the tsunami in Southeast Asia. I met Thai shamans who asked me to only work on tourists as they would take care of their own people. I was happy to oblige and glad to see so many doing the work.

I have learned that consciousness is all that there really is. Everything is conscious or it would not or could not exist. All matter is comprised subatomic particles given funny names by physicists to make up for all of the math they were required to learn. Each of these subatomic particles could be any of the other subatomic particles and their life time is very short. What causes them to be reborn as the same particle is consciousness. Without consciousness all matter would decay back into undefined dark matter. Consciousness is entirely fluid and can be attached to matter or it can be completely free from matter. Matter can't remain without consciousness reminding the particles who they are. Our power of creation is to imagine things that were not here previously, as they become conscious, they form.

This is the End

If you find this essay interesting and you would like to do some investigation on your own, ask to meet the Spirit of Humanity. All humans are part of the Spirit of Humanity so you don't have to journey or go anywhere in the spirit world. Just listen to a steady drum beat that is monotonous at about 200 beats per minute. As you listen to the drum, ask a question that you personally can't know the answer to, but some previous human does know the answer. Ancestral questions can work well, but it can be anything you really want to know.

Spirit has reminded me that I am still in their debt. I am grateful for this opportunity to present my experiences and hopefully many will find it useful.

Strive to live in harmony and peace.

Leon

BATTLE AT THE
WELL OF SOULS

———————— ✿ ————————

As AN ADDED BONUS I have attached an addendum that is a
work of fiction that I wrote to illustrate the problem of the vast
number of suffering beings. It is fiction and a work of imagination.
At one time I was trying to sell a TV series about shamanic work
and this would have been the pilot for the series. Note some
additions from actual practice for Hollywood.

A paved two lane country road followed along the river, which
was low even for this time of year. A flock of quail crossed the
road in front of him and he slowed and watched the little ones
run to keep up. After about five miles, the road forked. He chose
the right turn and began climbing along the side of a ridge that
led away from the river. He continued to climb in elevation and
the ridge he was following met and became part of a much larger
ridge that climbed toward a granite topped peak in the north. He

wasn't going that far. His goal was to reach the lake that lay at the base of the peak.

He turned off onto a narrow gravel road that continued to climb. After about a mile, the road leveled out and became a bulldozed parking lot that was roughly graveled with the broken rock that had been gnawed from the hillside. He slowed to a crawl and parked on the east side of the lot. The old faded red pickup that he drove did not lock securely but he wasn't concerned. Nothing that he had was worth stealing. He had a hunter orange backpack that was thirty years old, loaded with more stuff than he ever used. He looked around as he got his pack out of the back of the truck and prepared to start hiking.

This was not a difficult hike. He had been here several times over the years but it had been a long time since his last trip up here. There were few changes to the trailhead. The sign board was even more decrepit. If that was possible. This area was not a popular destination. That was why he came here. He didn't want to be disturbed. For him it was the destination not the hike that mattered. There was something about the trees and the color of the lake water and the quiet that told him there were special things going on here. He came here because it felt like the trees and the rocks were alive and talking to him.

He settled the pack onto his back and adjusted the straps. Being in the barn all of those years was not good to the condition of the pack. The clips were rusty and hard to maneuver, making sliding them difficult. Once the pack was firmly on his back and resting on his shoulders, a good feeling of being capable came over him as memories of the times he had carried the pack to the top of successive peaks came back to him. He shook himself like a dog and walked over to the start of the trail.

The first part was steeply downhill until you came to the lake. Old cedar trees were the primary tree in this spot. Their roots made steps where the duff was worn away on the trail that zigzagged down. He always stayed on the trail, even though there were plenty of places where others had short cut across the switchbacks. He took pride in walking without dragging his feet or scuffing the ground. He liked to make as little evidence of his passing as possible. It was a form of meditation to him this walking. He had enjoyed being out walking in the woods from the time he was a two year old. He drove his mother nuts with his wandering off. Was that what he was doing now, wandering off?

The sights that came as he walked, prompted awe. God, this place is beautiful. Why has it been so long since he came up here? Look at that lake. It is still as clear as it was. You can see over forty feet into the water, which is the most wonderful color of blue that gets darker as the water deepens. He shifts his pack and stops to take a break and drink a little water. He didn't bring much water but he has his filter. He had decided to sterilize it in chlorine bleach after finding it in his pack when he was preparing to leave. Was he preparing to leave or just go on a hike? Right now he didn't know.

What had his wife meant when she said get a job or I'll find someone who has a job? Did he care anymore? Maybe that was what he was here trying to figure out. Shit, he had a lot of things on his mind. The trail came almost down to the lake and then turned to the right and began following the first finger of the lake.

A map of the lake looked like a hand with the fingers reaching between the ridges that led up to the granite peak. The trail went along the side of the first finger and around the end then started climbing the ridge on the other side. When you crossed over the ridge to see the second finger, you were above a cliff of sheer stone that dropped straight down to the lake. The view here was of the lake in front of you and another mountain to the west on the other side of the lake. Here it was possible to see how deep the glacier had carved the lake. You were looking straight down into forever as the blue kept getting darker with the depth.

The trail continued on along the second finger, and did not descend in elevation but stayed relatively level. The trail was wide through this part and had the look of an old unused logging road. What could he have done to avoid being fired? He just didn't fit into the bureaucracy of local government. Made the mistake of thinking but not smart enough to keep his ideas to himself. He kept assuming that people want things to get better. The trail stayed high along the side of the ridge and where it went around the end of the second finger you could look down to the lake and a camp spot that was down next to the lake.

He never camped in this spot or even walked down to the lake here. It was real pretty but it wasn't his spot. Too close to civilization for his comfort. The trail became no more than a narrow footpath. There were places on the exposed rocky parts of the ridges where the trail crossed a steep slope of talus. Hard and rocky like his relationship with his sister. He couldn't afford to go to her funeral last month when she was killed in the car wreck. He had to borrow money from a friend to send flowers. They never spoke anyway. Why should it upset him that she was no longer there to judge and evaluate him? He was never as good or as smart or as dedicated or as organized or as any damn thing she happened to be talking about at the time. Did it bother him that he never said goodbye or was it that he wished they could have reconciled their differences? Whatever their differences were? He couldn't remember what led to their mutual disaffection.

He couldn't remember any time past early childhood when they did get along. Why did she die anyway? It was not smart of her to have been driving late at night in that neighborhood. As he remembered what he knew of the accident report that told of her death, the trail wound down into a deep green corner of forest that was firs and hemlocks mixed with the occasional older pine that usually stood high on the ridge. The cool green was a comforting tone that led him to stop and rest for a short spell. He did not take his pack off but sat so the frame was supported on the rocky hillside and made a back rest for him to recline into.

"It's too quiet," he thought. "Where are the birds?" As if to answer him two ravens began cawing back and forth as they flew high overhead and disappeared over the ridge. There was no room for a camp here and it was a long way down to the water if you did try to camp here. This was not his spot anyway, so he stood up and secured his waist strap. He liked the feel of the pack bearing down on his shoulders. He started up the trail. The ridge between the second and third finger of the lake was exposed and rocky with a few very old pine trees along the top of the ridge. He remembered these trees. They had gotten his attention on his second trip through here. How many years ago was that? It didn't matter. The point was the old pines on this ridge were maybe five hundred years old while the rest of the trees in the area were maybe two hundred years old at best. The whole east side of the lake had never been logged so what happened here?

He had been standing here pondering that question when the explanation appeared in his head as if a friend had just whispered a secret into his ear. The pines survived because their branches were up high and the thick layers of bark that covered the trunk insulated them from the lightening fires that were caused periodically on the exposed ridge. That time he shook his head and looked around. It made sense when you saw the evidence. It was all right in front of you but where had that thought come from. How did he know that? As the trips to the lake occurred over the years, he found that he sometimes got answers to problems that he couldn't understand otherwise. As he became more aware of this phenomenon, he started asking questions, deliberately trying to determine where the answer was coming from. He was never able to figure it out. It felt like the tree had said something or the words in his mind had come leaking out of the rocky outcrop he was admiring.

He remembered all of that now, as he looked at the trees, but he kept walking. It was not that much further to his spot. His special spot where he always camped. When you cross over the ridge and begin walking along the side of the third finger you are fairly high above the lake. This is the north side of the ridge and it is much more moist and green. New young firs and aspens compete in one area that you pass through. He follows the trail down into the woods and keeps going east until the trail turns to the north at the end of the finger and breaks into a wide clearing of old growth duff surrounding the base of well separated large old cedars. These trees are probably as old as the pines up on the ridge. This is his spot. It is down at the elevation of the lake so it isn't hard to get water for cooking and cleanup.

He always puts his tent in between these two particular trees that are off to the east side of the trail. There are two camp sites with fire pits just west of the trail but he likes to sleep away from where he has his fire and does his cooking. He was not planning on doing much cooking on this trip, just his corn soup. He didn't care that much about eating and unless this trip gave him some answers he didn't care much for living. He got busy putting up his tent and arranging his camp to suit his fancy. Nobody here to criticize or suggest that he could have done it better. Nobody at all. It was nice and quiet.

He planned to camp tonight and walk to the north end of the lake tomorrow morning. He wanted to see the large white pine that dwarfed all the other trees for miles around. He hoped it was still standing. After he finished setting up camp he began scavenging wood for a fire. It was safe even if the weather was dry and no one would see the smoke way out here anyway. He found that he had to go up the old dry creek bed for a ways to find much down dry wood. Enough people had camped here over the years to keep the close easy to get wood used up. He saw a fallen dead tree but had to climb over a large rotting log to get to it. As he dropped to the ground on the other side of the log something caught his eye. It was a hollow stump that was rotted away on the inside but was a complete shell on the outside. As he looked down into the hollow stump, he saw that the roots leading away from the stump were hollow as well. You could look down the roots as they twisted and turned into the mountain side. In fact, if you leaned over and put your head in the stump you could see a long way down this root. As he did this he was overcome with a feeling of vertigo and felt as if he was dizzy. He tumbled down into the root.

I'm falling, what the hell is going on. I am tumbling, rolling down this moss lined tunnel. At last, I catch myself and stop my headlong plunge. I am sitting on dark moss. Everything around me is covered with the same dark green moss. I stand up and look back the way I came tumbling down. It is dark that way. I can't see anything. I must have fallen past a corner. In the other direction is a faint glow. I am able to walk towards the glow as the floor is not slippery. As I travel around a bend in the tunnel that I am in, the light keeps increasing. I can see something up ahead. I approach a gate that is across the tunnel. It has a simple slide latch to operate to open the gate. A sign next to the latch says "You must choose to enter here. Please close the gate".

I stand there wondering why would I choose to enter and then immediately wondering why wouldn't I want to enter. Finally, I thought, "You don't really care what happens to you anyway. Go on in." I slid the latch and swung the gate open. After I had crossed through, I turned and pulled the gate closed and slid the latch home. "Where to next?" I thought and started down the tunnel. The light seemed to get brighter and the tunnel was opening wider. There seemed to be a path that led to the left side and as I walked around the corner on that side, the tunnel wall fell away and I was in a beautiful meadow on an open hill side. I looked across the meadow at something that was moving in the grass and flowers.

I moved towards the other side of the meadow to see what was moving. It was a bear eating the flowers of dandelions that were blooming in the patch of grass that covered the top of the hill. I was calmly watching the bear in fascination, when the wind shifted and instead of blowing towards me it blew towards the bear. The bear caught my scent and turned towards me and snarled a deep growl that shook my bones. I was trapped. There were no trees nearby and no other cover. The breeze blew again, pushing my scent right into the bear's face. Now not a growl, but a roar accompanied him as he stood up on his hind legs. "Oh, my god, he is two or three feet taller than I am." I felt my knees shaking as with three quick bounds across the space between us, the bear was on me.

I felt no pain and I watched in awe, as one swipe of his right paw removed my left arm from my side. I didn't fall because he clamped my head and face in his jaws and I watched my head come ripping off the top of my body. The bear dropped and tore my stomach cavity open devouring everything. Still no pain and I wondered how I could be aware of this. I'd seen my head crushed in a giant bear's jaw. I continued to watch in amazement as the bear deliberately went about the business of eating every last morsel that had been my body. As I was watching this, I became aware that I was watching this from the bear's perspective. I was in the bear. Not just my flesh and bones but me. My spirit was in the bear. I was a part of the bear.

When he finished eating, the bear, no I, no we, walked away.

I felt awkward moving on all four feet but we covered ground in a hurry, I wondered if I could talk to the bear. Was he conscious of me here in his body or did he only know the meat?

"Oh bear, where are we going in such a hurry?" I ask in some fashion that was more than thought. It had intention attached to it.

"I am going back to my den so I can take a nap. I just had a big lunch." the bear replied and again I wasn't sure how that it worked. It just did.

"Funny how you should mention that lunch. I was sort of attached to it. That was my body. Do you understand what happened to me?"

"You have merged with the spirit of Bear."

"Don't you mean a bear?"

"No, I mean the spirit of Bear. All of the bears, united and uninterrupted, in common, and in total. The spirit of Bear."

"How could you eat me and I can still be here talking to you? Where am I?"

"You are me and I am you."

"What is going to happen?"

"I am going to take a nap."

We had indeed come to the bears den. He ducked down and crawled under a fallen log into a grassy nest. This was not a winter den but temporary quarters that were good enough to take a nap. The bear did not seemed concerned about me sharing his head space as he curled right up and went to sleep. I didn't fall asleep as the bear dreamed. I went into his dream. The first dream came soon after the bear laid down. I was in the City Hall in my former boss's office. I could hear him talking on the phone but he was unaware of my presence. It was clear from his conversation that he was talking about me as if I had died not been fired. I tried to get his attention but I could shout and jump around to no avail. I thought that he should have clearly seen that I was not dead but he kept talking on the phone describing how fortunate he was in firing me because now my wife wouldn't get anything from the City's insurance.

I thought about asking the bear about this and I was transported right back to the bear. He was still sound asleep. I wondered how long bears sleep after a big meal. It was hard thinking of yourself as being a big meal. I next found myself in our house watching my wife cry. She was with her two best friends, who were trying to help her but she was inconsolable. I went up to her friend, Pat, and touched her on the shoulder so that she would turn around and see me. She gave a shudder and said "Should I turn the heat up? It seems a little cold in here."

"Yes, do turn it up. I haven't been able to get warm since they called with the news about finding his body." I walked around the room and stood directly in front of my wife. I wanted her to see that I was not dead. Instead I heard her say, "If only I hadn't said those things to him about leaving him for a man with a job. He wouldn't have gone on this foolish trip. I never wanted to leave him. I just wanted to be able to pay the bills again." She collapsed into tears again. I wanted to hug her and tell her that everything was fine. I wasn't dead. Maybe I was dead. I'd been eaten by a bear. I couldn't stand watching her cry and called to the bear.

I found myself back at the bear and he was grumbling about

being disturbed. "I don't want you to bother me until I'm finished with my nap so go away." I waited and looked around. He was quickly back dreaming and I was caught in that dream as well.

It wasn't something that I could suggest as Saturday afternoon entertainment. I watched my sister's car wreck. I saw her making her way carefully down the street while another car was careening down the cross street at a high rate of speed. Just as the light turned green and she slowly entered the intersection, the other car plowed into the driver's door of her car. She was killed instantly. I watched as the pieces of car settled out of the air and rained down onto the street. Her car rolled to a stop and I watched as her spirit rose out of her shattered body and wandered away down the street. She didn't even look back. It looked like she was trying to walk home as that was the way she went. I went back to the bear.

When I got to the bear's den under the tree, he wasn't there. Sitting in his place was a Native-American about my age, who was wearing a large headdress that fanned out across the top of his head. It looked like it was made out of cedar and was carved with strange designs. "Where's the bear?" I asked.

He replied, "You are the bear. Look at yourself."

I looked down at arms, covered with fur, ending in heavy claws. A sad heavy growl filled my chest and I roared as the sorrow of being dead and now being a bear overcame me.

"Easy," the native said. "It is not as bad as it seems. You came here seeking help. We just want to help you get through the problems in your life."

"Who are you? Why do you want to help me? I never asked to be a bear."

"I'm called Hnlamqe', which is bear in our tongue. I want to help you because you have been coming to this place seeking help and you have always respected our brothers the trees. Nobody asks to be a bear. It is a gift of spirit that is offered to those who have the wisdom and the power to use it correctly."

"I don't have any wisdom and power. What do you mean about trees being brothers?"

"The trees are, as all things are, brought into existence by the power of the inhabiting spirit. Therefore, they are another of our brothers. We are brothers in the bear so I will help you with what you need to do."

"What is it that I'm supposed to do? I came up here to figure out my life."

"You expressed three problems as you were walking up here. The loss of your job, the relationship with your wife, and the death of your sister. You have been given three visions to guide you in your choices."

"Those three dreams were visions to guide my life?" I asked. "I never wanted to leave my wife and I'm glad that she didn't really want me to leave but I don't want her to suffer like that. Why couldn't I make myself known? Wouldn't it help her to know I was still alive."

"You are still alive but you will never be the same. What you experienced in those dreams was what it feels like to be a suffering being. You watched your sister die and watched her become a suffering being. You know what it feels like from your experience in the dreams."

"What do you mean by she became a suffering being?"

"When a person dies a sudden traumatic death, their spirit doesn't have time to prepare and make the proper transition to the Upper or Lower world. They are trapped in the Middle world as a suffering being. In some cases, they don't even know that they are dead. You experienced what it is like. You are trapped and no one can see or hear you. You are there until some person who is still alive helps to free you."

"How can someone help to free someone they know? Can I help my sister? What happens to the ones who don't get help?" I was full of questions now. How could this be the way things were? Nobody had ever told me about suffering beings.

"Some people pray and offer prayers for their loved ones. It is effective after time. It takes energy to move a spirit from the Middle world. In the condition you are in now, you can go and look for your sister and take her through the barrier yourself. There is an area that the spirits go to and wait for someone to help them. The accumulation of spirits is in the millions because your modern man does not understand these things."

"What do I have to do to help my sister? I don't want her to remain as a suffering being. How can I find her? What is this barrier that you are talking about?"

"Easy, one thing at a time. I'll take you from here into the Middle world and I'll switch your appearance back so your sister will recognize you. Then you will have to search for her. You can try calling to her but she may not hear you or listen to you because she is still confused about her state of being. After spirits have been there for a few hundred years they start to figure out what they need to do. That is why it is so hard to help someone with just prayers. The person you're trying to help is so confused they don't know you are helping them. You may have to talk to your sister so she understands.

"Let's get started. You can explain things as we go."

"You are the shaman and I am the helping spirit so I follow your direction."

"I'm not a shaman. I want to help my sister."

"You are a shaman or you wouldn't have been able to turn into the bear. You have to be a shaman to be able to help your sister. If you were not a shaman you wouldn't be able to travel between worlds and here you are in the Lower world so you must be a shaman."

"I guess I will understand some of this some time. Let's go find my sister."

I felt more than saw that we were moving. The scene in front of me faded away to black and I felt a cool air moving past me. It was like being on an open elevator and you were moving up through layers of cloud. When I could see again, the world was a flat plain of drifting red sand as far as I could see. There was an orange sun hanging low in the sky. Somehow I knew that this sun never changed and this place always looked just like this.

"Why are we here?" I asked.

Hnlamqe' answered, "We are following her trail. When you saw her leaving the accident, she was trying to go home. Now she is just wandering. She came here but she is gone now."

Again it seemed to be dark and we were moving again through some type of cloud layer. "I want to find my sister, Elizabeth Miller, who was in a car accident," I pronounced out loud. I wasn't sure why I did that but all of a sudden I was moving fast. I don't want the chance to compare for sure but this felt like I was on the Space Shuttle on lift off. We were moving fast. What I saw made me think we were traveling into space. "Where are we?" I asked, as we slowed down.

"We are at the outer edge of the Middle world. This is where the spirits who can't cross over accumulate."

The view in front of me was gray. Gray as far as I could see. All there was, was gray. I went closer and I could see movement in the gray. I focused on one area of the gray that was closest and then I saw the movement was caused by spirits. Each spot of gray was another spirit who was a trapped suffering being. It was overwhelming to imagine. I could never find my sister in such a throng. I called out in agony "Elizabeth, Elizabeth, Elizabeth Miller."

My cry seemed to energize the spirits close to me. Suddenly all the spirits closed in around me. "Life, there is life here, set me free, help me, please. You've got power. You can help us. Set us free." It was bedlam. The voices came all at once and from all over. I reeled back from one side to have the noise double on the other side. There was no relief.

"Stop," I cried. "I will talk to one of you at a time. You," I pointed at the spirit directly in front of me. "What is your name?"

It was suddenly quiet. The moving cloud of gray in front of me calmed to reveal a middle aged women. "Mary Franklin," she answered. "Will you help me escape this place?" She looked at me with such a long pity me look that I couldn't look away.

"I'll help you, if you can help me find my sister. Her name is

Elizabeth Miller. If you or anybody else helps me find her, I will help everybody that helps me." Like a large rock dropped in a pond, my remarks started a wave of excitement that radiated in all directions. The mass of gray pulsed with ripples and then a ripple began coming back from one edge. I watched it build as it came toward me.

"She's here. Come this way." The ripple washed over me. I was amazed at how fast my request had been answered. I started in the direction that I had seen the ripple come from. The spirits parted in front of me and I was drawn to her.

"Elizabeth," I called out and she turned to look at me.

"How did you get here? You're not dead are you?"

"I don't think I'm dead yet. I really don't understand how I got here but I came to help you. I couldn't believe that you were killed. It was so sudden. I couldn't even go to the funeral. I wished we had talked more. We've been so distant and now I'll miss you forever."

"It's okay, now that I'm dead, I know you have to do something every day to stay in touch. I didn't plan on dying but I wasn't planning to live either. Now I wish I had filled every moment with something memorable, because when you are dead all you have is memories."

I tried to reach around her and hug her, but I reached through her instead. She started laughing and I realized that she was going to be fine. If I could get her out of this place, she was going to be fine. I could live with that. "Hnlamqe', what do I have to do to get her out of here?"

"You have to take her through the barrier surrounding the Middle world and then through another barrier into the Upper world. Once she is in the Upper world there will be people to meet her and take her through the processing that starts her on her path again. The bigger question is how are you going to help all of the people that you promised?"

"What is the nature of these barriers that you keep talking about?" I wanted to know. "How can I get through them.?"

"You are alive so you have enough energy to penetrate the barrier. Think of it as a semi-permeable membrane. Most suffering beings don't have enough energy to push through the barrier. The ones that slip through, don't have enough energy to get into the Upper world and they are taken by the dragons."

"What dragons? You never said anything about dragons."

The dragons are in the space of outer darkness between the Middle and Upper world. They wait to feed on the spirits that escape the Middle world."

"Why didn't you tell me there was going to be dragons?"

"You told me to explain it to you as we went along. We are coming to the point when you will have to deal with the dragons. That is why I mentioned it. If you are going to help all of those people you promised you can't take them one at a time. If you just had your sister you could carry her across and open the barrier into the Upper world for her. You promised to help a lot of people. You won't live long enough to take them across one at a time."

"Let's go look at this barrier you keep talking about." We start moving but it is not like when the way opened up for me to get to my sister. Now every spirit around wants to move with us so they won't miss their chance to get set free. When I get to the barrier, I am struck by how much the barrier is like a soap bubble. It seems to shimmer with waves of colors. The gray forms of spirits push against it to no avail. They can't penetrate it. I step up to the barrier and reach out my hand. I feel something that is similar to a balloon but as I push on it my hand goes through. I follow my hand as if my momentum carried me through. I find myself in dark space. When I look up above me thirty or forty feet, I see another membrane but this one is white and cottony looking. I turn back to the membrane that I just came through and in front of me are three large dragons. They actually look like the story book dragons I am familiar with. Their eyes are set wide toward the top of a narrow head with flaring nostrils and a large mouth. They don't seem pleasant. Noise appears in my brain that reminds me of listening to static on the radio late at night. Out of the whistling, whirling, screeching of the noise, thoughts emerge.

"We are not happy when a shaman sets a spirit free."

It is impossible to get a fix on the size of these dragons. They flow and expand around me. I am never sure where each one is exactly. "I don't think I care if you are happy or not. Who are you anyway?"

"We are the rulers of Earth and all must do our wishes." They don't seem happy. They float up in front of me and expand to an immense size.

"What does it matter to you if these spirits are set free?"

"You are denying us the opportunity of a snack. We enjoy the smooth taste of gray spirit."

"Then you are nothing more than a scavenger, like a jackal or a vulture. You don't sound like the rulers of anything." The whirring screeching static in my mind increased exponentially. I staggered from the volume of the noise in my mind. It was the worst form of tinnitus imaginable. I quickly realized that other than expressing their unhappiness, the dragons were actually powerless to hurt me. "If you like the taste of gray spirit why don't you reach through and help yourself. You claim are in charge. Show me your power and open up the barrier."

The noise drops and becomes a simpering "We can't. We have to wait for an unsuspecting spirit to slip through. That is why we hate it when one gets away."

"Then you are really going to be upset because I am going to help several thousand move to the Upper world today."

"If you open up the barrier, we will get every one of the spirits that tries to cross. You know you have to take them across in your body or some type of carrier for protection."

"I don't think I need to divulge my plan to you. You are nothing more than ugly hyenas. You just make noise." I turned away from the dragons and stepped back through the barrier to meet my sister and numerous anxious spirits.

"We never see anyone come back from meeting the dragons. You must have real power to talk to them," one of the spirits said.

"They have no power of their own. They have only the power that people give them with their fear. The same is true of all tyrants. Hnlamqe', can you help me to use my body to bridge the space between the two worlds? It seems to me that things like distance and size that are related to dimension are not fixed in this reality."

"That is so. I can help you. What are you planning on doing?"

"I want my body to be a funnel from this world to the Upper

world. If the spirits pass through me, they are not exposed and the dragons can't get them."

"I can help but you will have to hold the barriers open yourself. I can't assist in that. The spirits will be able to pass through you only as long as you can hold both ends open."

"Elizabeth, come here and hold onto me. I am going to take you to the Upper world. Dad will be there to meet you. I'm so sorry that I wasn't a better brother."

"Johnny, Johnny, you are wonderful now. I would have been trapped forever, in this gray mass if you hadn't come to me. I don't know how you did it but I'll be grateful forever. I'll send you some luck in finding a job when I get to heaven."

"Thanks, I don't know what I'm going to do but I feel a lot better about being able to choose what I want my life to be. I'll remember what you said about planning to live. Hnlamqe' is pushing me to get going and you get to be first. I love you, goodbye."

I reach up and push my right arm through the barrier. Elizabeth is with me in spirit. My hand reaches the barrier to the Upper world and touches the cloud like softness. I push through so my head and shoulders reach into the Upper world. My right arm is holding the barrier open. Hnlamqe' has anchored my feet in the Middle world. My legs are spread holding the barrier open. My body bridges the gap between the two worlds. Elizabeth flows up out of the top of my head and walks away into the Upper world. I can see her rushing to meet Dad.

As soon as she is gone, Hnlamqe' leads Mary Franklin over and through the opening between my legs. She flows up and through me and pops out of the top of my head. This begins the process of freeing as many trapped suffering beings as we can. Hnlamqe' leads them in and directs traffic. They pass through me as quickly as blinking an eye and pop out the top of my head and walk away without looking back. It is a struggle to maintain my focus but I have to concentrate on keeping my feet spread and my right arm opening in place. At times I get a glimpse of one of the spirits as they flow past. There was a period when the spirits who passed were all Viet Nam era soldiers from both sides. There was a group of Chinese who were killed when the railroad tunnel they were building collapsed. Mostly, I have no time to notice them all. At the end my right shoulder was cramped and locked into position. I stayed as long as I could but eventually I had to stop. I couldn't hold the bridge any more.

Hnlamqe' stopped the flow in at my feet and I collapsed back into the Middle world grayness as the last spirit cleared the top of my head. "How did we do? Did we get everyone through that helped find Elizabeth?" I questioned.

"You got a few hundred extra as well. They are going to be busy up there processing that many spirits. It is a good thing that you have done."

"I can't do anything for all of the rest of these here."

"You can come back sometime if your heart has compassion for these spirits. Now you know how to help them."

"I need to find my way back. I'm going to have to get home to my wife."

"I'll take you back to the tunnel that you came in. Remember, we are brothers in the bear. I'll give you a song so you can call me for help anytime you need it. You can also talk to the trees where you live. You don't need to drive all the way up to this lake. Although, I am glad you did. I've enjoyed meeting you. Not enough of my people come this way anymore. Here's your tunnel."

"Thank you for your help. I wish I could repay you some way."

"You can. Keep working as a shaman to help relieve suffering. It all makes a difference. You might not see the immediate results but if you are working in a positive manner something positive will happen."

"I don't know anything about being a shaman."

"You do what you just did. You act out of compassion with knowledge and the assistance of spirit. Your heart determines the outcome."

"If you help me, I'll do it." No reply comes and I turn and look back at the meadow. There is no sign of Hnlamqe' but I see the tail end of a bear disappearing over the top of the hill. I walk back into the tunnel and come to the gate. The sign on this side says "Please come again," and "Close the gate." I start to become apprehensive after going around the corner after the gate. I can't see what is up ahead. I am expecting to start climbing up the slope that I tumbled down. I held my hand in front of me when I couldn't see clearly enough. My feet were following the path, when suddenly I tripped over a root and pitched forward. I thought, "What the hell?" as I continued to fall without hitting the floor or ground.

Something furry and quick like a chipmunk ran across his

neck and he awoke with a start. He is lying next to a hollow tree stump. His mind swarms with memories. Had he been dreaming? It is going to get dark soon and it will be cool. He gets up and begins to gather wood for his campfire.

THE PRINCIPLES OF SOCIALIST ANARCHY

❋

By Hayward Crowell

There is a better way to operate human society.

We are witnessing the failure of the current human civilization.

THE TWO STATEMENTS ABOVE ARE true. What we choose to do about the on going failure of human society is up to every human on this planet. We all need to operate with a different relationship with the natural world if we are going to survive as a species. A new awareness is forming and the children of today are the beginning of a new understanding in how to a have relationship with a planet. The time will come when we recognize that the inventions of the means of commerce and investing are just that. Stocks, bonds, loans, deeds, insurance, trusts, mutual funds and every other scheme were invented as way for one entity to gain an advantage over another or to receive income without labor.

If we were to pattern human society on the laws of nature and not on the structure of human law we would be able to live in harmony the world over. The trees in the north never feel the need to wage war on the trees of the south. The reason is because the northern trees are not seeking an advantage over the southern trees. All the struggle in human society is over money and power. If we choose to grow in our understanding of nature and we begin the process of establishing a relationship to nature based on the recognition that all things are part of the conscious emanation of the creator, then we will start making the changes that are necessary if humans are to remain a viable species on this planet. Our current behavior is insuring our destruction as we pollute the air we breathe, the water we drink, and the soil we grow our food on. We are doomed to inherit the results of these practices for ever more. The pollutants become more and more widely distributed as the chemical factories continue to produce untold billions of gallons of solvents, paints, varnishes, resins, glues, weed killers, bug killers and people killers that we should stop immediately but won't. There is a way to live that doesn't require these things that are currently more harmful than useful. The sustainable permaculture type of approach should be adopted universally when doing any design or planning of new or improved facilities of any kind.

When a need is noticed and someone acts to fulfill that need there is an exchange on many levels. In the way our current economic system functions these exchanges have been designed to always take from the poor and give to the rich. That is the basis of capitalism. The rich claim ownership of the resources of the earth and then insist that the poor extract the resources at minimum wage. Then the moneyed class requires interest for the debt that the poor accumulate because they can never get ahead of the game for even a minute. They dream of winning the lotto as their salvation as it is the only thing that they know that will get them caught up on the bills.

Our goal of living in harmony with nature will be facilitated by adopting a means of relating to each other that does not give one person an advantage over others. This means that everyone is truly equal in all opportunities. It is hard now for people to envision this type of society. There are no prisons because no laws can be broken when there are no laws. Yet everyone has enough of what they need and they are free to spend a lot of their time in pursuit of learning or leisure. They are also free to create whatever they desire in art, music, gardening, writing, building, or anything else. It is not an impossible dream. It is the result of living in harmony with the laws of nature.

This type of society would be stable and unhurried without a time table or annual budgets. The primary axiom would be that nothing can be owned. All things are recognized as being a conscious creative part of the ongoing process that forms matter and creates galaxies. Every grain of sand is just as alive as every human being. Since everything is free and conscious in its own right it follows that nothing can be owned. Once we have an understanding of this first axiom then we can begin to realize that yes everything is but how that thing expresses itself is how well it serves the purpose for which it was created. Please note that in the previous sentence and from now on the word thing

THE SPIRIT OF HUMANITY

includes all things including humans, animals, plants, and rocks. It also includes everything man made such as concrete, telephone poles, and ice cream. As each thing grows in understanding of the greater purpose of the cosmos, the thing begins to consciously participate in the design of the future. That is my purpose here. You are already a part of the future by reading this and allowing a new idea to sprout in your consciousness.

How do we get to the end result of humans recognizing that the best that they can do to improve their own personal situation is to act to improve the situation of all of the people around them? We need to have some guiding principles to lead us in making the right choices. We will want to learn methods that work for us and then help others to learn also. It is necessary to educate everyone, as you can't leave out the ones you don't like if we are going to succeed in changing humanities relationship to the world.

What are the principles that we can use to think correctly about the situations we face? We need to change all aspects of human society, so how do we proceed to do that without descending into total chaos. First recognize that the way we are currently living is close to chaos already so we will be taking steps that are tending toward order because we are seeking harmony. The principles that we will use to guide us are called the Principles of Socialist Anarchy.

Why Socialist Anarchy? What is it and what does it mean? Socialist Anarchy does not exist as a political party that you can join. It is a descriptive term to denote a philosophy that is based on socialist ideas but without the imposition of the forces of a government. Abraham Lincoln talked about a government of the people, by the people, and for the people. Unfortunately, what we have is a government of the corporations, by the corporations, and for the corporations. The debates in Congress on health care made it abundantly clear that the interests of the people are not being represented. Even the President is so wholly owned by the corporations that he abandoned any thought of a public option. We do not have a government that is interested in the people. The people will learn to free themselves from the need for government as they learn to mimic the naturally processes in the way that they live.

To reach a place where government isn't necessary we need to begin free ourselves of the necessity of our fears.

Socialist ideas are based on the understanding that each person is as important as any other person. We were all born and we will all die. We are all part of the same creative energies that is forming the universe. We are all entitled by the right of birth to a share of the world's resources. This includes the right to clean water unpolluted by chemicals and wastes, the right to have healthy food, the right grow and be educated, and the right to create your individual way of being in service to the planet.

As we grow in our understanding more axioms will be recognized and added to the vocabulary, which people use to relate to each other. Some of the axioms likely to be in use are suggested below.

Axioms for a different way to operate human society

Nothing can be owned.

You can have more when everyone has enough.

All exchanges of services and goods are free.

The distribution of resources is based on need and fairness to all things.

If you are not taking care of what you have some else may claim a more beneficial use.

Decisions are made by a council circle of all the interested and affected things.

The Principles of Socialist Anarchy

Observation

Recognition

Definition

Participation

Agreement

Implementation

Evaluation

Correction

Contribution

Harmonization

These are the ten principles of implementing change. This process should be done for each aspect of society that needs changed. Currently, almost everything needs changed about how we live with respect to the rest of the planet. So we will have to begin slowly and build the system as we go. The technology currently exists for these changes to take place we just need to readdress the way things are currently programmed.

Socialist Anarchy is a growth process not an immediate result. Those who understand the principles will begin to make changes in their own personal lives. The understanding will spread as people learn to recognize the principles are a description of what they were already doing or something they already knew. Eventually as the understanding spreads the people will begin to implement change as groups. The groups will see their success grow and the groups will formulate change to develop greater organizing circles as the principles are applied to ever increasing levels of complexity. The process of growth is a growing understanding of the way things work and using the principles to reorganize our thinking about how to regulate activities.

Human beings currently regard themselves as in charge of the activities that are taking place here on the earth. When given the bountiful resources of the earth, the human response is to claim ownership and therefore the right of misuse. This doctrine has resulted in the abuses of capitalism which compounds the problem by assigning value to the use of money which requires interest. Subsequently, in order to pay interest a business must profit. These are long held illusions that must be dispelled as the falsehoods they are.

The three fundamental problems of our current economic system, ownership, interest, and profit are the economic plague on humanity. Socialist Anarchy solves the economic problems of humanity by negating and disavowing the validity of these three illusions. In order to begin to understand how we can effectively operate the systems of society without ownership, interest, and profit, we need to recognize that these are human creations. The means of commerce are a series of human inventions that have evolved over time to include trading on the future value of a contract held on some commodity. None of this is sacred. Nor is it necessary to continue to conduct commerce in the same manner in the future.

The beauty of the human species is the fantastic learning and growing capacity that they have evolved. Humans are capable of changing their understanding of the basic truth. It was once regarded as necessary and right to own slaves. It was once perceived as necessary to beat your wife and children and to treat them as property. It is appropriate that we grow in our understanding and change our definition of right and wrong. We will continue to do this in the future. Our survival as a species depends on it.

Ownership is not universal among human cultures. It is however, contagious. It begins in infancy and continues through a lifetime unless the particular human strives to eliminate the desire to possess. In cultures where ownership is not regarded as normal with respect to forest and fields, there are usually some forms of personal items or totem objects that are considered to be owned or possessed. The Socialist Anarchist view is that even allowing personal items to be owned is the beginning of the contagion. It soon spreads and more and more items are described as personal until there is formed a realistic basis of conflict. In order to prevent all claims of right of ownership it should be understood from the start, nothing can be owned. Everything should be used and taken care of as if it was owned in order to justify the continued use but there can be no ownership.

Viewed from a spiritual perspective, it is known that all that is and all that exists in form is an embodiment of the conscious spirit that causes the form to come into existence, therefore you can't own another spirit. When you have a conversation with the rocks that willingly gave up their individual existence to become concrete to create a new form such as a concrete arch bridge, then you can learn to respect that we all just are. It may not be a wonder that your roads develop pot holes if you curse them all of the time.

As a practical matter, it doesn't matter whether you own a TV set as long as you have one and can get a new one if necessary. The idea of lack of ownership means that no one person can have more than they reasonably need for their life to continue. In a society based on need and the economics of energy rather desire and the economics of greed there would be no way to justify having six TVs or a plasma screen TV in the door of the refrigerator. The mechanism to operate in this manner already exists. The process has not been applied with any kind of direction towards establishing a normal distribution of the goods. The allocation of goods and resources could be made on a rational basis with a more equilateral distribution using existing hardware and major adjustments to software. We only need to decide as a society to replace our current failed system.

Once we realize that we can choose the ultimate freedom of limitless opportunity by giving up the claim of ownership then humanity will be ready to step forward and do the right thing. The great thing about humanity is that no one lives forever so evolution proceeds by the death of the old who are committed to the way they are now. The youth naturally seek the next greatest thing that is happening. In order to save the planet it is going to be necessary to alter the way we use energy. The young people will be far more willing to adapt to new practices and understandings that are in harmony with the needs of the planet.

We will begin to grow in our socialist understanding when we realize that we need each other. We need each and every person on this planet to cooperate fully in order to slow the inevitable rise of the sea that threatens so many innocent people. We must get together in the future to efficiently proceed on shifting our energy use profile to more benign methods. Wind, wave, tidal, and solar power, as well as ways not yet developed are the future. The truth is the future starts now and we need to alter our decision making process now. I think we need to commit to the prevention of the rising sea levels now. The way to do that is with a complete change in our thinking. The solution to the Depression in 1930 was a completely different way of operating our society. We need a bigger more fundamental change now. We need to abandon the profit motive as a means of motivating activity.

Many people already spend their daily life in some kind of activity that does not profit them. In fact, many people desire to pay money in order to get to participate in some things such as archaeological digs or service projects with the Sierra Club. The point is, they have their needs taken care of so they are willing to work for the betterment of society without the need for profit.

Some people choose a life of service by the occupation that they use to make their way through the world.

These things are all good and if examined these ways of living would fit within the parameters of Socialist Anarchy and these people would probably have no problem adapting to the coming changes. The changes are coming. The question for our society is, "Do we recognize the coming changes and are we willing to make intelligent choices as to how we approach the implementation of those changes?"

Interest that accrues over time for the use of money is the next falsehood that has to be transmuted. We will find that our people enjoy enormous success when they are freely given the things they need to create their ideas. We currently limit the ability of people with ideas by limiting the availability of capital. Those ideas and those people who do not fit the description given to loan officers and bank managers as likely to generate a profit are not considered worthy of further investigation. No one with a heart felt desire to create should be limited by the access to resources if we wish to truly thrive as a society and a people.

The current crisis in the banking and financial world was brought about by the manipulation of the interest rates in a complicated scheme to sell inflated real estate to people who couldn't afford it. That would have been a bad thing but the big money boys like to make money on nothing at all, so they created worthless pieces of paper derivatives that they sold to each other and then took out insurance to cover their losses. The failures grew and spread through the banks to infest the entire economy driving down jobs and the value of everyone's retirement savings.

In 1929 at least some of the manipulators had the good sense to jump out of windows. Today's crop of fund managers and bankers still want their ten billion dollar bonus for the destruction they have wrecked.

The American people have not yet seen the light. They still continue to contribute to their deferred compensation or 401k plans or whatever payroll deduction that they have at work. The value of most people's plans is probably less than the amount that they paid in. The real increase in value for all of the years that they have been invested in the market is a loss. The desire for greater return or greed set in to motivate them. The deferred compensation investments for individuals were created to secure their future over the long term. It has turned out to be false hope and a giant rip off. If we examine the idea of saving for the future with the idea that our money will grow on its own we will find that it is false. Any interest accrued on savings has been canceled out by inflation. There is no real gain by letting money set because the basis of its value is subject to erosion.

The concept of profit means that you receive more for something than it is worth. The higher the false value can be raised the higher the profit. The creation of false values is the function of advertising. If you create a high enough demand you can charge whatever you want regardless of your cost in producing the item. This is fundamental capitalism. In a Socialist Anarchist society the value of an item would reflect the energy in the production and distribution including all of the environmental effects. This would lead suppliers to lower their environmental effects in order to compete for value. In the future the more evolved humans will have the benefit of having grown up without the expectation of profit and it won't seem strange to them.

There is a new way of thinking that is emerging. The end of profit, interest and ownership will change the way the human society works, opening the door for a balanced relationship with the earth that provides for us. This new way of thinking will be based on spiritual knowledge that is gained utilizing the techniques of shamanic practice. When enough people have developed an understanding of the relationship between the spiritual and material world, that is material is caused to exist by the consciousness of the spirit that inhabits the material, then humanity will begin to move forward rapidly to heal our relationship with our mother the earth.

The true and complete understanding that there is conscious spirit behind everything that exists means that you understand that the pavement of the road is a part of the divine creator. A stinking pile of manure at a stockyard is very close to the source of creation representing the exchange of life on many levels. The techniques of shamanic practice are available now to all of humanity. The techniques are taught by many different schools but the classes taught by the Foundation for Shamanic Studies are centered on what is described as core shamanic practice. These are the techniques that are common to the various cultures around the world and are not part of any specific traditional culture. These core shamanic practices are taught to people all over the world and thousands of people have been taught at least the beginning of the ability to learn directly from the spirit world. This is an important development for humanity. It is possible to have a direct relationship with spirit to learn whatever we desire to know.

When enough people begin to have this direct contact and the resulting knowledge about the true nature of our relationship with the creator then we will begin to move forward. The beauty of our current world is that our connection to the internet and television links the world quickly and things can happen in a hurry if an idea catches on. So which ideas are the ones that should catch on and move forward? If we think about the human relationship with the earth we will know what needs to be healed. Once humans return to a widespread acceptance of the spiritual nature of matter then it will not be a problem for humans to realize the foolishness of pretending to own property and we can start to restructure on the basis of the principles of socialist anarchy. There will be many steps along the way but the first will be the discussion of the ideas that will eventually be the foundation of a new society.

Observation is the first principle because that is where all learning begins. We observe and perceive the activity around us. This starts at infancy and continues through life. From a Socialist Anarchist perspective we observe human behavior in an attempt to understand the underlying motivation that is causing the particular pattern of behavior that we are studying. Once we understand the true motivation for people's behavior we can design our systems to function in a manner that we choose. An example is to study the traffic patterns to determine what regulates people's speed. It is not the signs stating the speed limit but the actions of the other vehicles in the traffic flow. If we were designing a traffic system according to the principles of Socialist Anarchy we would take this knowledge into account and allow the free flow of traffic to determine the safe operating speed.

Recognition is the second principle because we have to recognize the patterns correctly if we are to reach the proper understanding of the underlying forces that are operating. We will find that we may be in the observation mode for a long time in some cases as the true patterns of human motivation and interaction have not been studied with the intent of learning the underlying stimulus that is responsible for the reaction. We will need to observe carefully without judgment or expectation and repeat the same observations by many independent persons until we reach some conclusion. When we reach the state of recognition we are ready to move to the next principle.

Definition the third principle is the description of the recognized pattern from the observations. When this is done in the spirit of seeking harmony with the planet the result is a clear statement that easily understood and applied by ordinary people. The purpose of stating these definitions is that it builds a growing body of agreements. These agreements will be new ways for humans to relate to each other and the earth that feeds them.

Participation the fourth principle happens when those who have reached a definition begin to share it with others. The word spreads quickly as the clear statement's meaning is apparent to those who are in harmony with the upcoming changes. When the numbers of persons who are participating reaches enough of any circle of activity that circle of activity will change and begin to function based on a new agreement.

Agreement the fifth principle is when people come together and actualize the learning that they have been participating in. These processes are in use now but they are not recognized as such and the results do not end up being codified into an agreement. There is power in forming these agreements which concisely apply what we have so carefully learned about the way to move humans toward harmony.

Implementation the sixth principle is the plans and designs that bring forth our understandings of correct relationship so that we carry out our daily life in a manner in agreement with what we have learned. There is much discussion today as to whether education should be based on science or on faith, when in fact we need to utilize all of our knowledge and then implement congruent strategies that work towards our goal of harmony with the natural world.

Evaluation is the seventh principle and it is not that much different from the first principle except that it is ongoing and continuously in process when people are working towards harmony. We will always be looking to see if we can improve. To determine if there is a better way we may try some variations on the theme but we keep on evaluating. It is a part of our nature as humans.

Correction the eighth principle is the feedback response to the improvements envisioned from the ongoing evaluations. The corrections can be used to shape the programs to fit each of the individual areas or groups that may form. The cycle of evaluation and correction will continue to swing back and forth as we move closer to harmony.

Contribution is the ninth principle and it is essential that all contribute to the process in some way. All are equal and are of importance in the web of nature. We must learn to accept each person for what they are, exactly as they are, and then encourage them to do the best that they can. As we gain in understanding we will learn to see the contributions of others. When everybody is free to do all they can, we will be a marvelous society.

Harmonization the tenth and final principle is also an on going process. We will need to harmonize the various circles and groups that develop so that they connect and reconnect with each other in all of the ways possible. This process will help groups pass understandings and knowledge gained onto others until it has spread around the world. It is anticipated that many independent groups will form over the time of change from our current government by fear. These groups will join to pass on information but will remain independent and formless.

These ideas will be developed more completely later, for now it is important just to recognize that these principles exist and that there is a way for people to move forward in a logical simple process to cure the ills that we have allowed to run rampant over the earth for the last ten thousand years. These ills have been called by many names in their various incarnations but I would describe the ills as **the Four Afflictions of Humanity are Religion, Government, Banking, and Insurance.**

The cure of the four ills of will take time but it starts with the recognition that where we are now is the result of 10,000 years of building on a false premise. The truth of the existence of the falsity of our current civilization is the never ending need to wage war to defend the social structure that has been created by the rich to serve the needs of the rich. If the social structure of the United States was moral, fair, and just the country would not have a need for a military that dominates the existence of every one on the planet. The first step for the people of the United States would be to end the expenditure of resources on the military.

CONTAINMENT

— ❁ —

I FIRST BEGAN WRITING THIS LONG hand in a spiral notebook in the 1970's. At the time I had all of these ideas flooding into my consciousness and didn't know where they originated. The concepts of Socialist-Anarchy were from an inner resource that was tied to where I came from. I kept adding to it over time but never felt it was ready to publish. Here it is now.

The final version

Chapter One

The trail forks and I go left. The way less traveled. I long for the unknown and I descend the lower, less used, path that heads down toward the river. The alders are thick where they have sprouted up in the tracks of the logging trucks that passed this way many years ago. At times I have to dodge back and forth to make much headway. I am not going anywhere in particular. I just want to get out from the traces of humanity.

I don't think that I care much for humans. It matters not that I am a human. Too many rules and too much civilization are included with being human. I know that I am supposed to fit in and play a role in society. I just don't want to play the role that everyone has planned out for me. My dad is an engineer so I should be an engineer. I want to choose my own path without interference from societies expectations.

I had long since developed the habit of disappearing off into the woods by myself. I really hated school and the thought of being trained to do a job like my Dad had, and his dad had, and his dad had, back to the beginning of Containment. I wanted and needed something more than just doing my duty like everyone else. It was not that I didn't understand why, I just wanted something different. I loved to wander the old logging trails and game paths through the forests to the northeast of our home. The attraction to me of being in the woods was that it was natural and not concrete. You saw things and felt things that you never could where everything was sterile and clean.

Although the official rules about traveling through these woods did not include teenage boys going off by themselves, without telling someone where they were going, and when they would be back, I never worried about getting lost. The old logging roads generally go down from the top of the ridge and zigzag back and forth until they come down to the river. I usually don't go as far as the river. To reach the river, I would need a clear trail and a fast pace to get back before I would be missed. I would not be going that far today. I just want to wander in the woods and listen to the birds and maybe see some animals. This trail is anything but clear. The trees were logged a long time ago and now the road has grown thick with black alder trees. In some places, they are so thick that that you can't walk through them.

The alders have grown up much thicker in the middle of the road and I am picking my way, moving side to side, in what were once the wheel ruts from the logging trucks. As I move along the trail I am trying to not make much noise. I know that if I want to see animals I need to move through the woods as if I was an animal. Take a few steps, stop and listen, can you hear the squirrels chattering? I learned a while back that the squirrels would tell you what is going on in the woods. Once, I was also just slowly moving along and the commotion from several squirrels chattering behind me got my attention. I stopped and slipped off to the side of the trail and waited quietly. As I watched a small brown bear came down the trail sniffing and snuffling at the scent of my trail. On that day I moved quickly over to the left and found another path that I knew would take me back home. I wasn't afraid but I didn't want to chance an encounter with a bear even if it was a small one. As I moved along today I had no particular place to go, I just wanted to be out in the woods. It was a warm sunny afternoon and we had a break from school this week, my dad was working until five, and mom had just left to work the second shift at the hospital. I would have some time to myself.

I really much preferred the woods to the company of people. There were small flowers of several kinds growing at the edges of the trail. I recognized most of them as having seen them through the years but I didn't know their names. I wished I had someone who could teach me about them so I would not feel so unknowledgeable. I have learned the names of most of the trees in the area and can recognize some of the common plants but these wild flowers were so delicate and seemed so special that I wish I knew more about them.

As I was thinking about this, I heard noises down towards the river. Louder noises than I could imagine would be any wild animal. I started down the trail moving as quietly but as rapidly as I could. The noises sounded like something was smashing its way through the brush. I imagined it was a herd of elk. I had always wanted to see a herd of elk so I checked the wind direction to see if the wind would take my scent down the trail. At this time of day the breeze was coming up from the river so I was in luck. I might be able to get close to them if I was quiet enough. I kept going watching my feet as I stepped on the trail. I didn't want to step on a dead branch or dry brush and make sharp sounds that would let them hear me. I stopped to listen again. The sounds of breaking brush continued to come up the trail.

Then I heard voices. Someone cursed as if they had tripped over something in the trail. I stopped. Who could possibly be out here? What would they be doing coming up from the river? I slid off from the trail. Going a few feet into the brush I settled down and waited to see if it was a crew that had been maintaining the barrier. What they would be doing coming up this trail I didn't know but I did not want to be seen by a maintenance crew and have to explain what I was doing here. I lowered myself closer to the ground and lay among the buck brush and waited.

When I saw them coming up the trail, I knew they were not a maintenance crew by their appearance. Who were they? Six young men, maybe eighteen to twenty-five, walked up the trail breaking branches off of the alders and pushing brush out of the way as they went. They did not seem to care about being quiet and talked back and forth. The clothes they wore were not something that they had gotten anywhere in Containment. The shirt and pants were not any particular color but had patches of green and tan and brown without any pattern. The packs they were carrying looked to be made of the same type of fabric. It looked like they could have blended into the woods if they had had any idea of how to walk in the woods.

As I watched they stopped and looked around. One seemed to be the leader when he said to the others, "Let's get to the top of the ridge and find a clearing to camp for the night. Then we can scout out from the camp in several directions to see which way to go. We don't want to be found. We want to learn as much as we can without being seen."

They continued on up the trail, still making more noise than a herd of elk on the run. If they didn't want to be found, it was already too late. I was going to tell dad about them but I first had to get home without them hearing me. As I waited, I considered what they were here for and what they wanted to learn. I recalled so many years ago when I was listening to my parents in the night and knew this was more important than me getting in trouble for wandering in the woods without permission.

After they disappeared, going up the trail, I moved slowly off to the right, I knew another logging road was about a half mile in that direction. I followed a game trail through the brush trying to be quiet but I knew that they were making so much noise that it was unlikely that they would hear me. I needed to get home anyway, as my dad would be home soon. I reached the logging road and was able to pick up the pace. This old road saw some use through the years by hunters and picnic parties so that it was not grown up with alders and I quickly made my way up the ridge and headed down the road towards home.

Dad was not home when I got there, so I made myself a sandwich and waited. What would happen and whom should we contact was what I was thinking about when my Dad turned into our driveway. He looked tired and seemed as if he had already had a full hard day when he came into the house.

"Dad, I saw some strangers in the woods when I went for a hike today." I said.

"What? Where? How many were there?" He responded.

"I saw six young men dressed in strange outfits. I heard them talking about camping tonight and scouting around to see what they could learn." I answered.

"Did they see you? Do they know you saw them? Where were they?" He questioned.

One night when I was a small boy, I got up to go to the bathroom and heard my mother and father talking about something I didn't understand, so I hid around the corner in the hall. The floor was warmed by the heating pipes running through it, so I curled up and waited, hoping to hear something that would explain what was going on. My parents were excited but also seemed afraid. What was this talk of taking prisoners and a threat to the community from the outside? A threat from the outside, what could that be? I had always thought, had always been taught that we were the threat to the rest of the world. We had been chosen to protect the rest of the world from the threats that lie within the confines of Containment. Why would they be threatening us? Why would we be taking prisoners? I was young but I knew that things were not as they were supposed to be.

My name is Jason Nascent. My dad, who is named Ted Nascent, is an engineer at the big hydroelectric dam in the northeast corner of Containment and my mother who is named Tzaddi is a nurse at the small country hospital that served the people of the area. I can't think of a better combination but I guess that everyone who loves his or her parents feels the same way.

I found out later that a crew of linemen repairing a transmission line near the boundary wall of Containment encountered and captured wanderers from the outside. The line crew had no idea that they were taking prisoners. They thought they had found some people who had become lost and disoriented while on a hiking trip. The people must have been barely surviving when they were rescued. It was later at the hospital, where they were taken, it was learned that these people, who appeared so unfortunate, were actually people from the outside. The barrier had not been maintained in some time and they had wandered through it without realizing they were crossing the line into Containment.

They were hunting for food and had been following the trail of a herd of elk. They never caught up to the elk and were suffering from hunger and cold when they were found. They were taken in clothed, fed, and made to feel like they were royalty. Once the group of wanderers had established their relative innocence and all knew that they posed no threat they were taken back across the barrier and released. The gaps in the barrier were repaired and an inspection and maintenance program was started. Those in Containment felt duty bound to protect the rest of the earth as we had been charged so long ago.

Looking back it is hard to see how the action could have been changed. How could those in charge acted differently? Now we know that they should have killed them outright or never let them go. What we now know is that these people who we treated so nice returned to their village and told tales of being rescued by gods.

None of our administration had enough foresight to evaluate the people thoroughly. No one questioned them as to what they thought the world was like. We didn't learn until too late that they didn't have the latest in electronic marvels. Actually they didn't have much beyond the rudimentary radio and television. These people wasted no time in spreading their story when they returned home. Since they were a group, not just one or two, they could tell story after story and had no problem convincing the rest of their villagers that behind the barrier was a secret world that had everything. They told of a world that was inhabited by gods who knew everything and controlled the forces of nature at their whim.

As a consequence, a legend started and spread into the rest of the world about a place separated by the big rivers where the gods lived. The fact that the barrier was intact kept us from knowing that this legend was growing. We became aware of increasing attempts on the barrier only after several years.

I am older now, sixteen. I was a young man who had a chance meeting with another group of outsiders who made it through the barrier.

"They were on an old logging road that goes down to the river and I hid when I heard them coming because I thought the noise was from a herd of elk and I have always wanted to see a herd in the wild. When I saw it was strangers I didn't want to get caught so I stayed in the brush and listened to them talk. When they moved on up the ridge to camp, I came home to tell you."

"I am going to call the committee and report this. They will want to get a team out here right away. You are going to have to explain what you were doing and where to find them. I know you like to wander in the woods so I have not made a big deal about it since you are always home for supper but you don't know what some of the committee will say. You just tell the truth and I will stick up for you. Okay."

"Dad, I never meant any harm. I just like to see the plants and animals and listen to the birds. I like to be in the woods more than I like to be in a building or around people."

"I know, son. That is why I'll stick up for you. We will tell them that I knew you went for hikes and then it will be all right."

The committee sent out a group of men later that evening. A tall man in his forties led the crew. He was leader of one of the barrier maintenance crews. When Dad explained what I had seen they talked and made plans to come back in the morning with the idea of catching the strangers before they broke camp. I would have to go along to show them where the trail was and where to look, but I was not supposed to participate in any other way. Since it was the early part of summer, the sun would rise at about four am and we would be leaving the house at no later than five. Dad told me to go to bed early and get some sleep, but have you ever tried to sleep when the most exciting thing in your life is going to happen the next day.

I guess I finally went to sleep because I woke up when Dad was shaking my shoulder.

"Come on, get up, they are going to be here any minute."

"I will be right out as soon as I get dressed." I said.

"Do you want some tea and toast before we go?" He asked.

"Are you going too?"

"Yes, someone has to make sure that you stay out of the way. No, really I want to see what these people look like. You have seen something that not many have had the opportunity to see and I want to know what they are like. I told the patrol that you could not go if I am not included."

"I would like some tea and some toast, thanks Dad."

We had finished our breakfast and were waiting outside when three barrier patrol rigs drove up. Two were four door pickups and one was a large box van with small windows in the box that were covered with a heavy metal screen. They parked along the road and waited as the door to the first one opened.

"Good morning," the leader of the patrol said as he got out of his vehicle. He looked over at me and said. "Hello, my name is Chester Horstman but you can call me Chet. You did the right thing yesterday and I want to thank you for being smart enough not to betray your presence. Who knows what those fellows would have done if they knew you were there. Did you see if they had any weapons with them?"

I looked at this man who wanted me to call him Chet. He was a broad shouldered, well-built man with brown wavy hair and looked like a part of the wall he was responsible for maintaining. He was solid muscle and looked like he could handle any thing that came up in the way of conflict.

"My name is Jason. I did not see any weapons but they had backpacks and hiking gear and their clothes were all funny patches of color."

"That would be camouflage gear. Some people use it for hunting with bows. It probably means they didn't intend to be found and we should assume that they have some type of arms." Chet added.

"We are ready to go if you are." Dad said.

"Great, you and Jason can ride with me and show me the trail and then we will walk from there." Chet indicated the front seat of his patrol vehicle, which was a squat wide four –wheel drive with four doors and a pickup box on the back with various boxes and tools setting in it.

I wondered if he had any weapons but did not ask. I just climbed into the front seat between him and my Dad. It was a short drive to the place where the trail started down from the road. We parked and got out. I pointed to the way that I had gone and told them that I did not know exactly where the strangers were camped.

"Where is the trail that you came out on?" Chet asked.

"It is a little further to the north and is not as over grown as this one." I replied.

When the other two rigs emptied out, they did have side arms and rifles. There were a total of sixteen men besides my dad and me. Chet laid out his plan to his men. Chet, my dad, and I, and four other men with guns, would go down the trail that I had used on the way out, crossover and come up the overgrown trail towards the ridge. The rest of the men would spread out and slowly move along the trail through the woods toward where we thought the camp would be on the ridge. We would have them between us. Each of the patrol members had radios and would broadcast when they saw sign of the camp.

I was used to walking but really had to work to keep up as we headed down the trail. I showed Chet the game path that led through the woods to the overgrown trail. In less than a half an hour we reached the place where I had first saw them. Chet was impressed when I pointed out the place where I had hidden in the brush and listened to them talk.

"You really showed a lot of cool, kid. Not to move and not to panic and let them know you were less than ten feet away."

"Thanks." I said.

I knew from the look that my Dad gave me that he was impressed too but was also worried that I was that close. We started up the trail. It was no problem telling where they had gone as the brush had branches broken off all along the trail. I was able to move in the woods a lot easier than they seemed to be able to do. We did not go fast as the four men with weapons spread out on each side and kept pace moving through the woods. It was not too far until we reached an open area along the side of the trail where we saw their camp. There was a whisper of smoke rising above the remnants of a fire and four small tents that were also the camouflage colors.

Chet quietly radioed to his men. They were spread out around the camp and we had only to walk another one hundred yards to reach the tents.

"Stay here you two." Chet said to my Dad and I. "We will handle this part."

He had pulled an auto pistol from behind his back and waved to the four men with us to move in closer. When they got close to the tents, Chet called out in a loud voice.

"You men in those tents step out now with your hands up. We have you surrounded and there is no place to go." When there was no reply he called again.

"Those tents won't stop bullets so step out now or we will open fire."

"OK, OK, We are coming out. Don't shoot."

The door flaps on the tents unzipped and six sleepy looking strangers stepped out in their shorts and stood with their hands up, blinking in the sun.

"We are just exploring the countryside and camping out. We are not here to cause trouble." The one who seemed to be the leader said. "We don't mean any harm to anyone. We are just curious about this place."

The intruders were placed in a circle and guarded by four men with rifles, as their tents and belongings were searched. As it turned out they didn't have any weapons. They were then allowed to put on their boots and pants. All of the stuff was packed up and carried out by the patrol. My Dad, and I followed the four guards and the six prisoners and Chet back up the trail. Once we made it back to the vehicles, the intruders were loaded into the van. Chet dropped off Dad and me on the way. He thanked us again for our help and that was the last that we saw of the strangers. We were told that they were to be taken to Valley Falls in the south and held for investigation.

Chapter Two

The news came that Herman Ott, the programmer, was calling for a meeting of the general assembly. I knew from my school civics class that Containment functioned differently than any other society that had been formed on the earth. We did not have a government that was in charge of maintaining order. Our government is the program that operates the central network of computers that control the daily functioning of our society. Programs for minor functions or local decisions can be changed at a local level but the main over all program is accessible only to a few special programmers who are selected to maintain the code. Herman Ott was the one who was in charge of all of them.

The organization of Containment consists of various committees that have responsibility for a certain function or area. Any citizen was welcome to participate in any committee that they are qualified for. The general assembly was only called when critical decisions had to be made that affect the whole of our society. For Herman Ott to call the whole assembly meant that he felt that this would be a significant change to the way that Containment functioned. All citizens were eligible to express themselves at the assembly. Each person's input was valued and accepted. Decisions were made by consensus, and the assembly decided what consensus meant at the time. Only rarely did they decide to vote on an issue as they usually talked the issue over until even those who were opposed to the change agreed that it was necessary. Changes meant a change in the program that operated the main computers that functioned as the executive branch of the government. Herman Ott was responsible for maintaining and updating the code that was the operating system. He felt that a decision to resolve the crises of the intruders was needed.

As a practical matter, not all citizens showed up at the general assembly. Everyone was a part of different committees and each committee sent someone to represent their view or interest so any citizen who felt strongly about an issue only had to get one of the committees that they served to agree to send them as the representative for that committee. If you were an engineer working at a hydroelectric power plant like my Dad then you might be on the energy committee, the water resource committee, the dam safety committee as well as the committee for your village or town. Nearly everyone who was an active citizen was a part of two or three but there were a lot of people who felt like they didn't need to bother. They were content to let others spend all the time in meetings as long as they didn't have to. They spent their free time on hobbies or recreational activities like fishing or music.

The assembly would be held in the large town of Valley Falls about one hundred and twenty miles south of here. I knew my dad was going. I wanted to go too. I had no status. I was still a student and could not have any say but I wanted to know what was going to happen with the people I had found. I felt I had a right to know.

My dad knew that I wanted to go and said "I'll take you into the meeting hall but you don't get to say anything. Remember you are still a student and cannot be considered a citizen until you learn your skills and can perform your assigned useful function. Then you will have the right to speak out or vote at an assembly."

"Dad, that would be great. I want to see how Containment really functions and learn if I can change things when I do become a citizen."

"Don't be too smart. I am taking you because you showed good judgment out in the woods when you encountered the intruders and you should see how this is all worked out. Don't think for a minute that this or anything else is ever going to change the way Containment works because it won't. We are committed to maintaining the status quo for storage of the wastes for at least one hundred thousand years and Containment will still be the same then."

The assembly was held this time in a large facility that was usually used for hockey or basketball games or music concerts. The building held events that attracted a crowd. Normally the general assembly was not such a popular event. From the discussion that I was able to overhear from the people around me as we were going in, I was able to surmise that the event with intruders that I had participated in was not the only time such a thing had happened. It was only the last. I did not know how the business of an assembly was conducted and Dad was not able to tell me because he had never been to one but neither had any of the other people who were sitting around us.

At nine am right on schedule, someone came out on the stage and began addressing the crowd. It was a crowd too. I could not see an empty seat and groups of people were pacing the aisles asking if this seat was taken right up until the speaker started on the stage, then everyone just stopped where they were and listened. The speaker began with a brief history of Containment and how we came to accept our role as caretakers of the nuclear waste, and how this led to our constitution being expressed in the computer program that controlled the operation of our society. On and on he went telling what a great thing it was that our lives were so dedicated and responsible and therefore so controlled. This was the stuff I had heard so many times in school that I wanted to scream, "Shut up and get on with the program I want to hear about the changes."

Everyone else listened to this and nodded in agreement, yes, they were a special people, and yes, they had a hard role in life, but they accepted it and liked the controlled existence. Even my Dad was shaking his head and feeling the calming effect that the speaker's voice had. Was this some type of incantation that was putting them under some type of spell? I felt like I was the only one who knew that Containment was like a prison to all of us. We had no free will to express ourselves or to think thoughts that didn't coincide with the program. I watched the crowd and I realized that maybe I was the only one in the whole place who listened to the speaker's recitation and wondered why it had to be that way.

Eventually the speaker wore down and introduced several people who had some role in planning the function and one of them came up and went over the ground rules for the conduct at the assembly. There were microphones placed at numerous locations throughout the building. If one wished to address the assembly, then one went the closest microphone and waited in line until your turn came. The comments were to only be on the subject that was currently being discussed and not some old grievance. The limit was three minutes but everyone was asked to limit it to one minute if possible. If the moderator felt you were not being concise and clear in your thoughts or you were just repeating what someone else had stated previously you would be cut off. With maybe ten or twelve thousand people here, you had better be prepared and have something interesting to say if you were going to get anyone to listen to you.

Finally, the time came when the moderator introduced the Programmer, Herman Ott. My first thought when he came out on the stage was "He is old!" I could not believe that this thin white haired man was the one who kept the program and our society working. He began to speak and even with the microphone, you had to listen carefully to hear what he was saying.

"There have been events in the last year that makes it clear that the outside world has changed. No longer do they fear contact with Containment. According to our history the barrier was to keep us in and was not intended to keep the outsiders out. In fact it has only been in the last ten years that we have been maintaining the barrier. When the first group of wanderers entered by accident, they didn't know they were even in Containment. At that time we realized that if we were going to fulfill our commitment to isolate the world from the horrors that could be caused by the nuclear wastes we would have to make the barrier functional. We had in the past thought that was the responsibility of the outside but research has shown us that once the original wall was complete the builders moved away from Containment and no one came close to it again for a long time. The fear of dying from radiation or ingesting plutonium kept them far away. It has only been in the last one hundred years that people have moved back into the land that surrounds us. These people were at first hunters and then loggers who came into the area for the resources and then left. People started making their homes close to the barrier over the last years. Since the barrier was not maintained it was possible for the first groups of wanderers to enter without knowing that they were doing so."

"The real change has been in the last year when people started deliberately entering and searching out or making breaks in the wall. It is this change in the outside that I have asked you here today to discuss and find a response to the change brought not by us but by the people that we have dedicated our existence to protecting. What should we do now to meet our charge of isolating the wastes? I have some ideas, but I want to hear yours. Will the moderator please explain how we are going to conduct the comment period"?

"The procedure to follow if you wish to speak is going to one of the microphones that have been placed around the arena and get in line. While waiting for your turn, be sure that you have your remarks in order. Then when it is your turn, identify yourself by stating your name, your address, and what committees you represent. Then you can begin your remarks. We will rotate around the arena to each of the microphones in turn. Who wants to begin?"

There is general stirring from the audience and groups of people form at each microphone from the center of the floor comes a voice.

"I would like to begin the remarks by saying that we should do whatever is necessary to preserve the status of Containment."

"Excuse me," the moderator interjects. "You must first identify yourself and give your credentials."

"OK, I am George Allen Ratcliff from 1105 Basalt Drive in East Hanford. I am a member of the worker's health committee and the plant security committee at site 15. Our committees agree that the preservation of the current status is the only way that we can prevent these uneducated outsiders from doing something that could endanger all of us. We decided to maintain the barriers to keep these people out and if they insist on trying to infiltrate Containment then we must do whatever is necessary to keep them out. We have armed the barrier patrols and we should instruct them to shoot to kill all the intruders. When the word gets out that we are not welcoming them with food and clothes then the outsiders will stop trying to get in."

"Wait, wait, you can't do that." Erupts a loud voice from the left front microphone. "I am William B. Perkins from 2250 West Hill Road in the Central Project and I have farmed there all of my life. I understand that you nuke boys think that everything revolves around you but you could not exist if most of the rest of us weren't here making this society work. I have been a member of the supply committee for 42 years and we always have provided whatever was needed to make this place work. We cannot descend into violence. The very foundation of our society is that no one does harm to anyone else and we willingly provide whatever it is that someone may need for his or her existence. We must stay true to our values if we are to remain viable as a country. I will not support any plan that uses violence."

The next speaker begins and reiterates that the whole function of Containment is just that and if we are not able to prevent the outsiders from entering how can we protect them which is the charge that was given to us at the beginning.

The debate rages on and on, with each speaker extolling the virtues of Containment as sacred, but each speaker claiming a different virtue as the most important to maintain. However, everyone agrees that Containment must be maintained and the outsiders must be protected. Just how they would accomplish that is where there is no agreement. I wish I could speak. I want to say that we are wrong in thinking we are so special. I saw those young men who were captured and led away. I honestly believed that they had no evil intent they were just curious about the unknown. I certainly understood what it meant to be curious about something and I also knew what it meant to want to see something different.

At one o'clock, they announce a lunch break and give out numbers to the people waiting in line at each microphone. They intend to let everyone speak and it looks like it could take days to accomplish that let alone reach any kind of agreement. During lunch at a crowded nearby cafe my Dad and I talk about what has gone on. I ask if he is going to get up and speak and I am disappointed when he says that he doesn't have anything different to say than what someone else has already said.

"How do you think it is going to turn out?" I ask.

"I don't know," is all he says.

"Which way do you want it to turn out?"

"I think that if we had not let the original intruders go this would never have happened and now they think we are some kind of paradise. We have to find some way to convince them otherwise but I sure don't agree with shooting them."

"What if we were to educate them?"

"About what? They should know why Containment is here as well as we do."

"They don't seem to know the first thing about us. It is like the outside has forgotten why we were set in existence in the first place. If they don't understand that how can we convince them that they need to stay away?"

"Maybe you are right, but how would you educate the whole world full of outsiders?"

"We would only have to educate a group of them and they could go back to the outside and tell them that the first intruders had it all wrong. Why don't you suggest that this afternoon?"

"Since you can't speak out at the meeting you think I should, is that it? Maybe I should also tell them you don't like the way they are running the show and they should change it to suit you."

"Dad! Stop teasing. You know I am serious. These people aren't any different than us. They just live outside and if it is so terrible outside that they are willing to risk contamination then maybe we should be doing something to help the outside world. I don't want to destroy Containment. I just want to choose what happens in my life. So if nobody else suggests educating them then why won't you?"

"All right you win. I will get up and get in line. How do you think this education should work? We don't even understand what these people are thinking. How can we educate a group of people who may not even know math or science? We don't have the time to start out at the beginning and educate them all the way through school."

"Once again you have forgotten what school is like Dad. They repeat the same stuff over and over and over. It would be possible to have a special class for some of the smartest kids from the outside and teach them everything they need to know about Containment in one year"

We made our way back into the arena. It was not as crowded as it was in the morning because a large number of people milled around outside. They seemed to have formed into a couple of different groups surrounding loud voiced persons who dominated the group. As we passed by on our way into the arena I heard the largest group grumbling about how this wouldn't be a problem if the leadership hadn't been such weak willies and had killed the intruders as they came in.

I found a seat and Dad went up to the closest microphone and got into the line. I could tell that he really didn't want to be there but was just doing it for me. I began to realize all of the things that my Dad had done just for me. I remembered that he always tried to let me express myself and had let me wander in the woods when I thought that he didn't know about it. I began to feel that maybe he understood me after all.

When the session began the moderator got up to remind everyone of the procedures. This was part of what drove me nuts about Containment. These people loved their procedures. But then, the moderator asked everyone, who was in the lines to speak, to think back on the testimony that had already been given. "If you do not have something that is new and different then I would ask you to make way for those who do and please sit down."

I was amazed. People actually started out of the lines and moved away from the microphones. When it settled down Dad was only three back from the microphone for his line. He would probably get to speak this afternoon. Sometimes the professed Containment attitude of thinking of others and putting the group needs first actually works. The rest of the afternoon seemed to go quickly as the speakers identified themselves, gave their thoughts, which were not all original, and then sat back down. Before I realized it was going to happen, I heard my Dad's voice.

"Good afternoon, my name is Theodore, uh, Ted Nascent. My family and I live at 2156 Eleven Mile Road outside of Boundary Village. I am employed at the Dam and I am on the water resource committee, the energy committee, and I am on our village council. I have worried about the effect of the outsiders ever since I heard about the first group over ten years ago. At that time we restored the barriers and hoped that we could maintain our isolation. It didn't work. I have listened here today and I have to say that I have heard a lot of things suggested and not one of them is anything any different than what I have thought of over the ten years I have been worrying about what was going to be the solution. Then this afternoon I heard someone make an original suggestion, but it was not anyone who has yet spoken here today.

It is from my son, Jason, who found one of the last groups of intruders and is here with me to learn about how Containment works. He has always been somewhat of an original thinker and I never know what he is going to come up with but I think his idea has merit. At least he convinced me to get up and speak, which I never wanted to do. His idea is this. We ask the outside world to send a group of their best students about sixteen or seventeen years old and we have some of the best people in our society give them a year's education on the workings and history of Containment. This way when they go back they can spread the truth about Containment and not spread a lot of myths and half-truths that encourages the outsiders to want to come here. I think that the idea has merit and I propose that we begin thinking about implementing this idea and stop worrying about the intruders and definitely stop thinking about killing them. Thank you, I'll set down now."

The place was a buzz of turmoil as people scrambled from their seats and tried to get in line at the microphones. But when the next person spoke it was not from the floor. You couldn't hear his voice clearly at all when he began to speak but people quieted quickly as they realized who was speaking. I hadn't seen him on the stage and I didn't think he would respond to my idea but I recognized the thin white-haired man as Herman Ott.

When it was possible to hear what he was saying, I heard, "You ask how I can advocate yielding as a means of defense. Let me ask you to consider the behavior of wood. When faced by a nail, hard wood, the densest strongest variety, resists with all the strength of its fibers until it bursts asunder, splits, and becomes totally useless in its failure. Soft wood yields instantly; the nail pierces quickly through its fibers and bonds the pieces together in a useful harmony. The wood has yielded. The nail has won but the bond is made. We need to see that we are like separate pieces of wood. If we yield, and wait, the bond of the present adversity will bring us together in harmony."

Then he was praising my idea and saying that this was what he was looking for. He wanted a solution that would restore the balance between the outside and Containment so that we could exist in peace to perform our function. He also said that he personally would teach the class in history, as he was about as old as any one and knew it better than anyone else.

Then the floor dropped out from under me. He said that in order to make this work we needed to have some of our own students combined with the outsiders so they would have friends and not be treated as excluded strangers and he wanted Jason Nascent to be a part of the special class since it was his idea. He also thought that I could benefit from improved knowledge of the history of Containment. I looked around for my Dad but he had gotten lost in the press of people who were trying to get to speak. Was this possible? Would they adopt my idea now that Herman Ott had improved it? I needed some air and I wanted my Dad but I was stuck in this chair until things settled down.

When the old man stopped speaking, the rest of the speakers began anew, but with a different tone. It was now positive and glowing with praise for the idea that was on the floor. Finally, one of the speakers called for a question of consensus and the response was overwhelmingly in favor. When things settled down I saw my Dad waving to me. He had one of the coordinators standing beside him. He wanted me to come down and join them. As I made my way through the seats out to the aisle, people patted my back and said "Way to go kid." I never planned on anything like this. When I got to the floor and joined my Dad, he told me that we were supposed to go back stage and meet Herman Ott.

Chapter Three

It took more time to organize than I thought but eventually the class came together. You would have thought that the hard part would have been to get the cooperation of the outsiders, but no the people in Containment were harder to convince. They didn't want their children separated out for any special program. The ideas of Containment were so ingrained in the families that they had a difficult time having their sons or daughters change to something that may not be the way it always was. Eventually twenty-three homes were found that had an appropriate age son or daughter, and were willing to add an outsider as a sister or brother. These families would accept the outsiders as one of their own kids for the year that the education program was to exist. Most of the families had doubts that this would work but they were told that the outsiders had agreed to a strict set of rules and would be bound by a contract that would see them expelled from the program if they misbehaved.

I never knew how Herman Ott made contact with the outside and convinced them to participate. They selected the best and the brightest to represent their world. The outside seemed eager to participate and had no problem getting interested students to volunteer. They had a series of regional tests that were used to select the students. The tests were not just for how smart they were but also on how well they got along with others and on their powers of observation. They were supposed to report back everything they learned after all.

I was accepted into the program because Herman Ott wanted me in the program. We lived too far north to be a participating family so I would not be living with my parents. The outsiders were supposed to paired up with a student from Containment and live with them and share what we considered a normal life. This way they got educated even when they weren't in class. I would be paired up with an outsider but we would not be living in my home we would stay with Herman Ott. One of his granddaughters kept house for him. I didn't know what happened to her husband or if she ever had one but she had a daughter Elizabeth who was fifteen and stayed there also. She was not to be part of the program and would be going to the regular school.

The students from the outside arrived in September. They came by bus and all the host families were there to meet them. The formal school was not going to start for a week to allow the families a chance to settle in. I would use this time to say goodbye to my parents and take a last couple of walks in the woods. I would not have that type of freedom once the program was in motion. I just wasn't sure why I was selected to be in the program in the first place. Yes, it was my idea but why did Herman Ott single me out for so much attention. As we waited to meet the students we would be paired with, there was a typical long-winded program with speakers and introductions and great proclamations. I watched some of the strangers fidgeting and knew they were as bored with the program as I was. They didn't seem nervous or uncertain. They looked like they were calmly dealing with something that they were prepared for. I would have been so anxious in their shoes. Let's face it, I was so anxious now. I was very unsure of myself and didn't know what Herman Ott expected of me and now I would be living with him.

Valley Falls is the largest city in Containment and most of the families lived right in the city or close by. The students were introduced one at a time and then the family they would be staying with came up and they exchanged greetings. Each student then went to sit with the family while the next set was brought together. The twenty-three strangers consisted of twelve boys and eleven girls. Twenty-two had been paired up with their family as I sat watching wondering who would be left for me. He was tall, dark haired, and muscular, with a handsome face and a broad grin that seemed to just naturally reside on him. His name was Landon Holmes. My mom and dad went up with me and we shook hands around. Then Herman Ott came out and was introduced. He began to speak and explain what would take place over the next year. He of course felt that history would be the most important subject, but you could see the outsiders eyes brighten when he said that they would also be getting lots of science training as well.

After all the formalities were over, we went to a restaurant to get something to eat before the drive home. Landon kept looking around at everything in wonder as we sat down.

"What is it like where you're from?" my Mom asked. "Do you live in a big city?"

"No, we live in a rural area of small farms outside of Jamensburg." Landon replied.

"Well is the country like this? Do you have any brothers and sisters? What do your parents do? What are your hobbies?" Mom spilled out.

"Mom," I said. "Give him a chance to respond before you interrogate him."

Landon laughed. His smile never seemed to let up. "That is all right. It is very flat where we live. No hills at all. I have a brother and a sister and my dad is a gardener or small farmer who grows vegetables to sell and my mother makes things like quilts and candles and pottery to sell. My hobby is reading books. I read everything I can get my hands on. That is why I wanted to get into this program. I knew I would get to learn a lot of things nobody back home would ever dream of."

I was beginning to wonder why they had paired us up. I certainly didn't like to spend all my time reading. We didn't have much in common so far.

"Do you have interest in the outdoors? Are there any wooded areas around your house?" I asked.

"Oh, we have trees along the roads but it is an area of small farms and there is not any place that is a forest for a long ways. It is all in parks that you have to pay to visit."

"Well, you won't believe our place then. We are surrounded by forest for miles and miles. I can walk for hours and not see any one."

"Just the occasional group of intruders sneaking in. I hear." He says with an even bigger smile than usual.

"Did they tell you that that is how this exchange program got started?"

"Yes, you are somewhat of a hero to all the people in our country. That is why I am so lucky to be partnered with you."

"Do you mean people actually know about me?" I can't believe this.

"Jason Nascent is a name that is talked about as if you were the hope of our future. Everyone thinks that our life will change for the better once we get all the secrets of Containment. You are responsible for opening the door where so many have tried to sneak in. We need the knowledge of how this place is able to be so successful, if our lives are ever going to change. I don't want to hoe weeds all day like my dad and I want to take all that I can learn back to my people. That is why they sent me."

I had never thought about it like that. I just wanted to educate the outsiders so they would go away and leave us alone. Now I wondered if I had had a good idea after all. What if this didn't turn out the way it was supposed to? What did Herman Ott have in mind? I guessed we would find out in a week or so.

"We should order now so we can get going. I can't wait to show you the woods around our place. Did you look at the menu? What is your favorite food? I asked.

"I haven't looked at the menu. I have been too busy talking.

What do they have that's good? I really don't care what I eat just so I get to eat on a regular basis. That is one advantage of Dad being a farmer. We always have food."

"Well here's the menu you can have anything you want." My Dad finally spoke.

"There are no prices on the menu. How do you know what the items cost?" Landon asked.

"Here in Containment things do not have a price. We allow everyone to have what he or she needs to survive. The goods that are produced in Containment have always been distributed according to need." Dad explained as the waiter came over to the table.

"We have chicken a lot at home because we raise them. I think I would like to try the roast beef. If that's all right?" Landon said.

"Sure it is. I'll have that also." I wanted him to feel that he was accepted as an equal.

"I want the tofu and stir fried vegetables." My Mom added. "So go ahead and order, Ted."

"The roast beef does sound good so I guess that I will have it also." Dad said to the waiter.

"You can all help yourselves at the salad bar and I'll bring your orders when you are ready." The waiter had punched in our orders on a keypad that he carried and the order appeared on the screen in front of the cook.

After we had gotten our salads and set back down, Landon asked, "Are you a vegetarian Mrs. Nascent?"

"Yes, I am but please call me Tzaddi not Mrs. Nascent. I have been a vegetarian all of my life, but I married a meat eater so I have learned to cook some non-vegetarian meals as well. So don't worry about that. We will keep you from starving."

"That is an unusual but pretty name. What does it mean?

Mom explained. "It means star and it was my grandmother's name."

We continued to chatter back and forth getting to know each other and then left for the drive home. Along the way, Landon never stopped watching everything that we passed by and asking questions about whatever he didn't understand. He was impressed by the trees and farms that we passed on our way north. It was late afternoon when we arrived home.

The next day after breakfast, I wanted to show Landon what it was like to be out in the woods, and he wanted to see where I had found the strangers so we decided to pack a small lunch with us and spend most of the day. He was not used to walking long distances but was in good shape because he was an excellent tennis player or so he claimed when I asked him if he did anything besides read books. As we went along the road to get to the trail, I explained how to be in the woods and how to walk with as little noise as possible in order to see and hear what is going on around you. I wanted him to share the feelings that I had when out in the woods away from the rest of the people in the world.

"This is the trail I was on when I found them." I said as we stepped off from the road onto the narrow dirt path that led into the trees.

"Why were you going down this trail? It seems so over grown that you would not expect to get very far very fast."

"When I am in the woods I am not in a hurry to get anywhere.

The idea is to just be here and listen and look and wait and see what the natural world has to offer. Sometimes something happens and sometimes you just have a nice quiet walk in the woods. For me the most important thing is just to be here."

"I am not sure if I can understand what you are saying but I certainly like being out here with you. We don't have any wild places like this where I come from. Every bit of land is used for something and if you get off of the road you are in someone's field. Does this land belong to someone?"

"In Containment everything belongs to everybody. No one owns anything personally but they share in the ownership as a citizen."

"How does that work? Doesn't everyone just grab as much as they can for themselves? Who controls who gets to use what?"

"The interesting thing is that I don't know any other way. We talk about money and other forms of economy in our school. But I have never really understood how they work. Here the guiding principal is called beneficial use. If you can put something to a use that benefits society then you are allowed to have it."

"What if more than one person wants a piece of land or a house or the same car?"

"If two people want to claim the same piece of property then the local committee that is their friends and neighbors decides who can make the best use of the property. It almost never comes to that though. People are educated from the very beginning to think of the needs of the whole group. This started back in the beginning when everyone had no choice but cooperate or die because of the radiation levels that were not yet controlled. Things like cars are just regarded as tools and everyone gets the tools they need to do their job and live their life."

"What about rich people surely they don't want to share everything?"

"We don't have rich people because you can't accumulate wealth or gain at another's expense because the Society of Containment owns everything. You only have the use of those things you need. Look, we are making too much noise talking to see any wild life. I'm sure they will explain all of this so it makes sense in the classes. Let's go quietly and listen to the birds. Can you identify birds by their songs?"

"No. Can you?"

"Only the common ones. I can never tell which warbler is which or separate all the sparrows and finches by sound, but I like to try."

We had been walking for a while and I could tell that he was not familiar with how to walk through the woods in a quiet manner. He tended to break branches out of his way rather than bend them and flow past. He did not feel the trail with his feet and stumbled over sticks and rocks that he should have stepped over. I stopped and waited for him.

"You sound just like the strangers that I found that day. I don't think they knew how much noise they were making. It was just about here that I first heard them crashing through the brush. I thought that it was a herd of elk and moved on down the trail to see the elk but then I heard voices and decided to hide."

"Sorry, I really am a novice at being in the woods. I don't think could move through the brush like you. You seem to just flow along and I have to push to keep up. How did you learn to do that?"

"I have spent a lot of time out here since I was a small boy. I never seemed to get along with the other kids and we didn't live in town so I started going for walks. At first I would be angry or upset or lonely and would just start walking to get away from it all. Now I have learned to realize that for me the most interesting and valuable things are out here in the woods. At times it feels like the birds and the trees are talking to you and sharing their secrets. That is why I try to move as quietly as possible so I can hear them."

"OK, I'll try to be quiet as I walk."

"That's OK, I don't mind since this is your first trip in the woods. I don't expect to have you moving and thinking like an animal on your first trip. Here is where I hid when the strangers were on the path."

"Wow, you were that close! I can't believe they didn't see you. Were you frightened?"

"At first I was worried that it was a barrier maintenance patrol and I didn't want to be found and have to explain what I was doing here. Then I realized they were not from Containment and my curiosity took over and I wasn't afraid."

We spent the rest of the morning making our way down to the river. I had not been down to the river since before that day when I found the strangers and I was curious to see if I could figure out why they had been on that trail. There was an old abandoned mine at the edge of the river. I had not found this before. It had to be very old and there was not much left except some rusting rails sticking out of a depression in the ground. There was a pile of broken rock that must have been the tailings and a small bay off from the side of the river that would have suitable for landing a small boat. I remembered Chet saying that he thought that they had come down the river in a boat.

"Let's eat our lunch and take a break. It is going to be up hill all the way home." I said.

"Yes, I am starved." Landon agreed.

After lunch we went down stream for half-mile and went back up a trail that was more used so that it would be easier walking on the way back up the ridge. Along the way we saw a bald eagle sitting in an old snag. We were able to move slowly by and not spook him so we got a close look at him. It was the first time Landon had seen a bald eagle and he was impressed.

"I never knew they were so big and those eyes seem to pierce right through you. He is so powerful and majestic setting there."

"I know and if you ever get to see one catch a fish it is awesome. I was with my Dad at the dam one day and watched an eagle fishing below the spillway. He caught a fish that looked like it weighed twenty pounds. When he had the fish about a dozen sea gulls tried to harass him and he circled over and got in the updraft rising off of the face of the dam and he flew straight up like he had got on an elevator and left the gulls behind. Then when he was up high he just glided downstream to his nest, which is several miles away. All without flapping his wings."

"It is hard to believe that you get to see all these things. We don't have anything but flat ground and farms."

"You probably have birds and wildlife but you haven't learned to watch for them. Most of the people in Containment don't watch for them either, in fact I'm the odd person who doesn't fit the norm. I don't understand why Herman Ott wanted me to be a part of the class, because I am not the typical member of the society."

"Maybe he wants to straighten you out so you do conform to the norm."

"That's what I'm afraid of."

We continued to talk and compare views of the world as we went up the trail. I pointed to the things that I could name and explain, such as how to tell the different types of trees apart. He thought I knew it all, but I never pointed out all the things that I didn't know as we passed them by. We got back to the house as Mom was beginning to prepare dinner.

The few days we had before the class began passed quickly. Dad took us on a tour of the dam and we visited a small cave that is nearby. One day we checked out a boat and ski equipment and we went water skiing in the reservoir above the dam. Landon learned in a short time how to get up. He seems to be a natural athlete. I remembered how many tries it took me and how much lake I drank before I got the hang of it.

Then Sunday came and we were driving back into the city on the way to Herman Ott's house. I was apprehensive and Landon was eager. This was what he had come here for. He was going to learn all of the secrets of Containment and get the knowledge necessary to ease the burdens of his people. What was I going to do? I didn't have a clue. When we drove up to the house I was even more nervous and Landon was more excited. The house was huge and had a large yard of flowerbeds and trees that extended out in front of the house. The house was brick with a wide porch supported by stone columns and a wide front door that was carved with scrolls and figures surrounding a large letter O. The house was set on a hillside so that it looked down to the street where we parked.

We got out and took our bags and walked up a curving path that was made of brick laid in a pattern of squares. The four of us could walk side by side up the steps to the porch. Dad stepped to the door and raised a large brass knocker and let it drop. Once, twice, and on the third time the door opened. A young girl with golden blond hair, wearing a short green dress and white tennis shoes, greeted us.

"Hi, come on in. I'm Elizabeth and you must be the Nascents and Landon."

"Yes, I am Ted Nascent and this is my wife Tzaddi and our son Jason with our guest Landon Holmes. We are really amazed at this house. It must be really old."

"The house was restored after Containment was stabilized but the original structure dates back to the nineteenth century. It was in amazingly good shape because the roof never failed. Most of the other buildings of its time didn't survive the period of abandonment. Let me show you around. My Mom is out at the store and Herman is in his study. He will probably be out in a little while. He doesn't like to be disturbed."

"Do just the three of you live here?" I asked incredulously.

"Yes, but the back wing is all offices for the people that assist Herman and the formal dining room and the ballroom are used for official functions, which are catered by professional cooks. We have our own area that is private and not open to the public."

"There are big houses like this where I come from but I never thought I would be in one. In our country the rich have areas that are fenced off and guarded. You can only get a glimpse of the houses through the trees as you drive by," Landon added.

"Does your mom have to take care of this whole place?" my Mom asked. "I couldn't clean this place in a month." She is looking at the staircase that turns up from the back of the entry and thinking of dusting and polishing all that dark oak.

"No, we just take care of our private area and the staff takes care of the rest when there is a public function. I never go into the back wing and I don't know what they do. Really it is just like we have an apartment." Elizabeth says as she walks us through the large rooms. Then she steps through a door off from the hallway. "Come this way and I'll show you our part."

There is a small kitchen and eating area with an adjacent sitting room. It is really quite pretty with ivory colored wallpaper that has green ivy vines curling across it. The kitchen has a door that opens onto a patio and garden area that is in the back yard and closed off with a fence. The laundry and pantry area is in the back. There is another stairway, but it is only three feet wide not ten or twelve and Elizabeth leads us up.

"Here is your room, Landon and this is Jason's. My Mom and I are across the hall. You guys share a bathroom that is between your rooms. Herman has the third floor, with his study and office. He likes to be able see out across the valley. Don't go up there unless he asks you to."

"What is he like? Does he frighten you?" I ask.

"Oh no, he is a wonderful grandpa but he is so busy and has

things just the way he likes up there and doesn't want things moved around. I am sure he will be down in a little bit."

"Set your bags in your rooms boys and we'll go get the rest of your stuff." Dad suggests.

Chapter Four

On Monday morning, after Elizabeth left to walk up the hill to the neighborhood school, Herman said, "Come on boys," and led us around to the back wing. The back wing had a separate entrance from the street that was behind the house and was arranged more like a business than a home. The other students were arriving and being shown into a large reception room, we joined them there. When everyone was there, we were taken into a conference room that had been refitted as a classroom. Each person had a desk and chair and a supply of pens, paper, and notebooks. There were nameplates made up and setting on each desk. As we found our spots, a person stepped to the front of the room.

"Good morning I'm William Lyons, but call me Bill. I will be the coordinator for this class. I will teach some of the sessions but we will bring in various experts to speak to you on occasions when we are covering the topics that they are experts on. This is a large group to be in just one class so we will probably divide up some time in the future. For now we are going to go through a general orientation for the students from the outside world. I am sure that you from Containment have probably heard this before but bear with us. We will get to things that you don't know or haven't heard before."

"Containment began when the world tired of the problems associated with nuclear power and decided to eliminate it from the world. A place was chosen to house all of the radioactive materials and as they were shipped into the area that was chosen, the people who had a role in the nuclear industry were forced to go with the materials. They had no choice but to include their families and had to make a society that was separate from the rest of the world. Containment was designed to house the elements that were unfit for human companionship and many felt that the Socialist-Anarchists were quite right in insisting that they be included with the atomic workers in Containment. These people had a dream of creating a better world. They wanted a world that was free from the Corporate and Government abuse that controlled the world that they knew on the outside. They came into the area with the idea of providing the food and supplies for the atomic workers. Their leader was Hayward Crowell and he was the one who shaped the political and economic future of Containment. He was a marvelous man with incredible vision and insight and it is to him that we owe the success of our society."

"Imagine a man who could convince his followers to work hard not so they could profit but so that they could give it all away. It was his concept of the economics of energy that became the foundation of our system. The atomic workers needed to do their job to control the wastes and didn't have the time to produce their own food and supplies. The Socialist-Anarchists provided the food and supplies for the opportunity to live the kind of life that they wanted. The atomic workers became the technologists that make our world flourish and the Socialist-Anarchists became the farmers and loggers and other resource workers. Together they all became citizens of Containment and equal partners in a free society."

"The socialist part of the belief system was easier for the technologists to absorb than the anarchistic part of the belief system. They came from a world where everything was governed by laws and standards. An inch of lead would only stop so much radiation regardless of what your belief system was. The proponents of SA stated that they didn't seek to destroy the systems, which govern our lives and behavior but instead asked that we examine what it is that affects our own actions and stop pretending that the people who play political games have any right to affect our lives. In other words follow the natural laws and not the rules of power crazy men."

"Hayward Crowell, when asked, "How does one become a Socialist –Anarchist?" stated, "It is necessary to have developed a holistic view of the creation of the universe. As we look outward, we need to learn to know the world. Put your arms around a tree. Listen to the birds. Watch the flowers bloom and learn to feed yourself. Listen to your mother speak of dying. This is the source of our socialistic nature. Looking inward we come to know the way of service to the almighty creator and hence know no other law. This is the source of our anarchistic nature. We look outward and know that we are no better than the least of the creations and we look inward and know that we are no less than the best.""

"Let's take a break for a while. You should find that you are sitting near someone you don't know. After the break come back and talk to the person beside you. Find out who they are and where they are from. Learn if you have anything in common and then discuss the nature of SA. See if your partner can explain all of the ramifications to you."

The break was no more than a chance to go to the bathroom and get a drink of water for me. As I came back I saw Landon laughing with three girls who had sought him out. They seemed to think he was the most interesting person there, the way they hung on to his every word. I hadn't paid any attention to the person sitting at the desk next to mine and as I sat down, I realized that he was oriental.

"Hi, I said. I'm Jason Nascent and live north of here in Boundary Village. Do you come from China?"

"Yes, I am from Shanghai. My name is Chang Lee Rong. I have come to learn about your country and your way of life."

"Can I call you Chang?"

"That is my family name. In China we give family name first. You can call me Lee."

"OK, Lee you can call me Jason. I don't have any brothers or sisters and I live outside of a small village in the north. Do you have any brothers or sisters?"

"In China you are allowed to have only one child. I live in a large apartment building on the 23rd floor. Shanghai has almost 25 million people now."

"That is amazing. There are less than two million people in all of Containment. Do you understand the ideas of Socialist-Anarchy?"

"China has been a socialist country for several hundred years it is the only way that China can be. There are too many Chinese to be a self-centered people. Everyone must act for the common good if we are to succeed as a people. It is anarchy that I don't understand. How can you not have rules and not have disorder?"

"It is not rules that control people's behavior but their desire to be accepted by their fellow men. Do you have laws in China that everyone ignores?"

"Yes there are some laws that nobody agrees with but then they don't obey them."

"So are the people wrong or are the laws wrong?"

"There are some laws that everyone does agree with and they follow those."

"Yes, they do and they would behave the same even if there wasn't a law because it makes sense to behave in that manner."

"What about thieves and robbers? We have some of them in China and the law punishes them for their actions."

"That only means that China does not practice complete socialism. We believe that you cannot steal from yourself. Everything is the property of the Society of Containment. If you need something then you can have it. You own it as much as anyone else."

"I can see that I have a lot to learn to understand how this society works."

The class continued in a similar manner all morning. We had a short lecture and then a discussion sometimes the whole class and sometimes in a small group. Somehow I thought it would be more interesting when I suggested it. Then again I didn't think I would be in the class when I thought of it.

Lunch was served buffet style in the reception area. You had plenty to choose from to make your own sandwich and salad.

There were also a couple of soups. It didn't seem that unusual for someone from Containment, but I overheard several of the outsiders marveling at the selection and wondering how it could all be free. They still didn't understand that everything is free.

I saw Landon at lunch with a group of students from both the inside and the outside gathered around him. He seemed to naturally attract attention without really doing anything but keeping that goofy smile plastered on his face. He did not act as if he even thought about it. He was dark haired and handsome, with robin's egg blue eyes, but it was the smile that led people to him.

I was sitting outside on the porch eating by myself when I looked up to see Elizabeth going back to school after coming home for lunch. She waved as she went by and was quickly gone, but not before I noticed how her skirt brushed her legs as she walked.

In the afternoon, Bill introduced Herman Ott to the class and he began his discussion of the history. He had a particular way of presenting the history, not as a series of facts and dates but as a panoramic view of the interaction of people's lives. It became apparent that he believed in destiny. He felt that certain people were born to a certain time and they were given the experiences necessary to shape them to meet the challenges that eventually came to them in their life. He began by talking about Hayward Crowell but not in the manner that we had heard in the morning. He talked about the things that happened to him as a young man when he worked for a large corporation. Crowell had done well in the corporation until he worked there long enough to see the way people's lives were used up to feed the corporation. The continuation of the body corporate consumed people by extracting out all of the usefulness that they had to offer and then casting them away.

He became aware of the policies that caused people to be laid off before they could draw their retirement. He saw people whose health was used up by the practice of introducing new chemical products into the workplace before they were tested for the safety of the worker's health. He learned how the corporation forced the employees to surrender all rights to the patents and ideas that they came up with. As he became more aware of the way the inner workings functioned he had two choices. He could become a part of the body corporate or he could walk away. He walked away.

He then joined a government agency as a supervisor in a department that was on the face of it designed to provide service to the citizens. He worked hard to modernize the department that the politicians had underfunded for years. As he became more knowledgeable about how things were done, he learned that the service to the citizens was just a front and the real purpose of the agency was to assist the large developers. He learned of the way that the low-income sections of the population were manipulated to subsidize the developers providing income to the rich. When he protested and tried to change it, he was fired for conduct unbecoming an officer of the government.

These were the impacts on his life that caused him to start writing of the ideas of Socialist-Anarchy. He wrote and wrote before his ideas found an audience with the people whose lives had been consumed by the corporations or stolen by the government that was supposed to be serving the people. He was ready and his followers were ready when the opportunity presented itself to make a new society.

This was new I had not heard this type of history before and by the time the afternoon was over I felt that I knew Hayward Crowell and I knew how he felt and how his actions came from his deep caring for people. I also understood his deep mistrust of the corporations and the government and now I knew why in Containment there was neither.

After the classes were finished, I went for a walk in the large park that was nearby. It was a park and not the wild woods but there were trees and birds and some areas that you could walk undisturbed. Of course you had to ignore the sounds of the traffic that passed by on the streets surrounding the park. This was an old park and had been a park before the period of abandonment so there were trees here that were centuries old with large trunks and spreading branches that reached across the lawn. Not many of the trees were that old but enough so that you felt the awe of their presence. There were oaks, beeches, sycamores, and firs old enough to have been here when the Ott house was built. I could only guess at the stories they could tell.

Chapter Five

That night began what would become many sessions where Landon and I joined Herman in discussions that went beyond the regular classes. We began to affectionately call him the Old Man because he was willing to openly share the volumes of knowledge he had accumulated in over forty years of being the programmer. He claimed that his long tenure was not so much attributable to his abilities or to his tenacity but to the fact that no one else wanted the job. Our conversations were open and free spirited and he let us ask about anything and he would be able to explain it in a way that we could understand.

One evening, Landon asks, "How do you punish those who do evil, when you have no jails or prisons? I can't see how you ever make any one be good or obey the laws."

The Old Man answers, "We don't have laws that require punishment. First of all punishing someone does not make him or her a better person but a bitter person. Punishment is not necessary because it doesn't show the person, who is punished, the wisdom of a better alternative. Each act that a person commits carries its own fulfillment. No one in our society would bring the onus of violence or waste to bear on his soul. He wouldn't dream of having those things slow him down on his evolutionary path. Other acts are actually prevented by the system. It is impossible to steal if no one owns anything. You can have anything you like. If someone else has an item you want or need you only have to demonstrate a greater need and a capacity to use it and it's yours."

The Old Man continues, "Take for instance something as rare as a violin made in 1792. We have one here in Containment that has survived the 500 years in nearly perfect condition. No other violin in Containment has quite the same sound but there is only one of them. Obviously, the person who has this instrument can hardly claim to own it. It was surrendered gladly when he proved he was capable of playing it to the person who had it before him.

He would gladly give it to you if you needed it to play as well as you could."

Landon still looks puzzled and asks, "Don't you punish little children when they don't do as they are told. Aren't they spanked?"

"No, Landon we don't punish children. Jason since you were raised here, can you explain it so he understands about children?"

"Well, children may feel as if they are being punished but the aim is not to punish them for wrong doing but to prevent them from hurting themselves. The Anarchist system recognizes that small children need to be protected from themselves. The training system is not based on punishment but on positive reinforcement. The system provides for a graduated ladder of responsibility for a person to grow into full citizenship."

"OK, OK, what about an adult? Surely, not everybody is such a goody, goody that no one ever hurts someone. What about rape, murder, incest, assault with intent to kill? What do you do with the really evil people? Where I come from people are going to jail every day and here you don't even have a jail. That's what I don't understand."

The Old Man paused for a while and then said, "People are not really good or evil. In fact we try not to characterize anything as good or evil. We feel that most crimes that you speak of were caused from lack of material needs. We try to prevent the lack of material needs so that people can then meet each other's emotional and spiritual needs. If you grow up having your needs met then you are not likely to act in a way that is detrimental to you and society."

"There must be some people who just don't want to be a part

of this society and behave in a manner that is harmful. Can you say that in all these years you have never had to deal with a truly bad person?"

"I have had to deal with some one that I ended up thinking was truly bad but I don't like to be reminded of that. I hope that the society can prevent those problems from ever reoccurring. There have been some people who have caused problems by killing their wife's lover or something like that. There have been some people who truly don't want to belong to the society and they are usually drug addicted."

"So what happens then?"

"Some who have been found guilty of murder have been required to work in areas that are higher in radiation than would normally be allowed. They provide a service to the society and work until they are unable to do so.

Those who are drug addicts can still participate in society if they still perform their job. If they want to be free of the requirements of society, any person can choose the exempt status."

"What is the exempt status?"

"You are exempt from meeting the requirements of the society but you are also not eligible to receive any of the benefits of the society. You have to make your own way in the world. Grow your own food and provide for all your other needs, such as medical."

"Are there many who choose that option?"

"No, because once you make that choice it is for life. You can't change your mind if you decide that it is too tough to make it on your own. There are some who do make the choice but they are very few."

While all of this was going on, I went back to doing my favorite thing. I was looking at the books that Herman had collected on plant identification. I was becoming more like Landon in that I would read everything I could on plants, mushrooms, and wildflowers. I wanted to know everything there was to know about the natural world. Herman's library was extensive. The shelves covered most of the walls in the upstairs. He had collected many diverse subjects and was familiar with many of the things that I found fascinating. He helped me to get started in the wildflower books and spent time showing me how to key out mushrooms. He admitted that mushrooms were his real fascination for many years.

The days went on and we went to class and spent time talking to Herman but we also had our chores around the house, such as cleaning and laundry. We shared the kitchen duties with Elizabeth and her mom. I found myself looking forward to the times that I was around Elizabeth even if it was spent washing dishes. I began talking to her about my feelings of not really fitting in and I found that she had some of the same type of feelings. One day I was too bold and asked her what happened to her dad. She was upset and finally admitted that she knew something terrible had happened but she didn't know what. She had never known her dad. There were no pictures of him in the house and the only times when she asked her mom about him ended with her mom in tears and no information.

I gave her a hug and told her that it was all right. She was a beautiful person and her mother loved her very much. I wanted to tell her that I loved her also but didn't.

She occasionally went on walks with me to the park or down

to the river after school. It was a smaller river than the one where I lived and ran through a city but there were still places to go that were wild and unsettled. I would look for wildflowers and mushrooms and we would talk about the way the clouds blew through the sky and the patterns that the birds made as they flew.

Landon would usually have friends who invited him over to help with their studies. They were almost always girls. He also started playing tennis with the people at the local tennis club. I heard that he was really good and had no problem beating most of the local players. Then he asked Elizabeth if she wanted to learn to play tennis. She was thrilled that he asked her and said yes. He was a good instructor and she was fairly athletic so that it didn't take long before they were playing mixed doubles at the club. I was not inclined to try to learn to play tennis, as I am not very coordinated. I also didn't want to get into a contest with Landon for Elizabeth's attention because I knew that I would lose. Everyone liked to be around Landon including me.

The classes went on into the fall as we learned more about the inner workings of Containment. I became very interested in the way the programming was set up. The instructor for the programming class was not Herman. He claimed that although he was called the programmer he actually did very little with the actual program. He directed a staff that took care of the actual details. I was surprised to learn that there was no single computer that held the entire program. It actually wasn't just one program, but a series of programs on computers located all over Containment linked in a manner that let them operate as one.

THE SPIRIT OF HUMANITY

Anyway, the instructor was a woman named Helen Pendleton and she was responsible for the main program.

As the administrator she controlled access to the various computers that contained the actual running version. The way the system operated the processing was distributed as well as the data storage so the whole system functioned as one computer. It was not necessary to keep a pair of duplicate systems that were redundant with hot backup so that they were able to automatically kick in if needed. If one hub was down the program rerouted the data flow as necessary to other nodes that were in the same loop. Since the main program had been functioning for a long time there were few changes that needed to be made.

The activities of most people who had anything to do with the processors were to feed the processors the data of everyday life. Virtually everything about everything was recorded somewhere in the system. The agricultural production data was managed so that each farmer was producing just what was needed from their land. The whole system took in account the weather and seasonal variations, predicted which crops would do well where and allocated the production as necessary among the farmers. The farmers reported their activities and received updates as needed. Each aspect of the societies needs was managed in a similar manner.

Helen took us on our first field trip. We went to the basement to see her terminal. Her keyboard was connected to a series of monitors that could be switched to reveal different parts of the program that were operating at the time. The basement also had the large fiber optic switch that allowed the connections between terminals to take place nearly instantaneously. The way that she explained the arrangement of the computers was a series of wheels. The programs that were in each computer were only the ones necessary for that computer to do its work. The computer for our village didn't have information about any other village but was able to communicate information to other villages if needed.

I asked about the local controllers who do the work on each of the smaller systems and how they are prevented from doing more than they are supposed to. The answer is that in our system if you can figure out how you are allowed. I puzzled over this for a long time. I realized that this was truly a manifestation of the anarchistic principal at work. No controls whatever. The idea that if you were intelligent enough to figure out how to do something, then you were intelligent enough to figure out the right thing to do was somehow so scary and at the same time so reassuring that I spent hours pondering what the ramifications could be. Anybody could be the programmer from any location if they knew how.

I began to read the programming books in Herman's library and ask him questions about when he became the programmer. I never got him to talk about how he took over as the programmer. He continued to insist that the only reason that he was still the programmer was that no one wanted the job, but I began to realize that he did control access to the key elements of the program that even Helen Pendleton did not know about. He spent hours of time on his terminal in his study when no one else was around. When I asked him what he did, he replied that he was merely reviewing what the other programmers were doing.

One day when I was down visiting Helen after class, I got my first confirmation that maybe he did more that he let on. I was asking Helen to show me the way that she could contact the hubs of all the various wheels and we happened onto something that caused her to emit a gasp of surprise. When I asked her about it she muttered something about him being up to his old tricks again. When I said who is up to his old tricks, she replied you know Herman but then gave me no details when I asked for further information. She changed the subject and switched to a different location on her terminal so that I didn't see what had caused her surprise.

I spent more and more time on the terminals that they allowed the class to use and began to see where I could go and what I could do. I was able to make some changes in the program that were small but noticeable on a local level. When I saw that the changes went through I realized that it was true if you could figure out how you were allowed.

No one in the class complained when we started getting ice cream with our lunch as well as our usual choices. I didn't think anyone noticed until one day The Old Man said during our evening discussion, "I see you are having fun with your programming knowledge."

"What do you mean?" I asked.

"You know the change in the lunch menu." He replied. "That is fine that you have learned so much. Just remember the principles of our society require that you act for the greater good of all."

"I understand. This was just a harmless experiment. Besides, everyone likes the ice cream."

"No one objected to the change. That is why it went through.

I just want you to learn from this and think about all of the consequences of any action you take with your programming knowledge. I am proud of the way you have been able to learn this. No one else in the class has a clue that it is even possible to make a change, let alone figure out how to do it."

"Can you show me how to get past the local level computer?" I asked.

"Yes, I could but I am not going to. You need to learn more of how the economic system works before you begin messing around with something on the larger scale."

"Would you explain how you became the programmer?" I asked knowing that he hadn't wanted to talk about this in the past.

"I became the programmer when I wanted to make changes for my own selfish reasons. After the consequences came back to haunt me, I realized the error of my ways and have spent the last forty years trying to make up for it. That is why I want you to learn responsibility before you gain further access to the program. If you try to make selfish changes I will block them."

"I really have learned to appreciate Containment a lot more than I did in the past. I don't want to do anything that would upset the balance of the way the society functions."

"That is good, but enough for now. Let me be alone for a while."

I left knowing that he had told me more than he probably wanted about being the programmer. I didn't know how he got there but I knew that he had made changes that he regretted. What could they have been? I wished that there were some way of knowing. I was marveling at the idea that he knew that it was me who had ordered the ice cream when it occurred to me. Somewhere there is a log of the changes and who made them.

I had remained friends with Chang Lee Rong, who I had met the first day of class. He was the other student who spent free time working on the computer. I wondered what his level of interest was. I saw him the next day before class.

"Lee," I called out to him as he walked by.

"Oh, Jason How are you today?"

"I'm fine. How is it going with you?"

"I am liking the classes but I have trouble with the network links between the computers. I want to set up a system when I get home so we can become a more socialist country like here. I notice that you seem to get through the network. Can you help some time?"

"Sure, I wouldn't mind helping you. How about later today after class?"

"That would be great. I'll see you then. I guess we better go sit down for class."

"Good morning class" Bill said. He was standing with a short thin man with dark hair and a neatly trimmed beard. "It is my pleasure to introduce to you one of the direct descendants of Haward Crowell, Mervin Crowell from the great basin irrigation project. He will speak to you about the principles of Socialist-Anarchy and the development of Containment's supply system. This may take a while so be prepared to focus your attention on the not very exciting details of why this place works. Here is Mervin Crowell."

"Greetings, I will start out by saying that I never anticipated the need or the opportunity to speak to people from outside of Containment. It is our job in the supply section to predict the needs of our society and make sure that we can meet those needs. This was critical in the beginning and remains critical today. Initially, the emphasis totally focused on getting all of the nuclear wastes at least covered securely from the weather and not poisoning the people who were forced to deal with the wastes. The nuclear scientists, technicians, engineers, and operating personnel from around the world were not given any choice about being a part of Containment. When the time came that humanity could no longer tolerate the presence of the sudden disaster machines, when millions of people are affected and large areas of land are made uninhabitable again and again across the globe, the people eventually wake up to the lies of nuclear safety and insist on the removal of not only the problem but also the people that are perceived to have created and profited from the problem.

If you use a little bit of imagination, you can visualize about how long it would take for Containment to stabilize if the nuclear specialists also had to figure out how to live in this area and grow enough food for themselves as well as provide all of the other needs of a society. Remember the history of the area that became Containment. This area was once the eastern portion of Washington State which was home to the Hanford Nuclear Reservation. Where the Manhatten Project's plutonium bomb was created. After the end of the second World War, the corporations realized what a cash cow they had and convinced Eisenhower to create the civilian nuclear power program as well as build up a huge stock pile of nuclear weapons and missiles that continue to plague humanity. The production of vast quantities of plutonium polluted the entire area but the worst problem came about after the weapons production was shut down.

The plutonium was produced as a by-product of the nuclear fission process in a uranium reactor. The plutonium had to be removed from the spent fuel rods and separated from all of the other fission products and processed into a form that was usable to the weapons production people. In order to do this they built the PUREX Plant. Because plutonium is not a friendly substance to be around, the production was done using a series of glove boxes where workers performed their tasks reaching into glass covered boxes with long rubber gloves that were mounted on the side of the box. When the government shut down the PUREX plant production they anticipated restarting the process at some time in the future. There was no cleanup of the materials in the production line. They basically just turned off the equipment and walked away. Turned off the lights and closed the door.

"Good morning class," Bill said. He was standing at the front of the room with a gray haired woman that I hadn't seen before. "Today we are going to do something that is a little different than what we have done in the past. Dr. Shevnovski is the head of the Nuclear Safety Commission She has the responsibility for the function that Containment was created for. She is in charge of the safe storage of the nuclear wastes that we received at the beginning of Containment. It is because of the people who work for Dr. Shevnovski that we are able to exist in comfort and safety. I want you to know that this was not always the case. In the beginning of Containment, there were always people sick and dying of radiation poisoning. The nuclear scientists have solved most of the problems of long term storage in a way that protects us in Containment and meets our charge to protect the rest of the world."

Bill moves across the room to a large container sitting in the corner. "This container has samples of highly radioactive waste. If at the conclusion of Dr. Shevnovski's presentation, you feel that you could do a better job, you can have a sample to take home to play with. If you feel that you appreciate the work that has been done by the scientists then you can leave your sample here in the container. Each one of you have a sample and at the end of this portion of the training you need to know what to do with it and design a project to accomplish a safe use for your sample. If in handling your sample you get radiation sickness then you will have a feeling for what the first members of our society went through. I would now like to present Dr. Shevnovski."

"I will begin by telling you that I don't recommend anyone taking the sample home. It would probably cause a lot of consternation in your family. However, if at the end of this presentation today you feel that it would be safe then you certainly can take it home. You will learn first hand what we are going to talk about today. The effects of radiation poisoning do not become immediately noticeable unless the dose is high enough to approach fatal. There is usually a time delay depending on the dose before physical symptoms present themselves. When you receive a very high dose, death can occur rapidly."

"The shipments that were sent to Containment from the rest of the world had some items that were very high in radioactivity to some that were just barely radioactive. The first settlers of containment had no idea what they were getting or when. The barges came up the Columbia River or the railroad trains came in loaded to the maximum that the engines could pull. The first thing that was necessary was to evaluate what we had. You will have to do this with the sample that you receive. Then we had to make plans for long-term storage. Early on it became apparent that long-term storage wasn't an immediate option. The shipments had to be covered to prevent the workers from dying before they could even finish the assessment. A strategy for the short term was formulated. A plant was set up to manufacture precast concrete beams that could be assembled around and over the shipments as they came in. In some cases these concrete shells had to be covered with earth to further shield the highly radioactive spent fuel and reactor cores. These chambers would then be entered as time allowed by robotic methods and sampled and characterized. A long term storage plan could then be worked out."

I won't bore you with all of the details that Dr. Shevnovski provided us on that day. I knew that this was a major part of the education of the outsiders. The people of Containment wanted them to understand just what it was we had been charged with and how critical it was that we be allowed to meet our responsibility to the world. I had no idea what I was going to do with my sample. I didn't even want to look at it. Some of the other students were caught up in the excitement of dealing with something that was so dangerous. I was glad to leave it there and meet Lee to talk about computers.

"Jason, I am glad to see you didn't forget." Lee remarked as I walked up.

"I wouldn't forget. I'm happy to work with you on your network problem." I said. "Let's go downstairs and see if Helen will let us use her terminal. She has a much better connection and we will be able to do things a lot faster."

"I would never think of asking for special permission but you are a special student so she might let you."

"You still are not thinking in true socialist terms. We are all equal here. If we tell her we have a need then we should get to use the better terminal."

"I think you are more special here than you realize. I appreciate your reminder to think more socialistically though. That is why I am here. I want to learn how this place works."

"Well, let's go down and ask."

When we got downstairs, Helen wasn't there. I asked another one of the techs if we could use her terminal. He said no but allowed us to use a separate terminal that had the same connection speed. He required us to sign in and log our activity so that he would not be blamed if we screwed something up. With the higher speed and wider bandwidth it was possible to quickly show Lee the architecture of the directories and how the network was connected. As I was moving through the pages I was looking for something else. I wanted to know how the changes to the program were logged historically. I wanted to find out if there was fifty years of history. Lee printed out some of the directories that showed the links between the wheels and how the parallel processors were able to share information. This would be very important in setting up a system when he got back to China.

It was while I was gathering pages of directories for Lee that

I made another discovery that hinted at the way the programmer controlled the system. Since the various parts of the operating system were divided up and were modified at so many different locations to suit the local conditions, the real control was not in controlling the program but in controlling the communications between the various nodes on the wheels and between the wheels. I thought that I might have made a discovery that would unlock the hidden secrets of Containment if I could learn how to decipher the communication protocol. I had not found what I was looking for, however. I still wanted to find the historical files and gain access to them.

"Lee, do you think that now you can find your way around and through the system?" I asked.

"I understand better now. Thank you for taking time to show me."

"What are you going to be doing now with your new knowledge?"

"I want to continue to explore how it all fits together. I need to be able to make a similar system. Do you not think I should explore the system?"

"Oh, no. It is perfectly fine for you to explore the system. In fact you can probably come down here to use the terminal that we did today. That will make your exploration easier and I will help you if you need it."

"Thank you again, I am glad that you are willing to help me and I appreciate your reminders about socialism. How can I repay you? Most students here don't seem to be as friendly as you."

"I am not so friendly with most of the others either, but you and I seem to be interested in similar things. I would like to see the things you discover in your exploration if you wouldn't mind making me a copy."

"Yes, I can copy for you. Thank you very much."

"Great, don't send the copies to my terminal just make a paper copy and give it to me if you would."

"I can do that. I am going to my home now. Thank you again."

I went back upstairs and into the private residence part of the building. There was no one home except Elizabeth's mom. Landon and Elizabeth were playing tennis. I realized that I had never heard her called anything but Mom. We had been living there for over a month and I really didn't know her name. We had not had time for many conversations.

"Hi," I said as I went in. "Do you want me to help with dinner?"

"It is almost all done but you can set the table." She answered. "Landon and Elizabeth will be home when they finish their match and then we'll eat. How was your day today?"

"The lesson today was on radioactivity and on how to contain it. I wasn't as interested in it as some of the others."

"I know, Landon was excited when he came in to get Elizabeth. He said you each get a sample to play with. He sounded like he could hardly wait."

"I don't even want to see my sample. It is too scary to think about handling it."

"I agree. I told Landon that he better not even think about bringing that thing home. I have had enough loss to radioactivity.

I wish sometimes that we could be free of the whole charge and let some other part of the world have the responsibility."

She seemed to be so sad as she said that.

I wondered, "Did you lose your husband to radioactivity, Mrs. Ott?"

"Jason, I should never have said anything. Don't call me Mrs. Ott. Call me Julie. Ott is my maiden name. We never married. Elizabeth's dad died from a massive dose of radiation before anyone even knew I was pregnant. My dad died in another accident forty years ago, before I was born. He was Herman's son. Neither Elizabeth nor I ever knew our Dad. I shouldn't have told you all of this. I just was overcome by the sadness after all of this time." She cried softly and turned away.

I reached out and put my arm around her shoulders. "It is OK, I want you to know that I care a lot for you and Elizabeth. You have treated me well and I don't want you to be so sad. I won't say anything to anyone."

"Oh Jason, I didn't mean to burden you with this but I get so lonely at times. You had better finish setting the table. They will be home soon." She walked away dabbing at her eyes and went to check the oven.

The next day in class, the morning session was all nuclear theory. The good Dr. explained how the early nuclear technicians had to solve the basic problems of radiation and heat. The fact that elements that are radioactive are not stable and the mix of elements change as the decay progresses is one of the complications. The dimensions of the materials actually change and the shape of the vessels that hold the materials is also not stable. In order to have a long-term storage system all of this must be taken into account. Dr. Shevnovski was very proud of the way that the solution provided a useful output of energy and could be a benefit to the society.

They did have to provide constant attention and reprocessing and not just monitoring something in storage because of the useful yield of energy. Some of the decay products also had a beneficial use in the medical field. It was amazing to me to watch the excitement among the students as they learned about the possibilities of the nuclear energy. It seemed that many of them saw the nuclear energy as a blessing and not a curse. I couldn't forget the pain in Julia's eyes as she told me about her losses. I had no trouble leaving this section of the discussion when the morning ended.

In the afternoon, Herman's discussion of the history of Containment had to do with the formation of the constitutional program. The operating program for society is a computer that makes all of the allocations of resources and there is no bureaucratic government. This did not happen by accident. This is another blessing of the clear long range thinking of Hayward Crowell. He understood that the people had to have some way of exercising direct control. It is not possible for anarchy to exist in any type of government. The worst form of government is no worse than the best form of government when it comes to guaranteeing the freedom of the people. Herman explained in great detail how Crowell knew that even a good government thinks that it has a right to exist. It is not long until the projection is made that the government has the right to protect itself. This is followed by the assumption that anyone who doesn't agree with the government policies must have a criminal intent. If someone is a criminal then it is fine if the government violates their rights in order to protect the government. The final step is that it is good if the government commits criminal acts if it is doing so to protect its own interests.

The example that Crowell wrote about was the presidency of Ronald Reagan. The whole presidency was consumed with the idea that it was necessary to oppose communists and drugs. The fallacy of a president who preached, "Just say no," while importing cocaine to sell to finance his illegal wars was lost on his followers. They thought he was the great communicator. In reality he was an actor hired to play the part of the president while the corporations who hired him looted the federal treasury. The people who were hurt the worst were those that supported him the most. The poor and the religious, who were easily confused by his rhetoric that was geared to inflame their passions against drugs and communists, never realized that they were just pawns in the bigger game.

It was the brilliant writings of Hayward Crowell that convinced people to join him in founding the Socialist-Anarchists in the twenty-first century that laid the foundation for the success of Containment. Those people who had read his works and understood that all government is wrong were ready to step forward and voluntarily join the atomic workers who were being forced into isolation. This was the beginning of a new society and a new way of thinking. If the nation is to be, "By the people, for the people, and of the people," then there cannot be a government.

When the program was set up to operate Containment, Hayward Crowell was the first programmer. He made sure that anyone could modify the program if they knew how. The committees that were responsible for the various functions were given the authority to establish the algorithms that had to do with those functions. However, the architecture of the programs made it possible for anyone and everyone to have the option to modify the program partitions that had anything to do with them, if they knew how.

There is a set of classifications for the citizens. A full citizen was called a valid programmer and had access to any aspect of the program that they had the understanding to reach. A juvenile programmer was a programmer in training and could advance as fast as they were capable. They had to become a contributor to the operation of the society to get their full rights. An exempt status was a non-participant. This was regarded as an honorable status because the person who applied for exempt status agreed to accept full responsibility for their self. This was a lifelong decision and could not be rescinded so it was not done lightly.

Musicians and other free thinkers who were into the pursuit of knowledge through hallucinogens sometimes asked for the exempt status. The final status was used even less it was called invalid. A person who was given the invalid status was considered a non-citizen and was fully ostracized. They had no rights to any of the benefits of society and had to find some way to cope. This status was given to those who committed grave anti-social acts.

Hayward Crowell began with the concept that everyone was equal and had an equal right to the resources of the society if they were willing to contribute to the society. Therefore, every contributing person was assigned a citizen's number. This number was used in all transactions, whether you were contributing or using a resource. Once the main system of computers was set up, they acted as an accountant. The resources were inventoried and algorithms were set up for the distribution of the resources. As the society progressed the base of knowledge in the computers progressed. The amount of information grew exponentially and a new way of analyzing the information had to be developed. The solution was found in fractal mathematics. The analyses could be done on a small representative sample and the results extended to describe the whole. Eventually the complexity was such that based on weather analyses the computers were able to tell which farmers to grow which crops so that all of the needs of Containment were met.

We have come so far now that the processing the computers do is really transparent to the way that we live our lives. If you need something you go and get it. You do your job as needed and everyone's life goes on unimpeded by the thoughts of want. The day-to-day life of everyone in Containment is never concerned with anything more than doing a good job at whatever they do.

Landon and I left together that afternoon. I wanted to stroll up to the park and hang out with the old trees. He didn't have a tennis match and wanted to talk to me about the lessons that we had gotten on the computer program. We walked out of the back wing of the house and headed up the hill to the park. As we walked, he kept asking questions.

"Why would anyone want to work hard if all they get is the same as everyone else?" He questioned.

I thought about it and then replied, "People work hard because they take pride in what they do. It makes people feel good to know that they have done as well as they can. In many ways people are not equal and do not receive the same thing that everyone else gets. A person who is a good farmer gets to use thousands of acres to raise his crops but a person who lives in town only has the lot that their house sets on."

"If that is the case then what does it mean when everyone in Containment continually says that everyone is equal? How can you be equal and not be equal in what you have and get?"

"In Containment when everyone says that everyone is equal they mean that no one is more important than anyone else. No one has any more value as a human being and a citizen than anyone else. People have the same opportunity to pursue their goals as the next person. If you choose a different path then of course you will have a different set of things that come your way."

"In our country if you do more and are more successful then you get more in the way of worldly goods. But everyone doesn't have the same opportunities when they start out. I certainly could not afford to get a college education. I have to hope for a scholarship when I get back if I want to do anything except hoe weeds in my Dad's fields. My Dad could never afford to buy any more land to farm no matter how good he is."

"What do you think you will do when you get back home? Aren't you going to have to share the knowledge that you get here?"

"Yes, I will but at this point I don't know what that will mean. I haven't learned anything yet that will make me a fortune or even give me an opportunity."

"Have you found anything that interests you in what we have studied so far?"

"The nuclear studies I find fascinating but that is not something I am going to be allowed to pursue when I get back home. There is a prohibition against anything nuclear no matter how beneficial it is."

"Well, you can certainly understand that, after all of the problems that the world has had with the use of nuclear power."

"That was in the past. Look at what you people have done here. Your society is much better off because you have the use of the nuclear materials. The energy that radiation gives off is free. You don't have to do anything to get it."

"There is not a net benefit to our society from the use of the nuclear energy. We only have it because we were stuck with all of the waste from the whole world. The energy that we salvage as part of the storage process is a small percentage of the power that we use in our society. The largest source is hydroelectric and then solar power. We pay a heavy price to the nuclear materials in the health effects on the atomic workers."

"I thought that the health problems had been solved a long time ago."

"We solved the problem of the cancers that were killing a lot of people in the beginning of Containment but the exposure to radiation causes a lot of problems that haven't been solved such as genetic defects."

"I guess that there is more that I have to learn before I am ready to go home."

"Sure, such as do you know what is making that chirping whistle sound?"

"No, but I bet you are going to tell me."

"It is a quail. The quail have a system where one of them watches and chirps while the others eat. If the watcher stops then the others know there is a danger nearby and they head for cover. The atomic workers are similar in our society. As long as they keep telling us what a great job they are doing then we know it is safe. If for some reason they become quiet and concerned we know that there is danger."

"I'll keep that in mind when we take the field trip to the storage facility."

"That is why I shared that with you. I haven't been inside a facility either but it wouldn't break my heart if I never saw the inside of a nuclear plant of any kind."

"This is enough of a walk for me let's go home and get some supper."

That night after we had eaten and put the dishes away, Landon and I went upstairs to Herman's rooms to see if he was in a mood to share some more of his knowledge. I particularly liked to learn about plants and wild life from him. He seemed to have a lot of knowledge about the outdoors for someone who seemed to spend all of his time indoors. I decided to ask him about that, if he was in a talking mood. When we got upstairs, he called out, "Well boys, how are you doing? Have you learned all you need to know?"

Landon replied, "No, sir I have only just begun to understand nuclear science and the uses of nuclear power. I want to be able to take some useful knowledge home to help my people."

I jumped in, "I would really like to know more about the plant world and why do you know so much about them. Were you as curious about all of the living things as I am?"

"Those are certainly two divergent topics for one night's discussion. I'll tell you what Landon. I'll introduce you to someone who can teach you all the nuclear theory that you can stand. That is not really my area of expertise. You probably know as much as I do already. Those two topics really are the crux of Containment. You know that we were founded to safely store the nuclear waste and that the Socialist-Anarchists built the society because they were willing to farm and produce the goods for the technologists and give it away. So our society was built on plants and science. So tonight let's talk about plants and the natural world. Is that fine with you boys?"

"Yes!" I cried out. Surprised at my own outburst I noticed a grin on Herman's face.

"Well it is OK, I guess," said Landon a whole lot less enthusiastically. "But I really want to meet this scientist who can explain everything about nuclear science."

"You will. I promise to take you there soon. He doesn't live too far away. Tonight I'll show you something that you haven't seen right here in this house. Follow me."

He walked over to what I had always thought was a closet door and opened it. A flight of narrow stairs led up to what, I wondered as we followed him up. It was dark until he reached a light switch and turned it on. I was amazed we were surrounded by green growing plants of numerous kinds.

"Most of my free time is spent up here." He said. "I had the greenhouse added thirty five years ago. Jason you asked if I was interested in the living things and the answer is yes. I was always wandering in the woods as a youngster. I could not get enough time to spend out in the woods. When I became the programmer I knew that I would not get to spend the time I wanted out in the wild so I built my own wild up here.

The hard part was getting people to agree to tear apart the roof over this section. This house exists because of the slate roof was built so well that it would never need repairs. No one wanted to compromise its integrity. This would just be a dark attic if I hadn't forced the issue.

Let me show you around. The greenhouse is organized in sections with different climates being represented. There are partitions between the sections so that you can control the light, temperature, and humidity between the different sections. This section is a desert environment and is characterized by cactus from lots of different areas of the world. The next section is a temperate climate where I have trees like the citrus that won't grow this far north. The last section is a warm moist jungle and is filled with some of my favorite plants."

"How were you able to get plants from all over the world?" I was amazed that he had some of the things that he did.

"Some of the plants have a history that dates back to the beginning of Containment. When they set up Containment, the outside world knew that it would have to be self-sustaining so they furnished a lot of the items that you see here now. There are some of these plants whose history can be traced back to the beginning. However, not all of the plants are that old. Some are of a more recent acquisition. The general public is not aware that there has always been a means to contact the outside world. It was set up initially so that if there was a severe problem that threatened the existence of Containment help could be obtained. Initially the contact process was to be used for things like an outbreak of a contagious disease or shortage of a critical material that could not be obtained from within the boundaries. Eventually, the contact became an exchange of friendly gifts and the programmer of the time was able to obtain items that he would not otherwise have access to. I used this process to enlarge the collection of plants in our society. I do not have the only specimens of each species. There are other greenhouses and they are all open to the public."

"That is so fascinating. What is your most unusual plant?"

"I have many that are unusual but my favorites are the various cacti. They are so beautiful when they bloom and they can live in the harshest environment. In fact some of them have to have a harsh environment in order to flower. That is why I like them. The harder it is on them the better they do."

"Which plants are the hardest to get to grow?" Landon asks. "I never imagined such a place in this house. How do you do it?"

"The hardest to get to grow are the various jungle plants. Their normal home is so diverse that we don't know what the critical requirements for their propagation are. In the jungle, conditions change in just a few feet of elevation. Many of the plants are interrelated with many other plants some that we may not even know about."

"Do you use any of the plants for anything?" I wondered.

"I get fruit from the citrus trees but some of the other plants are medicinal herbs and there are some of the plants that are hallucinogenic. Those can only be used for special purposes."

"Do you use the hallucinogenic plants?" I asked incredulously.

Herman laughed and said, "Not any more, those are a younger man's pursuit."

"Why would anyone want to take such a thing? Those types of plants are not legal in my country." Landon questioned.

"In Containment every pursuit of knowledge is legal and using hallucinogens can help a person to reach an understanding of the forces of nature that they might not otherwise. Remember that people are responsible for themselves and no other person should judge what they do in the quest for knowledge. We believe that all of the things that are in the natural world have a purpose and were given to us to use. These things are considered a gift of the spirit."

"I still think that things are illegal for a reason." Landon argued. "Without rule and laws then everyone can just do as they please and no one would ever do anything that was right. I can't understand how this society exists without prisons to punish the lawbreakers."

"If there are no laws there are no law breakers. Our society is formed on the agreement of intelligent men not on the power of enforced laws to regulate behavior. The way to get men to do the right thing is to accept that the basic nature of man is to do the right thing and reward them when they do."

"I guess it is going to take me a long time to learn to think like that. I was brought up to think that man is basically subject to the temptation of the devil. We were taught to respect the word of God as given to us by the priest and to work to earn forgiveness for the sins that we were born with as well as the sins that we commit." Landon wanted the last word on this subject.

Herman looked at Landon and you could almost feel the

tension as he said. "So much death and destruction was caused by the preaching of the priests enforced by the power of the government that Hayward Crowell spent a lot of his writing to dispute the ideas of sinfulness. We know that a child is perfect when it comes into the world. We have to work to insure that the child's mind is filled with the positive and not the confusion taught by the churches, if the child is to grow to reach their potential."

"Do you mean that no one believes in God?"

"Oh no, nearly everyone believes in a divine power but they also understand that every man has to learn to make his own relationship with that power. No one would accept that anyone else could negotiate that relationship for him so we have no priests. We do have shamans who teach and help others to reach that understanding."

"I think our priests would say that everyone here would be going to hell and that they have no hope of being saved."

"As we have no prisons we also do not have a hell that we use to frighten people. I don't want to try to change your mind on all of the things that you were taught. I am just trying to explain the way that we have learned works for us here in Containment. Maybe that is enough for today."

The next day's classes marked the end of the fall period. The students were given a break for a week and Landon and I were going to use the time to visit my parents. I couldn't wait to get home and spend some unstructured time out in the woods. We were not entirely free as we were given a reading assignment that was to be the basis of our discussion when we were back at class. We did not all understand the nature of the assignment. Some of the group openly questioned the reason for the assignment. The assignment was to read <u>Eugenie</u> from the works of the Marquis De Sade.

Chapter Six

My mom was glad to see us. She acted like I had been gone for a year. She had made cookies and cleaned the house and had our rooms all made up with fresh linens. She kept asking questions about what all we had learned and were the Otts good people to stay with. She didn't think that we were getting enough to eat but we both assured here that we were never hungry. I think that moms are moms the world over because when we were alone Landon said that she was just like his mom so much so that he thought he was home.

Mom and Dad had both gotten time off and wanted to spend as much time as possible doing things with us. We of course had been doing stuff at a fast pace for weeks and wanted to lie around. We decided to go camping and kayaking down the river. This was a new adventure for Landon and he was a little apprehensive about sitting in a small narrow craft so close to the water. When we had everything loaded up and got started he quickly realized that the kayaks were stable and fast and he could handle it without fear. He really is a natural athlete. Our plan was to go down stream and find places to camp and not be in a hurry.

It was early afternoon and we were slowly moving along the shore of the river. We had fishing rods and were using flies that Dad had tied. Landon and I were trying to learn to cast the line out and get the fly to land with a proper presentation. It was hard enough trying to stay out of the overhanging tree branches and brush along the shore. Dad would show us again and again how to build a loop, how to shoot the line, and how to lay the line down so the fly just landed on the water. It seemed that no matter what I did the fly would land about twenty feet away in a splash with a pile of line around it. Landon once again started getting the hang of it quickly. He soon was making casts that were picture perfect. It is all in not moving the wrist he told me as if he had been doing it all of his life. Eventually, I let the pole lie along the side of the kayak and the line drifted behind as we moved slowly along. I wasn't that interested in making perfect casts anyway.

I found that I could paddle along and watch the birds in the trees. I wasn't that concerned with catching fish. The next thing I knew my pole jumped and I nearly lost it as a large fish hit the fly that I had been dragging behind me. I almost tipped over in my excitement before I began to play the fish and slowly reel him in. I had difficulty in keeping the kayak headed in the right direction as the fish pulled from side to side. If I stopped reeling to paddle I lost line as the fish took back what I had gained. It was only when Dad came along side and steadied my kayak with his and he used his net that we were able to get the fish out of the water. It was a big fat rainbow that was twenty-three inches long and weighed seven pounds. I had never caught such a fish nor have I since. I felt like all the things I had ever done didn't seem like anything important compared to the feeling of that fish and I fighting for over thirty minutes. I looked at the fish in awe. We had paddled over to the shore and it lie in the grass along the bank. I almost wished I had let it go as I watched its colors fade. Dad said lets clean that fish for dinner. I wasn't sure I wanted to.

While we were fishing, Mom had paddled ahead to the place that we were going to camp for the night. There was a small creek babbling down to river and a meadow that opened up along the side of the creek. Yellow willows that draped the area in long hanging streams of gold and green shaded the creek. Mom was gathering wild flowers and pressing them in a book when we got there. I was too excited about catching the fish to look at what she had found until later when she asked me, "Didn't Herman give you some books on identifying wild flowers?"

"Yes, he did. I brought one along and I also brought a book on mushrooms. He has quite a collection and he gave me these to get me started. I was planning on doing some hiking and looking around after we had the camp set up."

"I picked a few of these flowers hoping you could help me figure out what they were and if they would grow in the yard back home. It would nice to have wild flowers filling the back yard instead of the grass that no one wants to mow."

"The problem with growing wild flowers is that they need to have the same conditions that they grow in naturally and sometimes they don't even flower every year in the wild if the conditions aren't right, but let's see what you have."

"Herman has certainly taken an interest in seeing that you boys are educated in a wide range of interests. I am glad that this is all working out. I had my doubts about this whole program. I wasn't sure Herman would be up to coping with a couple of young men at his age and after all he has gone through."

"Do you know what all he has gone through in being the programmer?"

"No, I just meant that he lost his own son at an early age. I don't know any of the details. But once he was the programmer he kept himself isolated for a lot of years. I am surprised and pleased that he seems to get along with you so well."

"I am surprised that we get along so well too. I thought that he would be a scary old man, but he has helped me in a lot of ways. Like giving me these books. I don't know why he is interested in me though."

"I think that he must feel that you are a lot like he was when he was younger. He hasn't trained any one to replace him as the programmer and he is not getting any younger. I think he liked your idea for training the outsiders and decided to see what else is on your mind. He has been a recluse and I bet he enjoys the company."

"I don't know. I feel that he always has a plan. I don't think that he does anything without it being part of a greater scheme. He watches what all the programmers are doing and I know that he keeps control of the network although he pretends that he doesn't."

"Oh, I don't think he is all that diabolical. Why don't you and Landon go for a hike? Now that your father has our tent set up I am thinking of taking a nap."

I walked over to join Dad and Landon. "Do you want to go for a hike? I want to walk up the creek for a ways to see if there are any old trees up in the canyon."

"Sure, I'll go with you." Landon replied. "Do you think we will see any bears?"

"No, I don't think we will see any bears. It is possible but not likely. We might find some interesting mushrooms though since it was raining up here last week."

"I will go along too," Dad added. "We are through setting up camp. Maybe we will see some intruders."

"Will you two stop it? All I want to do is to go for a walk."

We follow the creek up the canyon and do a lot of back and forth, as we climb. There are a couple of places where we actually walk in the creek bed stepping from one large boulder to the next. The creek rumbles, gurgles and splashes over the rocks. It is noisy enough that you don't hear anything else. When this area was logged, which was over a hundred years ago, they didn't log close to the creek. When we get higher, we are beyond the willows and cottonwoods, which were down by the river and enter into a grove of large cedar trees. There are some Douglas firs and white pine that have reached considerable size. It is much easier to walk here because there is no brush or small trees under or around the large trees. You can't walk in the creek because it is thick with the large leaved thorny plant called Devil's club. The ground is a thick red duff that is soft under foot and we find what I was looking for, mushrooms. There are a large number of golden yellow colored mushrooms that have the gills descending down the stem. I get out the book that Herman had given me and spend a few minutes keying out the attributes and description. I arrive at the conclusion that they are Chantherellus Cinnabarius. The golden chanterelle, which Herman had suggested I might find at this time of year. It is a good edible mushroom with a pleasant flavor that makes a good addition to stir fried vegetables. We picked a couple of handfuls to take with us. We also found several boletes but they were always full of little worms so we left them there.

When we went back down to the camp, we fried the mushrooms and vegetables in butter and baked the fish over the campfire. It was a feast. I was not sorry that I ate the fish and I will remember how good it tasted just as I remember how well it fought when I caught it. We were careful to gather up all of the food scraps and bury them a long ways from the camp. The rest of our food was hung from the branch of a willow tree out of the reach of any bears. The chance of a bear marauding our camp was not great but it is better to be safe and careful when you are in their territory. We spent the rest of the evening sitting around the campfire waiting for falling stars and talking.

"This is certainly a wonderful experience," Landon said. "We don't have any place at home were you could go off and be alone in the wild. All of the parks that we have where people go to camp are by reservation only and they charge a fee just to stay in them. They are always crowded."

Dad replied, "We are indeed lucky to have this opportunity to sit out under the stars and smell the night air. If you think about it, we are no different than the first men on this planet. We caught our food and cooked it over a fire. Now we are sitting around the fire entranced by the dance of the flames. If it wasn't for our clothes and fancy camping gear we would be the same."

"Ted, I think we have made more improvements since the cave men than just clothes and camping gear. We have science and modern medicine and a civilization where all men are free of want." Mom answered.

"All men are not free from want where I come from." Landon interjects. "There are people who have an abundance but there are lots who go to sleep hungry and cold. You people in Containment have no idea how the rest of the world lives."

"That may be the best part of the program," I say. "I know that opening communication between our societies can only help all of us. As for comparing us with the cave men I think that the more time we spend trying to get in touch with the natural world the more likely we are to find a way to live in harmony. I wish I could know what the rest of the world is like. I have always felt closed in and surrounded in Containment."

"That is because you are closed in and surrounded you fool," Landon laughs.

"OK, OK, I know we are contained and that is what has bothered me in the past. I have always wanted the chance to do more than just do my job and be happy. This program has been the only time that I have seen a possibility to do more than what I am supposed to." I have never expressed this thought before and I wonder what my parents think.

"Regardless, of all the problems of the world we have a beautiful night and a great fire so everything is perfect." Mom says. "We should just enjoy this while we have it."

"Look at the stars. Did you ever see so many of them? The sky is so clear." Dad is gazing up to the northeast. "Look there is a meteor."

We all go silent as we scan the sky hoping to see another one. "What is that?" Landon asks.

"Where," we all say together.

"It is straight up and moving to the north but it looks like a star." Landon replies.

Dad sees it and says, "That is a satellite."

"A what?" Landon asks.

"A satellite. They were sent into space by the hundreds in the past for communication and weather observation. Containment does not have any satellite capability but doesn't your country?" Dad is puzzled by Landon's response.

"We don't have any advanced science beyond electricity and radio. There are only a few nights when you can see stars because of the pollution in the air. That is why I wanted to come here. I want to learn all of the science I can. Most of the students from the outside feel the same way. We need to learn what we are missing out on that you people take for granted."

"Now, I feel that we need to communicate more between our societies. I thought sure that you people were using the satellites."

"It is obvious that we all need to learn since it looks like there are satellites that are up there that nobody is using."

"I think I will ask The Old Man about this. If anyone knows about satellites he would." I say. "We should learn more about the outside world. It seems to be different than we have been taught to believe."

"We knew your idea would cause changes, Jason. I don't think we know just what they all will be." Mom is looking at Landon and I not at the stars.

The following day was much the same except I didn't catch a large fish. Dad and Landon got along well and spent their time casting into the holes on the bends, into the shadows under trees, along side partially submerged logs, laughing at the other if for some reason their cast wasn't quite perfect, and having a wonderful time. I drifted along with the line trailing behind the kayak not really caring as I watched the clouds through the spaces between the tree branches.

Mom and I didn't find many wildflowers as I think it is getting too late in the year. Most of what she wanted me to try and identify were well past their prime and dried up. Still it was interesting trying. At night we camped by a very small creek but this one had a waterfall of about fifty feet. The river canyon had very steep sides that forced the river to flow through a narrow zigzag that made the current fast with some rapids and eddy currents. There wasn't much room on the shore where we pitched the tents. The darkness came early because of the shadows of the canyon walls but there were few stars to see in the narrow band of sky above us. We sat around the campfire again and told stories.

"Landon always seeking to learn asks again, "What do you mean that in Containment your job could be considered as taking care of someone else?"

I volunteered an answer for that question. "In Containment everyone is recognized as having equal value to the society. If they are physically or mentally handicapped a way is found for them to serve. The best situation is when two people with different limits can be combined and help each other. We have people who are mentally needy combined with people who are not able to do everything physically and need an attendant. They both contribute by caring for the other and in many ways the society benefits."

Landon responds, "This really works? Are the physically

handicapped happy having to spend their time with some retarded person? Isn't it bad enough not being able to walk without getting stuck spending time with an idiot?"

Mom was shocked, "Landon, how do you treat people where you come from? Here a person wants to contribute and be of value to society and the rest of society values them for whatever they can contribute. From my work at the hospital I can tell you that many of these relationships form into life long bonds. There are no more loving caring people than the mentally challenged. They can do a wonderful job of helping someone who needs it. The physically limited are grateful to find a way to move through life and be a part of many things that they would not be otherwise."

"I guess that I still don't understand how this place works. In our society all of these people are a burden to the state and are either institutionalized or cared for by paid professional caregivers at great expense to the rest of the working people's taxes. Everyone hates to pay taxes, so these people don't get anything but the minimum of care. If they can live out on the streets on their own then that is what our society provides. No one thinks of them as contributing to anything."

Mom, Dad, and I are all shaking our heads. "That is so sad. It must be very difficult living in a world where no one thinks you are of value." Mom answers.

"Let's change the subject. I want to know how you and Mom met and decided to get married, Dad." I am hoping to break the maudlin mood.

"Why don't you tell that story, Tzaddi? You can tell it better than I can."

"OK, Ted but you don't get to interrupt and say that I have it all wrong."

"Just if you exaggerate how bad of dancer I was."

"You were a fine dancer. It was kissing that you needed to practice before you got the hang of it."

"Fine, fine, just tell the story." Dad is turning red in the firelight.

"Many long years ago when they were forming Containment my ancestors were forced into the area because my great, great, great, grandfather was a nuclear physicist. Our family was descended from a Brahmin and in the Hindu tradition regarded education as the most important thing to pass on to your children. His wife was also very well educated and had a doctorate in computer science. They worked together in the nuclear research project at Los Alamos. They didn't want to be a part of Containment and resisted inclusion but gave in when they were going to be expelled back to India. The population of India was skyrocketing and they felt their children would have little chance to be educated or employed in any kind of meaningful job.

One of the other Hindu traditions was the arranged marriage between families to strengthen the financial position of the families. In Containment there were few Hindus and even fewer that were Brahmin. But the idea of arranged marriages was a tradition that was impossible to break.

"I was a young girl going to nurse's school in Valley Falls when my brother approached me and said that he had some one for me to marry. I was not happy with the idea. My brother was four years older and not a serious student. He was working construction as a

302

carpenter building forms for pouring concrete. He wasted his time partying and causing trouble when he was not working. He said that a good friend of his would be the perfect husband for me. I told him that any friend of his would not be a husband of mine. I wanted nothing to do with alcohol drinking rabble-rousers. He insisted that his friend was a fine fellow and an engineer working on the rehabilitation of the dam where he worked and that he thought that he would be a great brother-in-law. I told him that that was it. No further discussion. I wasn't meeting his drunken friend."

"I was working that summer taking care of a doctor's children while they were staying at the lake cabin that the doctor used. It was a great job. I spent my time taking three kids swimming, boating, and teaching them how to fish. I insisted that we let all the fish go unharmed after apologizing to the fish for catching them. After a while it seemed like they were catching the same fish, so they children started calling them by name as they let them go."

"The doctor came up on weekends to join his family. There was a restaurant with a bar and a dance hall at the lake. The doctor and his wife took me with the family to go out for dinner one Friday. The table that we got was not far from the dance floor. The place was almost full of people so that was the only table that would seat all of us. The bar was on the other side of the dance floor."

"A tall young man was sitting at the bar by himself. He was tanned and muscular like he had been working outside. He looked up to see me and I turned away and went back to looking at the menu. The children soon noticed that he was staring at me and could not be quieted from their teasing whispers to me that I had a boyfriend. I was blushing and wanted them to hush. The waitress came over to get our orders and I hoped that we could eat and get out of there quickly. No such luck. The meals took forever to get there from the kitchen. As we were eating, the band started playing for the dance."

"After we finished the meal, the doctor asked his wife to dance, while the children were eating ice cream sundaes. I had no place to hide when the tall stranger walked up and asked me to dance. I said no but he kept asking."

"The children were giggling and chanting, "Tzaddi has a boyfriend, Tzaddi has a boyfriend," until I said yes just to get away from them. We must have been a sight stumbling around the dance floor because I was too embarrassed to pay attention to what he was trying to lead me through. I thought that the dance would never end but by the end of it I had relaxed enough to enjoy being in the arms of a handsome stranger."

"It would never do though. A proper Hindu woman would never let a stranger close to her. When the dance finished and he took me back to the table, I was surprised to see my brother standing there talking to the doctor."

"He looked over at me and said, "I'd like you to meet my friend, Ted." He is indicating the tall man I've been dancing with. Then it seems that the whole place is laughing and I am so embarrassed that I want to crawl under the table. My brother doesn't stop. He says, "Ted Nascent, I'd like you to meet my sister Tzaddi.""

"It seems that my brother had arranged the whole event including getting the doctor to take me out to dinner. He had also had the cook hold up our meals until the band started. So I was trapped and I was stuck with this arranged marriage."

"Tzaddi, you weren't trapped into this marriage. You could have turned me down any time I asked you out."

"And take a chance on who else my brother could come up with. No way!"

We were all laughing hysterically. When we finally calmed down we realized that it was late, so we stirred the fire and spread it out so that it would die out. Then we said goodnight and found our sleeping bags. I could hear my parents giggling as I went to sleep.

The next day we went fast in the kayaks because the narrow river channel caused the current to speed up. There were some rapids that you had to paddle through and there was no time for fishing. When we came out of the narrow channel the river widened out into the large impoundment in front of the dam. We went to the right and circled the edge of the impoundment until we got to the west where there is a large waterfall that drops over a hundred feet and is thirty feet wide. We paddled up to the base of the waterfall and let the spray drift over us. It was a warm sunny day for so late in the year and it felt good. We then paddled over to the boat launch where there is an official campground. Since it was so warm we decided to go water skiing one more time before going home. We checked out a boat and took turns skiing around the impoundment. It would be our last chance this year. The next time we would go skiing it would be on snow.

Then we loaded up all of the gear to return and went back home. Landon and I had some reading to do before we went back to class. The last two days of our break from school were spent around home reading and relaxing when I wasn't out walking in the woods. I read the assigned book for class but I also was reading in a book that Herman had given me.

It was called <u>Walking to Harmony</u>. It is a series of stories written two hundred years ago by Jacob Mem, a man who was like me and liked to wander in the woods. The stories seemed to speak directly to me and were very inspirational because he wrote about being picked on and teased or ignored by the kids in his neighborhood because he didn't belong or fit in. He would flee to the woods and spend his time alone watching the birds and listening to the world. Whenever he had a problem he would just start walking and he would walk until he found a resolution in his heart. It was so similar to what I had gone through as a young kid that I was entranced. He had made walking in the woods his method of getting through life and wrote this book in his fifties. His walking became a way of life for him. He was able to reach a meditative state by walking and walking until the inspiration would come to him. He said in his book that the greatest secret in life was to walk in all things contrary to the world. I felt good knowing that I wasn't the only person would had walked this particular path. I resolved to find out more about him.

Driving back into the Ott residence I remembered my earlier doubts and uncertainties. I felt that I had learned a lot and I no longer feared The Old Man but I was also aware of how much I didn't know about how this society operated. Such as how our society was able to provide to everyone what they needed but in Landon's world it was clear that there were a lot of people who never had any hope of having enough, while others had more than they could use in ten lifetimes. I also hoped that Elizabeth would be there to greet us like she was that first day. I missed seeing her each day that we were home. I didn't need to worry; she was at the door as before. Her mom came out and insisted that my folks stay for dinner this time and she apologized for not being there the first day when they arrived. It was a good meal. Julie had remembered that my mom was a vegetarian and had fixed a delicious meal that had nothing that Mom couldn't eat. Mom was impressed. I could tell that Julie really wanted my mom to like her and Mom seemed to get along with her quite well. I could hear in Mom's voice that she could relax and not have to worry about her son getting the right things to eat.

Herman sat in and had dinner with us. I insisted that he show my parents the greenhouse before they left. Dad went around checking out how everything worked. The automatic drip irrigation, the humidity controls, and the doors between the sections, that separated the zones, and he was most impressed when he saw the colorful little tree frogs in the jungle. He started to reach for one when Herman told him it that was a poison arrow frog and the secretions on its back could paralyze him. Dad left it alone and moved back to the temperate zone where Mom was drooling over the lemon and lime trees. Herman promised to send her some in about two months when they would be ripe. My parents finally left and we went to bed and got ready to go back to class the next day.

Chapter Seven

Dr. Shevnovski was there for the morning session. She brought with her some technicians and equipment for analyzing our samples. She went over the safety precautions that each student was to use to work through the diagnoses of their sample. We were not expected to be nuclear scientists by now but we were supposed to be aware of the risks in handling these waste products. Some of the students were attracted to the idea of actually looking at the sample rather than keeping it contained and using the instruments to determine what is indirectly. The technicians were willing to let them but they wanted to be out of the room when they did it and they suggested wearing lead aprons and respirators. I wanted to be out of the building if they wanted to play with their samples.

The large container that held the samples could be opened by removing the lid with a hoist that was part of the cart that the container was moved into the room on. As the hoist raised the lid the students crowded about eager to get their first glimpse of the samples. Each student had a sample that was numbered and assigned to him or her. They were to determine what it was. When the lid came off, the individual samples were in lead vials that were sealed. The technicians took out the vials and handed them out. We were given custody forms to fill out and were given another set of cautionary instructions. Each person had a designated time in the laboratory and would get help from the technicians in using the diagnostic equipment if they followed the cautionary instructions.

If they wished to open the lead vial and examine the sample

visually they were on their own. I checked the list to see when my time in the lab was and then placed my sample back in the large cask. I would not need it for two more days and I did not want anything to do with it in the meantime. Most of the students who were not scheduled for the lab that day did the same thing. Some however, kept the sample vial and carried it with them as they went about their day. Landon was one of those. I hoped he didn't decide to take it home and open it.

After lunch the discussion was held on our reading assignment. There were still plenty of the students who questioned the reason for asking us to read a book, which was filled with such debauchery. Bill, who was leading the discussion, asked, "Did any of you read the dialogues between the characters when they weren't in the process of abusing Eugenie?" Nearly everyone raised his or her hand. Bill then asked, "What did you think of the dialogues, Lee?"

"I was appalled that men who could speak so eloquently about freedom and the right of every man to express themselves could treat another human so viciously. It did not seem that they believed that the right to freedom extended to anyone except rich powerful men."

"That is correct. They did not consider women as being equal to men. This was written at a time when women were considered property. If we set that aside and consider the arguments, do they make a reasoned appeal for the total freedom that they advocate, Sarah?"

"I don't think that they do. There is no sense of any responsibility for their actions. The old men preach that they should be free to do as they wish without any restrictions and accept no liability for the consequences of their behavior."

"How does that make it different from what we practice as Socialist-Anarchy in Containment? Can one of you who grew up here explain the difference, John?"

"The principles of Socialist-Anarchy teach that you can be free to do whatever you like if you are acting with the common good in mind and you accept the consequences. We do not allow old men to debase young girls just because that is the only way that they can achieve an erection. That was really the justification that these people used. If it was necessary to do something weird to get off then it was OK. We have no rules or laws in our society that prevent people from pursuing deviant behavior. But our reason is to protect the people from having a government that has the power to enforce any prescribed ideas as law. We still expect that people will behave in a manner that is acceptable to the majority of the people."

"Does that mean that we have a set of behavioral practices that are acceptable and a set of behaviors that are not acceptable and how would you tell the difference, Susan?"

"That is a good question. I don't think that there is any defined set of behaviors that are forbidden. That doesn't mean that they all would be acceptable. I think that our society has a set of mores but needs no moral laws. The difference would be felt in your heart. If something you want to do feels good and makes the other person feel good and you would not be afraid to have other people find out that you did it then it must be acceptable. If you don't feel good or the person you are with doesn't feel good and you don't want anybody to find out about it then it is not acceptable."

"Can we say that the sexual acts that were committed with Eugenie would be acceptable if she was a willing participant?"

Landon jumps up and says, "No, these acts could never be acceptable. They are despicable. That is why we have laws in our country. There is no doubt about it when something is wrong. Some of these men were priests and bishops and no one would believe that men of God would ever behave in such a manner. I think that this book is the vilest piece of writing I have ever seen. I don't know why we were made to read such filth."

Bill is somewhat taken aback and replies, "The reason you were asked to read this book is because we wanted to foster a discussion of the ideas of liberty. This book spends far more pages discussing the right to liberty and the ramifications of granting men that liberty than the book has pages describing the sexual debauchery. This book was written at a time when just talking about the right to be free was a crime. The priests and bishops of the time were engaged in many things that were abusive of the people they were supposed to be serving. The government was servant of the rich and powerful and abused that power. The Marquis DeSade wrote about the things he knew about in a manner that got people to read his books. There would always be a chance that they would learn to think as free men if they read the whole book and not just the exciting pages."

"I think that this society is full of dangerous ideas and lacks the controls that a good set of laws would provide. Laws that would protect the citizens. Laws that would safeguard the women and children from filth such as this book promotes." Landon is seething.

Bill starts to reply but several of the students are waving their hands. "Go ahead," he says and waves his hand in the general direction of a group of the most excited students.

"I am not even from Containment and I can tell you that I feel a lot safer here than I ever did at home. We have laws against rape but women and girls get raped. We have laws against beating your wife but they didn't help my mom. I have been fascinated since I got here by how well this society works. I think that because people here are free then they don't act out of rebellion and get started down the wrong path. In my country, if you break a few laws like drug possession then you are branded as a criminal and your life is ruined forever. A mistake of judgment or hanging out with the wrong crowd can cost you your whole life of opportunity. Then you are forced into a life of crime because once you are jailed you are schooled by the career criminals in the jail. You never have a way to restore you self-worth and become a good citizen because you can't get a good job with a criminal record."

"That was good. Anyone else?" Bill asked.

"Yes, I also am not from Containment and I agree with part of what Landon says. I can't see how this society prevents child abuse, pedophiles, and other deviant behavior without laws against that behavior and jails to hold the law breakers."

"The word prevents that you used is the key. We provide everyone with the basic needs of life and we guide the children as they grow into adults. We try to prevent any person from being abused as child by not allowing unfit persons to be parents.

Hopefully, if someone has a problem they will get help before they hurt someone."

"Then if someone does hurt a child what is the response in this society?"

"Containment has always made the choice to act for the good of all. If a person is not capable of acting for good then they are separated from the rest of the society but not by putting them in jail. They are assigned to a work location that prevents them from being in contact with vulnerable persons such as women and children. If they committed a violent act that caused others harm then their work assignment will be one that has a high exposure to radiation and they will fulfill their work contract relatively quickly."

"Does that mean that they die?"

"Yes it does. Let's get back to the discussion of the freedoms that our society allows. Can any person control the lives of others in Containment? What do you think, Susan?" Bill asks.

"Yes, there are many ways that a person can control what others do. The prime example is Herman Ott. He has the power to do anything to anybody because he is the main programmer. He could write the code that would get you assigned to the worst job imaginable and you would not be able to change it. Lower level programmers have control over the distribution of resources and could keep you from getting what you need like food or medicine."

"Do you know of any time that that type of thing has happened in containment?" Bill questioned her in response.

"No, I don't but it would be theoretically possible in our system."

"Do you think it is theoretically possible, Jason?"

I had been daydreaming about the unlikely possibility that Herman would mess with the code and assign someone to the worst job possible and woke up responding. "I think all decisions are reviewed on several levels so that it would be impossible for someone to have a vendetta against another person and use the computer code to get them in some way. All decisions can be appealed to the various committees that have jurisdiction, which prevents the abuse of power."

"Does anyone else have a question about the administration of freedom here in Containment?" Bill asks.

"Yes, I do," Melinda, responds. "You said that unfit persons are not allowed to have children. Isn't that contrary to your ideas of freedom?"

"Children are not a right. They are a privilege in this society. Early on in the beginning of Containment many people had been exposed to too much radiation to be able to be a biological parent. There was a time when the population of Containment was threatened with a rapid decrease because too many children were dying. The decision was made to make reproduction of the species a function and parenting a separate function. Each function was licensed by the society. People who could reproduce healthy children were given that responsibility. There were those who had been irradiated and couldn't produce children but they would be fine parents and they were given that responsibility. As it is now the population is stable and we do not need people just being producers of children. Most people in Containment apply for and receive a license to produce and raise one child each. That means a married couple could have two. Some people who have special qualities are licensed to produce more to make up for the people who can't or those who choose not to have children. If someone can't demonstrate good parental qualities they are not licensed to have children. There is no sacred right to produce children and young couples are prevented from having children until they demonstrate the necessary maturity to properly raise a child. There are required classes in child rearing that must be taken and passed before the license is issued. Our society regards children as our most precious resource and everyone in the society takes properly raising and educating children as an important duty. They must receive positive reinforcement and no negative input from their parents and teachers. Does this guaranty a happy child and perfect child? No, but we have no people raising sociopaths by beating or abusing young children."

"I am a student from the outside where in our country it is not unusual for teenage girls to become pregnant. If young people are not licensed to have children then how do you stop them from having sex?"

"They are educated to make proper choices but in Containment there is required chemical birth control for all people of all child bearing ages to prevent unlicensed children. If you have produced your children and you so desire you can choose a surgical option and no longer have to take the medication. Therefore if they do have sex they do not have children. Remember that in Containment we do not prohibit any type of behavior but most young people realize that they are making a momentous choice and choose wisely."

I was glad to get the day's classes behind me and I headed on out to the park for a while before going home. I was lucky and met Elizabeth coming home from school. She joined me in my walk up to see the big trees. The afternoon spent in class discussing sex of the most debauched kind had my hormones raging or was it just that I was a teenage boy. I was so attracted to her I could hardly stand it. I had not had a girl friend or even a girl who was a friend before. I knew that I wanted to be close to her. I hoped she didn't mind spending time with me.

"Let's go sit under that giant fir tree." I suggested. I had been under the tree before. It was so large and the branches were so thick that they draped down to the ground in a circle about thirty feet in diameter. Inside the circle of branches was a thick blanket of needles that had built up for over two hundred years. You had to squeeze through between two of the branches but once you were in it was a closed space that was covered by the overhanging branches. There was an outcropping of basalt on the west side of the trunk that the tree had grown into. It was also covered with the needles. This shelf of needle-covered basalt formed a nice couch next to the trunk. When I found this spot I knew it was magic. You could lie on your back and look up through the branches and watch the squirrels at play overhead.

"Who would know this space was here," she said as I held the branches apart for her to enter. "It is like a chapel. The light in here is so green. It's almost like swimming underwater in a lake. This is so beautiful. Thanks for showing me this."

"I hoped you would like it. Come over here and sit down and then look up." I led her to the west side.

She started to look up and then said, "How many squirrels do you think there are?"

"I have never been able to count them because I can't tell when I am seeing the same one." We settled back and lie there on the rock. It was fascinating watching the squirrels chase each other up and over and around and along the branches. The game that they played soon had us laughing. "I am going to bring some peanuts the next time I come to see if they will come down a little lower."

"I want to come too." She said. "Please remember to ask me."

I thought to myself now that is not going to be hard to remember. I looked over at her and saw that she was looking at me. "It is so nice that you like it here. I was hoping that you would. Your eyes are so green in this light. I love looking at them. It is like gazing into a pool in a mountain meadow." We were lying side by side on the cushion of needles. I wanted to reach over and touch her but I didn't want to frighten her.

"Jason, you are so different from everyone I know. No one else would ever find a place like this or think to share it with someone like me. Thank you. I love it here."

I could only think but she doesn't love me or at least not yet. I will bring her here again and with some peanuts. We stayed a little while longer not talking, touching or moving before we both stirred and said "We better get home for supper."

Landon and I went up to visit the Old Man after we finished eating and putting the dishes away. Landon immediately said, "Can we go meet your friend who can educate me about nuclear science? I want to ask him about my sample."

"I have been anticipating that question and I talked to him

earlier. So the answer is yes. We can walk over there from here." Herman replied.

We went out the front door and walked left along the road. The road curved and followed the edge of the hillside past several large brick houses. Herman remarked as we went by, "All of these houses were built before the period of abandonment but the only thing that was left was the outside shell because the roofs failed and then all of the wood rotted away over time. It took a major effort to salvage them but it was worth it, don't you think?"

"Yes, I do. The brickwork is so interesting. The patterns that they used to lay the brick are very intricate." I replied.

"Who gets to live in these houses? In my country only the very rich could afford something that looked like these and they would be surrounded by walls and fences to keep the poor people out of the neighborhood." Landon inquires.

"You know that no one owns anything in Containment. A family can apply for any house they want and it is assigned based on need and how well they can put the resource to the service of the society. The question of how well the family takes care of the resource is also a factor. If you don't take care of what you have someone can claim to be able to better use the resource and get it."

"So only those who can afford the upkeep can have one of these houses?"

"Landon, that is true but what you are missing is that everyone can afford the upkeep on these houses and on every other house in Containment because nothing costs money because we don't use money. People pay with effort and caring. If the house needed a new roof it would get a new roof no matter who lived there. All it takes is the resident caring to see that it gets done."

"So who lives in that house with the beautiful flower gardens?" Landon asks.

"That was a good one to choose as an example. The resident there is a garbage collector. He picks up all the refuse in the neighborhood and sorts it out to the various recycled material centers."

"You mean a guy who picks through garbage for a living gets to live in a place like that instead of a doctor or lawyer?"

I interject, "The garbage sorter provides a very useful service to society because we are a closed loop system. We can't keep importing more of any type of material so we reuse nearly everything. The food waste and organic materials are composted back into soils. A garbage man is as good as a doctor in our society but the funniest thing is we don't have any lawyers because we don't have any laws."

Herman also laughs and says, "The garbage man gets to live in a nice house because he does a nice job of taking care of it. In our society if you provide for the needs of society then the society provides for your needs. Here is the home of my friend."

We had been walking down the street talking about big fancy houses and had walked past most of them to a street of smaller brick homes with much smaller yards but they were still well cared for. This house was a craftsmen style bungalow with a wide porch across the front of it. We walked up the steps and Herman reached for the large brass knocker on the door. The person who opened the door spoke with a stuttering lisp.

"Come in please," and gestured into the room. "I'm Mike. Who are you?" he said staring at Landon. "I know Herman. I don't know you."

"My name is Landon and this is my friend Jason." Landon answers.

"Do you know John?" Mike asks.

"No, they don't know John." Herman adds, "I have brought them over to meet John."

"John told me that friends were coming over tonight. I think he means you. We go into see him in his room."

"Thanks, Mike." Herman followed him and Landon and I trailed along. I noticed that all of the doors and the hallway were wider than normal as we stepped into the room at the end of the hallway. Inside the room was a man in a motorized wheel chair. The chair seemed more alive than he did. It had a computer screen mounted where John could see it as he reclined back into the folds of the chair. He had tubes and wires draped across his chest and a bag of urine on the side of the chair so he must have had a catheter as well.

"Good evening," a mechanical sounding voice came from somewhere on the chair.

"Good evening, John." Herman replied. "I have brought the two young men that I told you about. This is Jason Nascent and this is his friend, Landon Holmes. Landon is from the outside and is one of the students in the program that Jason recommended at the last general assembly."

"Yes, I see." The voice ground out. "Landon, I hear that you are eager to learn more about nuclear science. Is that so?"

"I want to learn all I can before I have to go back home. There is no program to teach about nuclear science in my country."

"Why of course not, why teach something that you are not going to use. What use do you plan on for the knowledge that you gain here?"

"I don't know that I have a use planned for the knowledge that I am seeking. I just want to know as much as I can. I can't believe that where I live they have let knowledge degrade to the point that there are things that people knew two hundred years ago that we don't know now. Mankind has been going backward for over two hundred years because we decided that something was too dangerous and put it away and out our minds."

"I can see where a bright young man with a thirst for knowledge would feel that way but the people of the world had their reasons at the time. There were many deaths caused by nuclear power plant failures. The lives of over ten million people were affected when the Diablo Canyon plant failed when the earthquake struck. The plant had been protested from the beginning because of its location near a fault. The designers insisted that it was safe because they designed it to withstand an earthquake of 8.0 on the Richter scale and the highest recorded quake had been 6.5 but the quake of 9.2 made all their designs seem foolish as the two cores went critical and melted down following the rupture of the cooling water piping. This was not the only plant to fail. There were two in France and three in Russia and one in Japan and people could no longer drive by and see the cooling towers in the distance and not think about dying a horrible death from radiation. They had seen it too many times in the news."

"I have heard all of that so many times growing up, but here in Containment the people live and work with nuclear energy every day and I think it makes their lives better because they don't pretend that something is too dangerous to know about."

"Jason, what do you think about the nuclear energy situation and what do you want to know about it?" John asked.

"The nuclear power situation is a curse that caused Containment to be formed. We were forced to take all of the world's waste and our lives have been dedicated to protecting the world from it ever since. We will never be rid of this curse for at least a hundred thousand years. And I don't want to know any more than I have to in order to get my sample identified and my report written."

"It is clear that you don't think of it as a blessing. What is this sample you are talking about?" John asked.

Landon jumped in. "Here is one. We were each given one in the class to identify the contents and to provide a report that gives a use and a solution for the waste that is contained within."

"I see." John said. "Did they not give some cautionary instructions on how to handle this sample?"

"Yes, they did." Landon replied. "I think they are just trying to frighten us from really learning about what it is."

"Well, do me a favor and go set that on the front porch until you are ready to leave and you might not want to carry it in your front pants pocket if you want to have normal kids." John waves him out of the room. "Come back in when you are rid of that. Herman, what is the idea behind these samples? Are you trying to make the kids sick? Aren't their parents going to be upset if they become sterile or develop leukemia?"

"John that part of the program is under the direction of Dr. Shevnovski. She was told to educate the students in the problems of dealing with hazardous nuclear waste. I had no idea that she was letting them carry the samples around. Jason, is everyone carrying around a sample?"

"No, I put mine right back into the cask. Most of the rest did also. There were some of those who didn't put it right back that had the lab session that morning. I assumed that they would. I thought Landon might have had the lab that day. I didn't know that he was carrying it around with him."

Landon comes back into the room and asks. "Do you really think that the sample is that dangerous? What do you think it is? How can you tell just by looking at the sample?"

John replies, "Those type of sample containers are filled and sealed by a robotic sampling device that can go into high radiation areas and take small core samples by drilling into whatever is radiating. The core drills are diamond coated so they can drill into anything. The cores are automatically done so that people are not exposed to the high radiation levels. What you have is a sample from something that was emitting high levels of radiation. Didn't they tell you that?"

"Yes, they did. We are supposed to figure out what is in there. I don't think it can be all that bad."

"It could be. I always error on the side of caution. Getting too little radiation can't hurt you. The first thing you should do is put the sample into a counter and measure the amount of radiation escaping before you do anything like carrying it around. It could be a gamma source. You don't know."

"Why would they give us something dangerous?"

"They gave you instructions on how to handle the sample and you didn't follow them. Are you someone who doesn't learn by teaching but only by making your own mistakes? If so, I am not sure I can be of any help to you."

"I can learn from teaching but I thought that they were exaggerating just to impress us. I want to learn from you because I feel that I can trust you."

"I am not so sure that you can trust me. Maybe you should put that sample back in your pants and you can impress all the girls when you show them your glow in the dark prick."

"What do I need to do to get you to help me learn all about nuclear science?"

"Why don't you come over for the next several evenings and work with Mike. He could use some time off to visit his family. If you can learn from him what he does and then fill in for him while he is gone, that will give us time to talk. If you can't learn from Mike, then there is no reason for me to waste my time with you. Is that OK with you, Mike? Will you teach Landon to fill in for you?"

"Yes, I can teach Landon. I need to see my mom."

"What about you Landon?"

"I will come over every night after supper."

"No, come over after your classes. You need to learn how to fix my meals if you are going to fill in for Mike."

"Then I'll be here at 4:30 tomorrow afternoon."

"Great, what about you Jason do you want to learn nuclear science?"

"I think that I will just accept what they teach us in class as being enough."

"I am tired out for tonight so Mike will show you out. Don't forget to put that sample back into your pants as you leave, Landon."

We made our way out and Landon picked up his sample from the porch. He didn't put it into his pants and spent some time trying to figure out how to carry it with the least amount of exposure. Herman finally told him to hold it as high as he could over his head and to walk at least five feet behind us. We walked back home and did not discuss the evening's events further. Landon stopped in the classroom and left his sample on top of the cask since it was closed for the day when classes had finished.

I knew that the next day would be an opportunity for me to spend some time with Elizabeth because if Landon was going to work with Mike then he would not be playing tennis. She would have no reason to spend time with him. I went to bed planning the next day or at least dreaming of all the things that I wanted to have happen. The next day's morning class began with Dr. Shevnovski remarking that she noticed a sample that had been returned unopened. She commented on the fact that the sample was left out and could have picked up by someone for whom it was not intended and who had not received the cautionary instructions. "This sample was assigned to an individual. That individual is responsible for this sample. This class was all given instructions for the safe handling of these samples. You were told that these samples contained radioactive waste and you were told that technicians were available to help you determine the nature of that waste. I received a phone call last night that was highly critical of me for allowing untrained individuals access to waste sample containers. I had been told that the students in this class were highly intelligent and I am disappointed to realize that this is not the case. When the technicians talked about opening the sample to see what was in it they were joking. It is unfortunate that one of you did not listen and understand the instructions that you were given but instead contemplated a joke as real. Nuclear technicians have a type of gallows humor that keeps them from the dread that is inevitable if you only concentrate on the dangers. They comment on the dangers in a lighthearted manner so they don't have to think of the very real doses of radiation that they are receiving. If I had my way this individual would be sent home, however, in Containment we allow a person the right to be stupid and to learn from their mistakes. So that you understand the samples are to be stored in the cask except when you are using them in an actual laboratory procedure. Is that understood?"

I looked around the classroom and noticed that everyone else was looking around the classroom trying to figure out who the guilty party was. There was only one person who wasn't looking around and he was missing his normal smile so it didn't take long for the class to figure out who caused them to sit through a scathing lecture. It would be a while before the class treated Landon as the beautiful young god that they had thought of him as before they heard him described as unintelligent. Now they would question if he were smart enough to be with them. These were the best and the brightest where they came from.

The afternoon session was a continual drone about the economy and the way that it functioned. Nobody cared. Or at least nobody really paid attention. This was the bland old boring stuff that actually made Containment work. We still followed the principles that were set in motion by Hayward Crowell and they still worked. If no one owns anything and the public owns everything and nothing costs anything, there is no need for money. The rest follows from there. People are encouraged to do a good job and rewarded when they do by an increase in privileges. It is always your peers that decide who is doing a good job and not the foreman or supervisor. The person who works with you always has a better idea of who is doing what. I know that I should pay more attention to this facet of how Containment works but I have a hard time summoning any interest. I keep thinking of being outside and it is getting darker sooner every day it is hard to be outside when it is cold and dark. The winter will be here soon enough.

The class finally ended. I saw Landon and wished him luck with his next learning experience. I was glad it was he and not I. I walked over to a small neighborhood market and picked up a bag of peanuts. I also got some fruit drinks and some fancy candies that were wrapped in gold foil. Elizabeth had agreed to meet me in the park and I hoped to do more than just watch the squirrels play. After I left the market, I hurried up the hill to the park and saw her standing next to the large fir tree.

"Hi!" I said as I came up to her. "Have you been here long?"

"No, I just got here. I have been listening to the squirrels chatter. It sounds like they knew we were coming and they have been waiting impatiently for their treat."

"Then let's give it to them." I said as I held the branches apart for

327

her to slide between. I followed her in to what I considered our secret space and the closeness of her let me feel the warmth of her body and smell the aroma of her hair. She went over and sat on the rock on the west side and I climbed up into the branches and laid rows of peanuts along the tops of the branches as I climbed back down. I hoped that the squirrels would follow the nuts and come down lower where we could see them clearly. I finished laying the peanuts on the branch just over our couch of rock and joined her there.

"I brought you a treat as well." I took out the juices and gave her one. "And you have to try these." I unwrapped one of the candies and held it to her mouth. The candies were made of honey and berries and melted into a creamy sensual delight as soon as soon as you had them in your mouth.

"Mmmm, oh that's good." She responded. "Here you try one." She unwrapped one and held it to my lips. I felt her hand linger on my face as the sweetness filled my mouth. We were not watching the squirrels and were startled when the shells of peanuts dropped beside us.

"Oh look," she laughed and pointed. There was a row of squirrels on the highest branch that I had placed the nuts. They raced to see who could eat the most and then jumped down to the next branch where the race was on again. There were at least a dozen of them lined up along the branch.

"I wonder how close they will get to us before they notice us. I want them to get the ones on the lowest branch."

"Then you'll have to be quiet and not talk." She unwrapped another candy and held it to my lips. I did the same for her and then we settled back and lie on the rock looking up. It was hard not to laugh as the shells rained down and the chattering got closer. We held our breath as two squirrels came down to the lowest branch. The others were not as bold or had gotten enough to eat because they scampered off. These two started at opposite ends of the row of peanuts along the branch and worked their way to the middle. When they got to the middle there was only one peanut left and instead of squabbling over it they held it together and each nibbled on it. Then they sat and looked down at us before running back up the tree trunk.

We looked at each other and at the bag of candies. There was only one left. We unwrapped it together and placed it between our lips. Our lips met around the melting sweetness. I held her close until the candy had melted away and we licked each other's lips to get the last of it.

"Oh my, that was good." She said at last. Her voice had an unusual throaty tone to it and I could not speak at all. "We must go. It is getting dark. I don't want my Mom to worry about where I am."

I gathered up the debris and placed it all in the bag from the store and then as I held the branches apart for her to leave I kissed her lightly as she passed.

She only smiled and said, "I didn't know that watching squirrels could be so much fun."

We went home and at supper I could not keep my eyes off of her. Her mom must have suspected something.

She asked, "What are you two up to?"

Elizabeth replied, "We are not up to anything. Landon is gone to John Eagleton's so I went for a walk in the park with Jason instead of playing tennis."

"Well, you both look like the cat that ate the canary."

"We don't have a cat or a canary, Mom. We went to the park and fed peanuts to the squirrels."

"Fine, but I think you two are up to something. Neither one of you has hardly eaten a thing. That doesn't seem normal to me."

"We ate some of the peanuts too." Was the only thing that I could think of to say.

"If you are finished eating then put the food away and do the dishes. I want to know that you are doing your school work because I am going down to the club to go swimming with Hazel."

"Yes, Mom."

"I'll be upstairs with Herman after the dishes are done," I added.

Later, I went upstairs and saw Herman sitting at his keyboard. He looked up and said, "I was having a conversation with John over the network. He is looking forward to working with Landon but said that Landon is having a little difficulty understanding Mike. He thinks it will be good for him to spend time with Mike because he has a strange idea of the handicapped being useless. John doesn't think of himself as being handicapped or limited in any manner but he is totally dependent on someone being there constantly."

"Who normally fills in for Mike on his days off?"

"He hasn't had any days off in years. His family can't come up here to visit him anymore because his mother has a heart condition and can't take the stress of travel. Mike is worried about her but can't leave John. This will be good for all of them. What did you want to talk about today? You seem to a have a grin tattooed onto your face. Have you been messing with the program again?

"No, I haven't made any changes lately. I find it is too boring to work through all of the permutations that are necessary to diagnose what the result will be. I have learned that you can't just make changes. The result may not be what you intended. I was hoping that you would explain how you work with the creative process to make the society to be what you want it to be."

"The beginning of all creation is observation. You can't change what you don't understand. So begin by watching. When you are watching don't judge or evaluate just try to understand what is happening. This is true in all things whether you are watching the behavior of people or a scientific experiment. Observation is first and then definition will follow. When you have a definition that you think correctly describes what you have observed then you begin again by watching and testing your definition. Only when you are sure that you have validated your definition can you then ponder what you would change and then like you said you have to work through what the permutations of that change would be. It is always an unknown at some level. The programmer works best when the programmer is not revealed by the changes that he makes. You did well with the ice cream because most of the students never even noticed that something was changed and those who noticed that the lunch was improved had no idea where the change came from. The really big changes in the way society works sometime have to be announced out loud to the public. This class of outsiders is an example of that type of change. I was glad when you got your dad to suggest it because then the idea did not come from me. The people could accept the idea of bringing outsiders in and educating them because the idea came from a young man who had no motive to do them harm. It was just an expression of his caring for the society and the people of the world. If I had stood up in front of the crowd and announced that this was my program they would have wondered what I was up to and resisted the idea without considering it."

"You didn't know that I was going to make the suggestion, did you?"

"No, I had no way of knowing that you were even there but I wanted someone to make a suggestion of a similar nature that I could then confirm and implement without being the originator of the idea."

"What if I hadn't got Dad to speak up?"

"If no one had voiced the idea then I would have had to get someone to make the suggestion. I had intended all the time that the morning session was going on that this would be the result. I just had to be patient and wait until the idea jelled in someone's brain."

"So the whole general assembly was a staged event to build public support for something that you had already planned to do?"

"In a way, yes but also no. I did not know how it was going to turn out. I just knew how I wanted it to turn out. It could have been a completely different result if someone else had made a different suggestion that captured the mood of the public that was there."

"I heard many people advocating violence outside the arena.

Would you have accepted a violent solution if there was a groundswell of public support for violence?"

"Most of the advocates of violence were outside and did not have a legitimate committee that they represented. I knew that there would be some who wanted to use force and we had to make sure that those who were passionate advocates of peace got to speak as well."

"But would you have accepted a violent solution?"

"No, if the general assembly would have overwhelmingly supported violence then I would not have been the programmer any longer. Someone else would have been controlling the outcome and I would have been forced out."

"Is there someone who is actively trying to force you out as the programmer?"

"Yes, there are always a few who are dissatisfied with the way that the society operates but there is no one who actually has the ability at this time to make the changes that would be necessary to force me out. It is mostly due to inertia that I remain. Most people do not like to make changes in their lives."

"If I promise not to make any changes without discussing them with you will you show me how the network links are controlled by the communication protocols?"

"Not yet first decide on something that you would like to change and then we will work on it together if I agree that your change deserves implementation."

"That is fine, I don't know what I would change now anyway. Would you loan me another book similar to the <u>Walking to</u>

Harmony that you let me read. I really want to understand that type of thinking."

"Sure, I will look to see what I have that is similar. You can keep that book since you like it."

"Thank you. That way I'll be able to reread some of the parts I didn't totally understand."

"You will notice that there are some places that I read several times as well. I'll see you tomorrow. We probably should talk about some of the things in that book."

I went downstairs and ran into Landon who was just coming in. "How did it go with John?" I asked.

"I didn't even spend any time with John. I was trying to understand Mike all evening. He has been doing the same things for so long that he doesn't even realize that he is doing something that I don't understand. He learned to take care of John in a certain way and he has to do it exactly that way. If I stop him and ask questions, then he has to start over at the beginning of whatever he was doing. I ended up just watching him and recording what he did in my notebook. He can repeat the steps over and over without making a mistake but he can't stop and explain what he is doing. The worst thing is I don't think John knows what all he does because he can't see what Mike is doing most of the time. I tried to ask him to explain what the procedures were and he said that I had to learn that from Mike."

"It sounds as if you will be going over there for a while."

"I know. I didn't want to learn how to baby-sit a quadriplegic from a moron. I wanted to learn nuclear physics."

"I am sure you will get to learn nuclear physics. John Eagleton is the leading thinker in theoretical physics in the whole world. Just because he has a crippling disease doesn't mean he can't explain the way the universe works. A lot of people would like to have your opportunity. You just have to be patient."

"I know. That is something I'm not very good at. By the way what is up with Elizabeth? She was all smiles when I came in and when I asked her what was up, all she said was, "Nothing.""

"Maybe she got good grades on her tests at school."

"OK, I see you are not talking either. I might as well hit the rack."

"Yeah, I've got some reading to do. See you in the morning."

The next day was my turn in the laboratory with the technicians from the waste handling facility. I didn't want to do any more than what was necessary. I wanted to identify my sample and leave but the technician who was named Joseph insisted that I complete each step along the way and understand what we were doing. He felt that if it was important enough for him to be there then it was important that I commit to learning the process. He got my attention by engaging me in solving a mystery. We had a sample that was taken by a robot from an area of high radiation. Now we had to learn all that we could about that sample.

It soon became apparent that the sample would be changing as we studied it. The radiation was caused by decay and as the decay was the result of several different reactions. We had to determine the distribution of the reactions. I began to sense that this was like solving a jigsaw puzzle that changed pictures every time you came close to finishing it. I finally realized that probabilities and possibilities are not the same thing. We could only determine the contents of the sample within the probabilities that the testing could resolve. I learned how hard it is to be exact when there is not an exact answer. Yet we expect that the nuclear scientists and technicians to protect us one hundred per cent of the time with one hundred per cent certainty. We do not tolerate failure on their part.

I began to realize that what they were teaching us was not nuclear science but logic. We had to learn that in the world of sub atomic particles there is no exact anything. In a brief corollary of the Heisenberg uncertainty principle, the more you know about a particle the less you know about where it is and the more you know about where it is the less you know about what it is. I didn't see why Landon found this stuff all that fascinating.

Each night for the next two weeks was much the same. Landon was over at John Eagleton's and I helped Elizabeth with the dishes. I hadn't been able to be alone with her for more than a moment since we fed the squirrels. Her mother seemed to be making sure that she had something for Elizabeth to do after school every day and even now she kept darting in and out of the kitchen as if she thought she could not trust us alone. I finished with the drying and putting away and then went up to visit the Old Man.

I was beginning to tire of some of his mystery when I asked him direct questions about what he had done to become the programmer and what he did to remain the programmer for so long. I was not able to get him to show me how to access the files that controlled the communications between the hubs. I started working with Lee again after class trying to unravel the codes that held the secrets of how this whole program was held together. It was beginning to look like nuclear science in that the closer we came to understanding one part of the program the more we didn't understand about how the parts fit together. I decided to ask Helen for help.

I went down to the lower level the next day and found her at her terminal." How are you doing?" I asked.

She replied, "I am doing just fine all things considered. How have your programming excursions been going?"

"I have been stuck on a couple of things that I don't understand and Herman is not willing to explain. He thinks that I will not learn if I don't figure it out for myself."

"What is it you are trying to change?"

"I am not really trying to change anything. I have learned that it is so much work going through all of the permutations to see the effect of the changes that I haven't tried to change anything lately. I have just been trying to learn about how the program works. I have been trying to access the core of the program that controls the communication protocols between the hubs. I think that I am encountering some type of security routine that is blocking my attempts at getting in to the core program."

"Why do you think that you are encountering a security routine?"

"Once I get past the initial screens and do a search function it is as if the search function had a random response generator. I can search for a subject but that subject is never what comes up in the results. The results of the search can be anything at all but never what I am looking for. I have been working with Lee and he encounters the same type of thing when he is searching for something that is part of the core program."

"Yes, it appears that something is blocking your access. That doesn't happen with me but I am only doing my assigned functions. I don't go exploring where I am not supposed to be. I learned a long time ago that exploring was not the way to get promoted. My suggestion would be to do a search for what you are not looking for and see if what you are looking for comes up. I am only kidding of course. I am sorry that I am not more help."

"Do you have access to the communication protocols between the hubs as part of your assigned tasks?"

"I do, but only when I am working on a task that requires that I modify or use the protocol for a specific hub. I can't access something that I am not working on and I have never worked on the central access protocol. I don't think that has been modified since I have been here."

"Who set up the routines that control access and that engage this random search response?"

"The routines for the access control have always been there and I have never heard of this random search response until you asked about it. I told you I don't go wandering beyond where I am supposed to go. If you have a reputation that you can be trusted to do your job then you get promoted and then you get access to more code but only as you need the access to do your assigned tasks."

"I thought one of the fundamental principles of Socialist-Anarchy as set up by Hayward Crowell was that everyone was to be able to have the ability to access and modify the code."

"It is one of the most sacred principles of SA but you can't let someone who doesn't know what they are doing just mess around with the code. There are routines that only let you change the code when you can demonstrate what the results of those changes are. You have encountered that already. That is why you have to figure out all of the permutations first."

"I wonder how all of this came to be. It doesn't seem as if Hayward Crowell would have set it up this way. It effectively blocks access by anyone who is not part of the system already and you can only work on it if you have been assigned that task. I think changes were made that modified the access sometime after Crowell was the programmer."

"Who can say for sure? It was so long ago that there is no way of knowing."

"There must be some archive of the history of the changes that are made to the code."

"Well I have never been assigned to log any changes that I make."

I am beginning to sense reluctance to any type of exploration or discussion of the history of how the code has been altered over time. It is probably of no use to continue this discussion with Helen. "OK, then how did you know that Herman had made changes that day when you were first helping me out?"

"I saw that something wasn't the way that it had been when I left it. It looked like his style of action and I just guessed that it was him because it would take a high level clearance to override the routine that I had set up."

"Thanks, for talking with me. You have been a lot of help. Although, I still don't know how to get into the communication protocol."

"Just remember that you can only access what you have a need to access. It was good to see you again. Come by sometime soon."

As I walked away I pondered what she had said and didn't say. Somehow I had a feeling that she had told me more than she knew. What was it she said? "You can only access what you have a need to access." That had to be part of the puzzle. Who or what was deciding what the basis of need was. How could the interrupts be set in the program to kick in the random response generator? Was there something to her joking suggestion that I search for what I am not looking for to find what I am looking for? It might be worth a try. I could set up a program that would randomly search for subjects and then screen the results against another criterion that would reveal a match if one occurred. I would be able to get Lee to help write the programs and we could have several programs operating that continually tried the search mode. They could operate with different matching criteria so we would in effect be looking to solve several puzzles simultaneously.

Something else occurred to me as I walked back upstairs. Helen did not seem her optimistic self. She must have something on her mind or had something happened. She never spoke before about not exploring in order to get a promotion. I wondered if someone had reminded her of that recently.

Did someone resent the help that she gave Lee and I in our quest to explore the system? Who would be aware or know that she was helping us and why would they care? If Containment was governed by the operating system of a computer program was the programmer the government?

Then a thought struck me. I was reminded of the history lesson about Hayward Crowell and his thoughts on how government acted to preserve the government even if the rights of the people were trampled in the meantime. Was someone acting to preserve his or her power? Who had power to protect?

These questions would go unanswered for now. I found myself in our living quarters and nobody was home except for Elizabeth. She was in the kitchen when I went in. "Hi, how's it going?" I asked.

She turned around startled and said "Oh, hi."

"Is something wrong? Are you deliberately avoiding me? It seems that you and your mother are going someplace or have something to do all the time so that we never see each other."

"Mom doesn't think I should be spending time alone with you anymore."

"Why? What did I do? Did you tell her what happened with the squirrels?"

"You didn't do anything and I didn't tell her anything about what happened that day. She came to me and said that I was growing up and that it wasn't appropriate for me to be spending time with an older boy who was looking to take advantage of me."

"Do think I am just trying to take advantage of you?"

"No, I love spending time with you. You talk about so many things that are different from other boys. You see things that other people don't even notice. Like the patterns the birds make flying in the sky as flocks. I told Mom that you were just being friendly. She said that Grandpa warned her about what could happen if we spent time alone together. She also said that Grandpa doesn't want me distracting you from your studies."

"Who said you were distracting me from my studies? I don't understand what is going on here. I admit that I am attracted to you. I feel so good when I am close to you. I have never felt that way before and I want to be able to keep feeling that way. I miss not going on walks and talking." I kept rambling on.

"Look it is not my idea to avoid you. My Mom is the one who is worried. She hasn't left me alone for days. She will probably be in here any minute. She is just outside in the garden. I miss not going for walks with you also but I can't defy her. I am all that she has to hold on to. She lives her life for me and she cried and said that she doesn't want me making the mistake of loving the wrong man like she did. She said we can't defy Grandpa or something terrible will happen."

"Did he threaten something?"

"No, she just knows that he controls everything and if he says that you should do something you are better off doing it."

"He must have said more to her than you are telling me. I think I'll ask him what is up."

"Oh no, don't do that. He'll know that we talked. I don't want to be sent away to another school so just pretend that everything is fine. We'll find time to be together but we won't have a chance to see each other at all if they think that I told you about this. You need to leave. Here comes my Mom."

"OK, see you later."

I went upstairs to my room. I was confused and angry about the thought that Herman wanted to keep me away from Elizabeth. Why should he care? I am just a student in his program. He is not my Grandpa. Why should he be trying to decide whom I spend my time with? I wanted to be with her under that tree again. I wanted to taste the sweetness of that shared candy again and again. I wanted to feel the warmth of her body next to mine and smell the scent of her hair as it brushed over my face. I tried to forget but I was not able to get this out of my mind before I heard the call to dinner.

The dinner was a strained affair. No one really spoke. Landon was still over at John's but this was his last day. We could have used his smiling face to break the somber mood. After dinner I went up as usual to visit with Herman. We had been having good discussions on the subject of being in the moment and tuned into the natural world. I didn't want to lose the closeness that we had been building but I resented his interference with my relationship with Elizabeth. I wanted to tell him to butt out and leave us alone but Elizabeth had insisted that her mother would move her to another school if the Old Man wanted it. I decided to keep quiet and try to see Elizabeth when I could.

Chapter Eight

"How are you doing with your studies?" The Old Man started the conversation.

"I am bored with the economics, finished with the nuclear science, and I am interested in the history of Containment which I never was before. I know what you taught us about Hayward Crowell and the beginning of Containment but I want to know how we got from there to where we are now."

"Do you mean how the economic system enabled us to function as a society? Herman asked smiling.

"No, I mean how the program evolved. What is the history of the changes that have been made since Crowell started the program? There doesn't seem to be any record or discussion of what those changes have been in our textbooks. I know that the program has constantly evolved and changed but the books act as if it is still the same program that Crowell started."

"I don't think that the changes that have been made are any more than administrative adjustments to keep the program in line with the changes in the population and the level of involvement with the storage of the nuclear waste. I think that the principles established by Crowell are still in affect unchanged. That is why the history books do not mention any changes."

"That is the thing that puzzles me. There have been enormous changes in the way Containment functions such as the way children are raised or in the assignment of duties to people who fail to act in the best interest of the whole. I don't think that Crowell had even thought of these things and yet you tell me that they follow the principles that he laid out."

"The changes follow his original concept and are only administrative."

"But who was the programmer that made each of those changes? There is not even a record of who was the programmer when. Don't you think that history should have recorded who made what changes and when those changes were made?"

"I don't think that any one wants to think that the program that governs their life is subject to being changed by any person that is a contemporary. People want to think that the program, put in place by Crowell, is alive and well and doing its job. The history of Containment doesn't hinge on who was the programmer when. That would be against the principles of Crowell. He did not place any importance on who was in control. He felt it was necessary that anyone could be."

"You are the programmer now. Don't you think that it is important for people to be able to find out what you have done as the programmer and credit you with the improvements you have made in the way that Containment operates?"

"Definitely not. I know what I have done. I know what I have had to do to keep this all working. The people don't want to know those things."

"If the people aren't knowledgeable about what you do, how can anyone learn to replace you?"

"Exactly, I would not be the programmer nor would anyone else be for very long if all of our actions were out in the open."

Did the previous programmers all the way back to Crowell feel the same way and act in secrecy?"

"As far as I know, yes."

"I guess that there are some things that we will never know."

"Yes, and it is best that way. More important than the history of Containment are your studies of the plants and inhabitants of the natural world. How are you doing in your studies there?"

"I have been reading the books that you gave me but I don't have a lot of time to actually get out into the woods to try and identify any new plants. It is too late in the year for a lot of things to be out there any way, especially any mushrooms."

"Have you tried any of the meditative techniques from the book by Jacob Mem?"

"I don't know if I am getting anywhere with that either. I seem to be frustrated all around. Do you have something else that I should be doing or reading in that direction?"

"Do you have a music player with headphones?"

"Yes, I do. That way I can listen to music without disturbing anyone else."

"I am going to give you a disk with something to listen to. It is not music, however. This has a series of drumming recordings. There is a ritual to follow as you listen to the drumming. This is described in a book that I will give you. You should read the book and then practice the rituals as you listen to the drumming. This is a visualization technique that should be practiced on a regular basis. If you are able to complete these exercises then you should make progress in understanding the natural relationships between plants and animals."

"Humans being one of the animals to which you refer, right?"

"Yes, we are no more important than any other animal species. You need understand that to make progress on the spiritual level."

"I did get that understanding from reading the writings of Jacob Mem."

"Well, take the disc and the book, when you have practiced the rituals and think you know what you are doing, come and see me and then I'll talk to about what you have learned. Until then keep working on all of your studies."

"OK, I'll give it a try."

I made my way downstairs and back to my room. I knew

that he wanted to add, "and stay away from Elizabeth" to his last sentence. I could hear it in his voice. It was all I could do not to talk about his edict to Elizabeth's Mom but I wasn't supposed to know about it and I didn't want to make matters worse for Elizabeth and I certainly didn't want her sent to a different school. I lay down on my bed and began to read.

The book was <u>An Introduction to Practical Shamanism</u> it was written as a beginners guide to the spiritual ideas of Shamanism. The purpose of listening to the drumming was to induce a mental state that caused the brain waves to shift from the normal alpha wave pattern to a pattern called the theta wave. This wave pattern was typical of a trance or meditative state. The brain was freed from the normal program that caused it to see the world in a rational manner and allowed new experiences to occur. These experiences were described as being visionary and not of the ordinary reality. In fact the writer called these experiences the worlds of non-ordinary reality. Non-ordinary reality consisted of three worlds the lower world, the middle world, and the upper world. The writer also said that from a shamans viewpoint these worlds were more real that the world that we normally think of as the real world. I was confused. How could something that you only imagine in your mind be more real than the physical world that you can see, touch, taste, hear, and smell? This was going to take some getting used to.

The next day was classes as usual and then afterwards I saw Landon and Elizabeth leaving to go play tennis. This was the first time that they had played in some time and I wondered why Julia and Herman didn't object to them being together the way that they did with me. Maybe they thought that he would be leaving here at the end of the school year so they would be separated anyway. I don't know but it bothered me. I hadn't really talked to Landon during the time that he was taking care of John because he was over there as much as possible. I wondered if he would start joining me with Herman or what he intended to do.

I was on my own till dinner so I decided to walk down to the river and spend some time in the natural world. I recalled one of the meditative methods of Jacob Mem was to walk as hard and as fast as you could for as long as you could focus your thoughts on the thing that was bothering you and then find a place to sit in the natural world. You were supposed to sit quietly without thinking or talking to yourself in your mind and watch the world and wait to see what would happen.

I walked as hard and fast as I could down to the river and headed east along the trail that was for biking and jogging that followed the south side of the river. I went about three miles and then got off of the paved trail and went down to the bank of the river. The shoreline was made of large oval boulders about three or four feet in diameter of granite and limestone. There was also some large chunks of basalt but these usually had edges and were hexagonal not round. I sat on one of these. It was warm from the sun that was going down and I watched unsure of what I was watching for.

I waited. I tried to keep my mind still. I focused on my breathing as Jacob Mem had suggested for when you are having trouble shutting down your mind. I saw a large bird on the other side of the river that blended in to the color of the rocks. It was standing on one leg with the other folded up and its head was down along its back. I shifted my eyes and it became invisible again as it blended into the rocks. I refocused and I could see it again. The bird remained motionless standing right at the edge of the water.

Suddenly the long beak plunged into the water and then the neck stretched out above the body and the sharp bill held a fish about eight inches long. The bird flipped the fish so that it went head first down that long neck and the fish was gone. The bird resettled into its resting position and quietly disappeared. It was a blue heron. I had seen them down by the river but had not seen one catch a fish before. Why was that fish swimming so close to the shore? How had nature provided a blue heron just what it needed when the heron was only waiting quietly? I realized that I had just received a lesson. Wait quietly knowing what you are waiting for and if you remain undisturbed it will come to you. The things we need in life are provided. I needed to know what I was waiting for and be patient. I made my way back up to the trail and jogged home so that I wouldn't be late for dinner. I could be patient and wait. I knew what I wanted. There would be a time that Elizabeth and I would be together.

The mood at dinner that night was jovial as Landon regaled us with stories about learning from Mike. It had been an eye opening experience for him as he gained the knowledge that the handicapped really could contribute to the whole of society. After spending several evenings with John he became aware of how totally dependent John was on Mike. It was Mike who kept things organized and functioning. John could explain in mathematics the formation of a black hole but he was not able to balance his peculiar dietary needs. Mike had to keep John's body functioning and cared for. What goes in goes out and Mike had had to teach Landon how to deal with the whole process. Landon spent a week caring for John while Mike was down south with his family during that time he was worried the whole time about making a mistake and causing John to suffer.

"What was the worst thing that happened, Landon?" I asked him.

"The worst thing?" he replied. "I'll tell you the worst thing. It was the third night that I was there by myself. I thought that everything was going well. I had fixed his dinner and he and I were talking about nuclear physics and how the small world of the subatomic particles related to the massive stars and quasars of the world of astrophysics. You know the same forces govern the behavior of all particles, no matter what the size of the particle. Anyway John is talking and giving me the description in mathematics when he just stops speaking. His eyes get wide and he is looking at me with a questioning look. I don't know what he means or what is going on. I just sit there waiting for him to start talking again. His eyes get wider and he is blinking rapidly. I finally realized that he couldn't talk because he couldn't breathe. His respirator had quit. About that time alarm bells started going off and the control panel on his chair was nothing but flashing lights. I panicked. I didn't know what to do. Mike didn't tell me about this. I looked at John. He was unable to do anything except look back and he was turning blue. I knew I had to do something fast. I started reading the alarm lights. They all indicated that various functions were disconnected. I looked down at the floor and saw the main cable between the chair and the computer that controlled the chair. It was disconnected. How I don't know but I quickly reconnected the cable and the lights stopped flashing one by one. I heard a rattle of breath and looked at John. His color was coming back and I swear he had a smile on his face. I waited until he had caught up on his breathing and I said, "Are you all right?" He laughed and replied, "I am now." That was the worst thing that happened."

"How on earth did the cable get disconnected?" Elizabeth asked.

"I don't know for sure. I didn't trip over it and I certainly didn't pull it apart. John can't move but he can control his chair and change its position but I didn't notice him doing anything before it happened."

Julia said, "That must have been very frightening. John could have died. You wouldn't think he would have been laughing at the thought of dying."

"I know," Landon replied. "It was almost like he was laughing at me, at seeing me panic."

I added, "Those connectors should be made so they can't just be pulled apart. They should have lock screws or something."

"I found some tape and taped the joint so that it couldn't come undone."

"That's good. I wonder why that wasn't done a long time ago."

"John saw me taping up the joint and said Mike never had that problem. It almost seemed like he was testing me. I guess I passed because he is still alive and as cranky as ever."

"If he was testing you, he sure would have paid the price if you had failed. I can't believe that he could have done anything to disconnect the cable." I was doubtful.

"I know I have puzzled over this ever since it happened. I can't come up with an explanation for how it could have happened. I asked Mike if he ever had trouble with the cable and he acted like he didn't know what I was talking about. He said that he never messes with the electrical stuff, that's dangerous."

"Are you going to be going over there in the future? Julia asked.

"Yes but not to stay for any time until Mike takes a week off in the spring to see his family again. I will just stop in now and then to talk to John. He actually has a busy schedule of visitors who come to ask him questions about all kinds of scientific studies. He is able to sit there and just puzzle out the answer. He has amazing concentration powers."

After dinner Landon and I went upstairs to visit Herman. I anticipated that the discussion would continue to be more about the relationship between John and Landon. I was right. Herman wanted to hear all about the knowledge that Landon had received while sitting at the side of one of the great minds of the century. He asked shortly after we went through the door, "Did you learn all there is to know about nuclear physics?"

"No, I don't think that I could ever learn all that there is to know. I learned enough to know that my country has a long way to go to get back to educating the students about science. We have been backward for too long."

"Did you get John to help you with your sample?"

"No, I didn't even dare to bring that up. I followed the

procedures and did that through the technicians at the school. I won't make that kind of mistake again."

"That is actually what we are trying to communicate with this program. We don't want the world to make that kind of mistake again. The problems of nuclear waste far out weigh the benefits of nuclear power. The people of Containment have accepted the responsibility of dealing with the results from the last attempt to supply the world's energy needs with nuclear power. We don't want all of the suffering of our ancestors to have been for naught."

Landon replies, "I think that I understand what you are saying but our country is going to have to reverse the trend that started with the abandonment of nuclear power. We can't continue to ignore science. Our students need to learn how to use science to make a better way of life."

I interject, "The people of Containment don't want your society to continue in a backwards slide. We didn't even know that the outside world had forsaken technology with the loss of nuclear power. We just want the outside world to realize that you can't expect us to meet our task of isolating the world from nuclear waste if the outside world does not leave us isolated."

"Isolation is not necessarily a good thing. You need some of the things from the outside in order to improve your lives in here."

"Like what? All you ever talk about that we don't have is jails and religion and we certainly don't need those. What is there that you have in your world that would improve our existence? Name one thing."

"Chocolate."

"What is that?"

"Chocolate is what makes life worth living. It is the basis of all the good candies. It is smooth and creamy and melts in your mouth. It comes from the cocoa bean, which grows on trees in the tropics. You people have been isolated for so long that you don't even know what you are missing."

"I don't think that one kind of food could make all that much difference in the value of our life."

"It is not a food. It is ambrosia. You can have chocolate cakes and pies and ice cream as well as a thousand types of candy. Herman, do you think that my mother could ship me in some chocolate for Christmas. I don't think I will be able to get through the winter without at least some chocolate."

"I guess we will have to have some kind of exchange between the families. You are not the first to ask that question. We don't have a big deal about going out to buy gifts for everyone you know because we don't have a consumer economy and we have people from all types of backgrounds so we have a holiday associated with the winter solstice, which is where Christmas originated. However, I have gotten lots of families inquiring as to what we are going to do for the holidays. One thought was to let the outsiders return home for a week to be with their families, another thought was to let the parents come here and visit but there doesn't seem to be a lot of support for that idea. May be your idea of just exchanging gifts would be the best. We could arrange mail and package exchanges a lot easier than having the students go home for a week."

"I didn't know going home was an option. I am sure that all of the students would like to go home for a week."

Herman grumbled, "I didn't say that it was an option. I said that the thought had been suggested. At this point nothing has been decided. In any case it won't be an option to the students. They will be told what is going to happen and that will be that. This program and its goals are the most important thing that the world has going on. If twenty kids miss Christmas it's not the end of the world. If we don't successfully convince you and the rest of the world of the vital necessity to leave Containment as it is and to not pursue nuclear power then it may well be the end of the world as we know it."

I hadn't spoken in some time so I thought that my opinion would be of value. "My personal preference would to be to try some of this chocolate that Landon is talking about. So I think an exchange of some sort would be the right way to go."

"Well, it is good to see that I convinced you that there is something of value outside of Containment."

"I just think that if the only thing you can think of that we are missing is candy then it must be really good and I want to try it."

"Once the people of Containment get a taste of chocolate then it is all over. You would surrender this whole place to get some more."

Herman laughed, "Then that leaves me no choice but to block all of the exchanges with the outside to prevent the spread of chocolate."

"When do you think that we will know what is going to happen? Landon asked.

"It will be as soon as the arrangements are made." Herman answered.

Chapter Nine

In the end, security arrangements could be made for a package exchange, so that is what happened. No one in Containment wanted any more people coming in and they didn't want the students to leave before they had a sufficient understanding of the need to keep Containment secure. Not all of the exchange students were Christians. Lee wasn't. However, they all seemed to have practiced a ritual of gift giving that was foreign to those of us who grew up here. People in our society valued the time spent with someone more than the idea of spending money on someone. Landon's mom shipped in enough small boxes of chocolate so Landon could give them as presents to everyone that he knew. I think that everyone agreed that this was something that was missing from Containment.

We made a big deal out of exchanging gifts so that Landon and the rest of the outsiders would feel a little less like outsiders. Regardless, the lessons went on. The students learned about the history and the necessity and the functioning of Containment. It was in class one day that Landon got to express his feelings about our lawless society. He was asking about our traffic signs and thought that they were proof that we really did have laws. Bill pointed out that no law required a person to obey the traffic signs but people did so out of courtesy. No penalty existed for running a stop sign but if someone did fail to stop and caused an accident then they would be held responsible for the consequences of their choice. Bill pointed out to Landon that people in Containment were raised from the beginning to appreciate that they were making choices with each thought and action they took.

Landon states, "In our country people learn to respect the law from the beginning and they know right from wrong and how to choose between the two."

"How do you know that they respect the law in your country?" Bill asks

"You respect the law by obeying all of the laws," Landon asserts.

"Do the people obey all of the laws?" Bill continues his questioning.

"Why yes, certainly they do. Except for the criminals, who don't respect any authority."

"Do you include traffic laws as something that everyone respects?"

"Yes, everybody knows that all laws are equal in importance."

"What's the speed limit on the highways where you live?"

"The highest posted speed limit is 90 kilometers per hour."

"Does every body drive 90 kilometers per hour?"

"No, everybody drives about 100 kph."

"Why is that?"

"Nobody wants to hold up traffic and be considered as an oaf. Everyone drives a little faster than the speed limit so their fellow drivers don't get upset."

"So, the opinion of the people driving around them is more important than the law?"

"No, the law is the most important but people know that they won't be arrested for speeding unless they are at least 10 kph over the limit. So they all drive 10 over the limit, it's expected."

"Then the speed limit is a minimum speed not a maximum speed?"

"No, it is a maximum," asserts Landon

Bill stops and looks around at the class. "I think you can see what I am illustrating here. In the outside world they have laws that everyone pretends to obey but they are governed by the opinion of their fellow citizens"

Landon raises his voice, "No, no, that is not at all what I said."

"Landon, it is not what you said but it is what we all see. In Containment we have eliminated all of the pretend rules and we allow the rule of public opinion to hold sway. No one is a criminal because they don't want to obey traffic regulations.

"You are a criminal if you don't obey traffic regulations in my country," Landon insisted. "Laws are necessary to enforce the proper behavior."

"I think in your case that might be true." Bill gives up trying to convince Landon about what controls people's behavior. "You might try reading some of the original works by Hayward Crowell, Landon. It might help you to understand what we are doing here." The rest of the class had seen a demonstration that clearly indicated that people are more influenced by opinion than law.

That night after supper, Landon and I went up for a visit with Herman. Landon couldn't wait to tell Herman about the traffic laws. "I still think that I proved that Containment has laws or rules that govern the people's behavior." He said, after explaining what went on in the classroom.

"What makes a law or rule be a law or rule?" Herman asked. He answered his own question. "It is the requirement to comply and the threat of punishment, if you don't, that makes a law or rule. We have regulations here in Containment but they are not accompanied by any demand for compliance or punishment. However, we do have something in Containment that comes close to being a law. That is the building and zoning codes. They do have requirements for compliance. They do not limit people's behavior but they are designed to foster energy efficiency, long term stability, beauty, and care for the environment." You could try to prove your case about the codes if that is what you want but I think you might want to take Bill's suggestion and read some Hayward Crowell. I have them all here."

"OK, I like to read. It might help me to understand how this place functions. Let's see what you have."

"His first books were all written before he had solidified his ideas of Socialist-Anarchy. You should try Implementation of Socialist-Anarchy. It is written about how people can learn to make choices and accept responsibility. The first people who joined Hayward Crowell did so after he published this book." I added.

"Why did people want to join Crowell? What were they doing?" Landon asked.

"They were advocating for changes in the government and being branded as criminals when the decision to clean the world from the nuclear fiasco happened. The creation of Containment gave Crowell the opportunity to try his ideas."

"Then that is the one I'll start with."

Herman walked over to one of his cabinets. "I have an

autographed copy that has been handed down in the collection of the Programmer direct from Crowell. You can read that if you wish but don't take it out of the house." Herman lovingly removed a volume and handed it carefully to Landon.

I hadn't known that original works from that long ago existed. I guess I never thought about that. I crowded over to see what Crowell had written in the book.

Landon opened the book and on the frontispiece he saw Crowell's hand written script. He began to read, "I hope that each person who reads this book will come to the same conclusion that I did before I began writing it. There is no evil. The things we think of as evil are only choices. Helping people to learn to choose wisely can eventually eliminate those choices that we currently describe as evil. We can create a better world not by fighting evil but by helping people to live better through more conscious choices." Landon closed the book. "I will read it but he has a long way to go to convince me that here is no evil."

"Just give it a try," I say

"Take care of the book, Herman adds.

We spent the rest of the evening talking about the beginning of Containment. Herman knew some of the myths and mysteries about Hayward Crowell but he couldn't determine if they were all based on truth. Eventually he said the truth is whatever you believe it to be and it is beneficial to Containment to believe the stories about Crowell because it gave our lives more meaning than if we were just taking care of the nuclear waste. We had the higher purpose of creating a society built on a new way of relating between humans.

The next morning at breakfast, Landon said, "You have to read the book by Crowell. I was not able to put it down after I started reading in bed last night. I didn't get to sleep until three this morning."

"You are probably right I should read his books. I never really thought about how he managed to interest people in joining him." I replied.

"I want to go back and read some of the parts again so I can understand them better and then I will give you the book. I am sure the Old Man won't mind if we both read it before he gets it back."

"Thanks, I probably won't be as fast at reading as you are. I can't believe you read it in one night."

"It was a long night and I need to go back over it to make sure I didn't miss something. In a way the concepts of socialist anarchy are more valuable to my people than I thought nuclear power could be. I can't wait to report back to the government what I have learned."

"Landon, I hate to tell you but that is the part you missed. Your government is not going to want you to spread the ideas of socialist anarchy. Governments will act to protect the interest of the government in all cases. Look at some of the other books by Crowell if you want but you need to know that before you go home."

"I was sent here by my government, Jason. They are expecting me to give a report about what I learned. They are not going censor what I have to say to the people."

"OK, if you say so but I can tell you that all forms of power act to protect themselves. It is inevitable. I am encountering it here as I try to learn the history of the changes to the program. There is a vested interest to your government in keeping the ideas of SA from being broadcast to the public in your country."

"You might be right about that. I had to sign a contract before I was sent over here. One of the provisions in the contract was that I had to report first to the science committee of the Defense Department before I made any public statements."

"Anyway, give me the book when you are done. I want to see what you think is worth missing sleep over. Let's get to class before we are late."

The day passed like several days had passed before. We sat in class. We had lunch and then we sat in class for the rest of the day. I longed to wander somewhere where the trees felt the wind without the stench of humanity filling the air. I wished to be free to wander the hills to the south where I have heard that moose are frequent visitors. I day dreamed through most of the day, not paying attention and not realizing that I was missing the point of the educational process that I had envisioned. Much of what they covered was about the utilization of the nuclear wastes as part of the process of dealing with them. There was one interesting discussion that had to do with the radioactive asphalt used in paving some of the roads out in the country.

In the outside world's previous understanding of nuclear waste everything had to be contained or buried or sealed away in some manner but the early engineers in Containment had such a huge volume of low level waste that someone suggested using some of it to pave the rural roads. The benefit in the winter is that you don't have to plow snow. It melts off. They picked rural roads where there were few people and no long distance commuters who spent hours on the road every day. That way no one was exposed too much in the way of radiation. Roads were kept safe in the winter without the expense of maintaining snow plows in remote areas. It was a typical Containment solution to the problems that the early settlers had to face. Make what you were given work to your advantage some way. I went back to thinking about hiking through green trees and moist forest environments.

It was a cold windy day that Saturday and Landon had given me the book from Hayward Cowell so I settled into a big warm chair and began to read. The <u>Implementation of Socialist-Anarchy</u> by Hayward Crowell is a small book with less than two hundred pages. It was written in 2012 the year that time was supposed to end.

Are you happy with your current economic situation? Do you feel secure about the future of our planet in the face of the limited response we are making to the changes in climate? Is confident the word that you would use to describe your feelings about being able to afford the medical care that you currently need? What is the possibility that capitalism will come to any solution to the wars that continue to plague humanity when money is the source of the problems?

It is the intention of this book to illustrate the failures of the current capitalist system and demonstrate an alternative way of operating the distribution of goods and services in society. The purpose of an economic system is to regulate the distribution of the resources that are available among the needs that are requiring the resources. In a capitalist system money is used as a means of determining who gets what services and goods. If you have enough money you can do whatever and get anything regardless of the laws. The power of money congealed into the hands of a few very rich has resulted in the bankers picking the leaders of countries. Please take the time to consider the history of how that came about with a brief history of recent times.

Once upon a time not so long ago, there was a land where people were happy and successful and felt that they could solve all of the world's problems. This land was the greatest power in the world and its people felt blessed by the creator because they had just won another major war after emerging from a long deep economic depression. The people of this country lived the Biblical passage of be fruitful and multiply. The people had plenty of kids and saw that the kids went to a good public school and to church on Sunday. In the schools the children were taught the history of Manifest Destiny and How the West was Won. There was a feeling among the children that all things were possible. The world was available to them. All they had to do was follow their dreams.

Underneath the veneer of the perfect white world was an underbelly of the things not discussed in polite company. The conditions of the natives who had been forced onto reservations colored the childhood of those who grew up in the West. Others experienced the various sides of the remnants of slavery if they grew up in the south or the industrial north. The south and west also saw no reason not to discriminate against those from south of the border. It was possible to see these things if you looked but most of the people were happy not to notice.

The people of the Great Generation as they came to call themselves had so many children that it was called the baby boom. Many of the children grew up with questions that they couldn't answer. Such as, "Why hide under your desk if a nuclear bomb is going to go off?" Some of the children grew up to face their own war in Viet Nam, some of the children chose to refuse to go to Viet Nam, but the majority of the children did a little protesting so that they felt good about being in opposition to the war, then they used their college deferment and got an education so that they could get a good job.

A good job became the key as pragmatism replaced idealism and the boomers settled down to the job of raising their own kids. Oh they mouthed a few words of protest as Reagan's policies were put in place. But not for long or loud as they were making real money now and that progressive income tax was a thing of the past. People were entitled to their earnings. They didn't kill any one directly. They were just smarter or better connected or had the inside news or the early opportunity. What they did was not criminal and they deserved to keep their earnings.

It is possible to view history in several ways but it has been said that history is always the story of the victors. This contest appears to have been won by the one percent who claim class war fare if someone has the audacity to suggest that taxes should be raised on the rich. The end is very nearly in sight. The peoples of the world will all be enslaved to the corporations through the feeding tube of the job that doesn't quite pay enough. We do have the possibility of remembering and doing our own recall. Do you remember that Jimmy Carter had an energy independence program that was canceled by Reagan? Reagan even had the solar panels that Carter had installed as an example removed from the roof of the White House. Can you recall that we once had plans for efficient mass transit and high speed rail so that we wouldn't be dependent on cars and airplanes for transportation? The truth is that every person has their own experiences and they can choose to color the experience any way that they want to. You may not have chosen to aware of the process where the rich have systematically plundered the earth in every way possible, but that doesn't change the outcome of the last fifty years.

Some people remember it as a good thing that Reagan's hence men secretly traded missiles to Iran preventing the release of American citizens held hostage by the Iranians at the time. They prevented the release until after Carter was no longer president. Do you recall that there was no investigation or action to restore justice by Congress? Those of us who are old enough to remember have a duty to the future to not just let this all go by the wayside. Regardless of how you have acted in the past the possibility of acting differently in the future is always available. What do you want your children, grandchildren, and great grandchildren to think about your actions as the world faced the crisis of global warming and economic collapse?

Prior to 1970 there was an alignment of understanding and values between the working class people and the Democratic Party based on the works of Franklin Roosevelt. Unions knew that there were two sides to politics and the business owners were on the other side. If you choose to remember George McGovern, that election is when the separation of values started becoming based on emotional issues. If you worked in a factory, mine, refinery, or steel mill, or drove a truck, or worked in a lumber mill, what you heard was, "I don't care if he is a Democrat, I won't vote for some peace loving faggot from South Dakota." The negative advertisements that were broadcast about McGovern were false but they succeeded in preventing his election.

Newt Gingrich built a career by extending this separation. People were vilified as Liberal. Democrats were denounced as tax and spend. The issues of guns and abortion were used to drive a wedge between the thinking process and the vote. If you are angry about something it is easy to steal your interest and your vote. What happened over the last fifty years was a country wide shift in values regarding money. The process of eliminating programs for the needy and replacing them with more opportunities for the rich to avoid taxes continued into and through the Clinton presidency, accelerated through the Bush years and hasn't missed a beat with Obama in office.

It is now appropriate to close schools and fire teachers and eliminate medical care for the disabled because you can't raise taxes. Many of the people that are currently so excitedly Tea Party have a good heart but this was a movement that was constructed and systematically planned and built over time. There is not a single overwhelming conspiracy so much as there is a single underlying motivation, which is greed. The greed is coupled to the constant fear that someone will take something away from them. The majority of the very rich have long since learned to shunt their guilt into the belief that no one else has any value as a person. Therefore, nearly all of the rich and powerful people tend to act the same way. With the same values, they make similar choices. What are the values that have been installed over the last half of the century? Based on the rhetoric of the current crop of candidates and the actions of the leading business men for the last few years here are a few of society's current values.

1. It is good to be rich.
2. If you are not rich it is your own fault.
3. Taxes are not to be paid by the rich.
4. Public moneys should be used for programs to benefit the rich so they can trickle down on the poor.
5. Periodical stage a scam requiring a bailout.
6. Encourage all of the possible investment by small investors through payroll deductions and then dump the value with a scare and a sell off.
7. Buy all of the market at bottom dollar.
8. Repeat steps 4 through 7 about every eight to ten years as frequently as public memory will allow.
9. Operate a continual war economy so that the defense budget is never questioned.
10. Create a climate of fear to keep justifying increasing restrictions on personnel freedom.
11. Vilify anyone who voices opposition to the conservative agenda as unpatriotic.
12. Block any meaningful changes in health care by including insurance companies instead of eliminating them. The result is the United States does not have a public option for health care.

13. Preclude any meaningful election reform so that we still have the best government money can buy.

14. Block all attempts to value the poor or the immigrants or the migrant workers as human and restrict their access to health care and opportunities for citizenship.

15. Initiate referendum petitions in as many States as possible blocking the power of the States to raise taxes effectively hampering the ability to govern.

16. Insist that social security wasn't intended to provide for people and everyone has to have their own retirement and medical to take care of their own future.

17. The bankers will continue to foreclose on homeowners in spite of getting billions in bailout money that they awarded to themselves in bonuses.

These values are not restricted to the United States, they would be familiar around the world where capitalism has held sway as the economic system of choice, the choice often forced by invading businesses. Many more things can be added to the list of values that have permeated the world society of commerce. These would include moving jobs overseas and ending employment here and then sheltering the money so no taxes are paid to the US. The CEOs get a big bonus for that as well.

The point is if you look around you will see that the humanity is already in a total war for resources. The corporations are at war against the indigenous peoples all over the world. The war is over in many places in Africa and South America. The people don't own the resources. Some dictator or warlord sold them to a mining conglomerate. This is also true in the US with oil, coal, and natural gas leases of mineral rights that preclude the property owner having any control of the removal. It could be a British or Chinese registry, but it will be a multinational company with power invested into several governments. The power of the local government will be used to insure that the people work under brutal conditions at low wages. They will then be taxed to pay for the International Monetary Fund loans that the country was forced into to pay for the development of the roads, bridges, and dams, that the corporations wanted for access to their development. This has been and is the model of development that has been followed since the British perfected it in 1600.

The United States has a long history of going to war to protect the interests of business men to exploit the holdings of the indigenous people throughout the Americas. It started with the formation of the first settlements. It was always appropriate to take whatever the white man wanted. The US history includes such glowing examples as the Trail of Tears when the Cherokee were forced to move to Oklahoma and the trail of broken treaties with every other tribe in country. There are still tribes today that are fighting a continual battle in the courts in an attempt to regain the lands and rights that they have lost.

Businesses began to use the governments as enforcers against the peoples of the undeveloped areas of the world. The United States expressed the policy of Manifest Destiny as an excuse for the policy of removing or slaughtering any natives in the way of the discovery of riches. Having been a British colony the United States businessmen were quick to secure the trade in coffee, sugar

THE SPIRIT OF HUMANITY

and bananas with the use of US forces securing a local dictator who supported the businesses in proportion to the graft payments he received.

The United States assassinated Allende, the legitimately elected president of Chili in 1973 while I was in Venezuela working at Guri Dam. That was just another cog in the long history of picking dictators in the banana republics for Dole and United Fruit. There have been those in the US political system who have suggested assassinating the current president of Venezuela, Hugo Chavez. The US has continued the pattern of using armed force to prop up corrupt leaders in Iraq and Afghanistan where we have added a new twist by using private corporations like Blackwater to do the dirty deeds for us that we don't want to get into with official US involvement. Is there any hope that peace will have a chance to prevail?

It is apparent that our country will continue to be business as usual for as long as some type of stability can be maintained. Rachel Carson was sounding the alarm about climate change and had documented sea level changes over eighty years ago. If the common man was going to use some common sense, they would have by now. Unfortunately, the common man needs information that is reliable and complete in order to be able to make a correct judgment. Many of the things that everyone should know are currently considered classified and top secret. We should know where the trillions of dollars spent for the war in Iraq went. We should know why the Democrats are not willing to investigate any of the criminal activity of the Dick Cheney cabal. We should know why speculation is allowed for critical commodities like gasoline. We won't learn these things under our current system that allows government secrets.

The continual use of emotional issues to occupy the time and mind of public debate rather than discuss the real issues results in getting people to vote against their own best interest. It continues to work again and again as the issues of guns and abortion will never change. This ploy of playing who's more conservative may actually work against the current group of candidates trying to get the public to vote for them. Once a candidate has assigned a value that they support to their campaign rhetoric, the other candidates can criticize the position as not conservative enough, or not valuing the unborn, or not protecting the second amendment. So far the strategy is working as there is no acceptable candidate that can unify the people. The people are grouped into tight little knots of clinging to your own belief and criticizing everything else. There will be no chance of a leader emerging from this pack of dogs.

The things that aren't being discussed in the process of deciding which of these political whores will lead the United States are the really important issues facing humanity. The population of humans on the planet is increasing rapidly. In spite of the rapid rise past seven billion, the thought of limiting people's reproduction is verboten to discuss. The corporations are waging wars with the countries that they control. However, the attempt of trying to limit the massive expenditure of resources on destruction will see one labeled unpatriotic. The climate changes are accelerating but the pressure is on to drill more oil wells and burn more coal. The issues of race, immigration, and gay marriage will continue to divide people and prevent progress towards solutions.

The likelihood that a solution will be found to society's problems when as a society we never have any better information than what is served up by Fox news and Good Morning America is small. It is possible now because of the changes taking place rapidly in the way the world communicates. We are learning that the internet can cause changes in a hurry if people are informed and the issue is something that gets the attention of enough people who to care to respond. As we are learning new ways to communicate, we can choose to learn other new skills as well. Let's keep that in mind.

In the book 1984 by George Orwell he describes a civilization that consists of three main powers that are at continual war with each other. The actuality is not that simple. There are several countries that are manipulated by the bankers into continual conflict. There has been an increasing growing alignment of power centralized in the hands of a few who alter elections and use the power of money to buy whatever country they need. The people who understand this trend are too frightened about their personal situation to speak out in any meaningful way. In some places in the world where the situation has been extremely desperate for around fifty years, the population is so determined to change that they have begun to demonstrate in the streets where some of them are killed by the powers in place. Many of the powers in place are rich families that got that way selling their countries resources for pennies to the corporations.

What I want to suggest is a different way of looking at the world and if enough people around the world start to change how they look at the world, then we have a chance. If I was to ask for one thing from these writings it would be for enough people to understand and care enough to change. Just read these words with an open heart and an understanding mind.

What I will describe is a new way of operating the world. Since many of the world's problems are caused by the relationship to money I will begin with a brief history of money. Money is an invention that was conceived originally as a means of facilitating commerce. While the direct trading for goods and services suffices for the local area, it doesn't allow for trade over long distances or across the seasons of time. Gold and silver and jewels were used to facilitate the portability and accumulation of wealth originally. While they had the advantage of having actual intrinsic worth, they have the disadvantage of not being dependable and subject to fraud. Various other items were used for money in places around the world, there were shells and beads that were often manipulated with a lot of labor but many areas settled on coins of some type that had actual value like the Spanish piece of eight. These were in use for some time but eventually gave way to paper and coins that represented value without any intrinsic value of their own.

The first fraud was to use fake gold or silver. We know the story of Euclid because of a kings concern with being cheated. The process of civilization became a process of using the power of the government to enforce the power and validity of money. The coins of Rome were respected and accepted for value because the image of Caesar was stamped into them and they were backed by the power of Rome. In one of the oddities of commerce, the money of the United States is not issued by the government but by the Federal Reserve. Printed on the paper is the government's promise to back the currency and it says this note is legal tender for all debts public and private. You are not given the choice of whether or not you wish to accept this piece of paper for payment for your services.

This revelation that the purpose of government is to protect the value of the currency of the country may be a surprise to some, but this is actually is the original purpose of government, to make the world safe for commerce. The Greeks and Romans extended the reach of their armies on the strength of the taxes they imposed on the conquered territories to pay for the services that they received. The British Empire extended the concept of using the force of arms to extend the greed of business for cheap resources across the entire world.

This continues today in South America, Africa, Afghanistan and Asia. Oil is the main resource that is extracted but it is far from the only one. The catch phrase of "Making the World Safe for Democracy" is a euphemism for subduing the natives for profit.

More ideas of commerce were invented with the concept of debt and interest. This was followed by stocks and bonds and notes and pooled mortgages. The process of inventing new ideas of commerce continues to this day.

What is important to note is that every step of the process was subject to fraud and criminal acts by the participants who were skilled in the art of deceit. This continues today with one Ponzi scheme after another being uncovered. This is where the history you were taught in school leaves out some of the facts.

At each step of the subjection of humanity to commerce, there were people who objected and tried to explain that this was the step that doomed humanity to a life of servitude. Little did they recognize that it was the first step, the idea that money could represent value, that is false, incorrect, wrong and doomed us to failure.

Socialist-Anarchy is the promise of a new life on this planet.

If you are reading this you will want to know something of the circumstances that have led to it being written. We are in the first half of the Twenty-first Century and the planet is in turmoil across the globe with conflict and wars across the entire planet.

This serves a two-fold purpose. It allows the patriots the opportunity to feel good about their self as they hate the people who have been designated to be hated and they get to kill off some of the population. The process is not new. It has been practiced for about ten thousand years. Most of the people in most of the countries are in a daily struggle to earn enough money to pay the bills, pay the loans, pay the doctors, and pay the grocer for the food they eat. The situation is not improving as the politicians who operate the governments are chosen by the corporations.

So a brief look at history is sufficient to demonstrate that money is an invented commodity with no intrinsic value. The value of the money is its ability to serve as a means of facilitating commerce. Money is used to facilitate all commerce without respect to purpose or social need. In that respect, money has no moral value and does not discriminate between the truly, meet, right, and proper and the spawn of the devil. Spoken differently as far as money is concerned a drug deal is a drug deal whether you are buying from your neighborhood pharmacy or your friendly local pusher.

As seen in recent history, the value of money is the value of the government behind the currency. For many years the US dollar was regarded as the standard. All other currencies were valued in relation to the dollar. One of the ploys of the multinational financiers was to end the reign of the US dollar as a standard, forcing it to float among the rest of the currencies. The resultant devaluation of the dollar caused many changes to take place in the world economy. The rise of China as the world's leading industrial and financial nation is one result.

Therefore we see that the link between money and government is the problem we can fix easily. If we eliminate money the need for government goes away. So let us begin to envision a way to facilitate commerce and the exchange of goods and services without the use of money.

I have spent considerable time struggling with this concept. I have reached the conclusion that it is necessary for humanity to back up and start over again. The first step is to abandon the idea that it is possible to own any item as property. This is the tricky part. The idea that nothing can be owned does not mean that you have to give up your possessions. It means that you have the use of those things that you need but you do not own them.

There is a spiritual understanding that many of the native cultures had about the nature of reality. Many native cultures considered everything to be alive. Rocks, hills, trees, lakes, rivers, frogs and mosquitos and all of the rest of the world were a part of the universal spiritual connection to the creator of the universe. This understanding is teachable because there are specific techniques that anyone can use to achieve the experience of this knowledge. These techniques are written about in many texts with a shamanic connection. The person who utilizes the experience will feel their spirit rise up ascending into the far reaches of space to encounter the creator. Once the contact is made the person can merge their conscious understanding with that of the creator. The resultant experience will remain with the person because of the depth of the feelings that they have.

It is this experience that enables a person to understand that nothing can be owned because it is a spiritual being in its own right. After you are able to communicate with the spirit of an object you will realize that objects liked to be used to fulfill their destiny the same as all other spirits are on a quest to find a way to express their talents and destiny. The resultant cooperation between an object and person is responsible for many expressions of great art and music. Think about Michelangelo and the piece of marble that became David or BB King and the guitar he calls Lucille as examples of this. There are billions more examples as all people have a talent of some kind and they express that talent through some type of material relationship.

As I kept reading the book of Hayward Crowell, I realized that if Containment had not coincided with the creation of a society founded on the principles of Socialist-Anarchy it would have never have happened. I knew that the power of government was prevented from interfering with the operation of Containment just because of the high radiation levels that were forced onto the scientists and technicians kept them from doing anything but work on the problems. To have a group of people volunteer to work to feed them so that Containment was possible was a miracle. That the process worked so well and lead to such a high level of success as a society was only due to the diligence of the people who volunteered.

As I read on I came to where I dropped the book. When I picked it up and read it again I saw that Hayward Crowell had predicted just what we were doing now. He knew we would have to deal with the outside and he suggested education as a possible solution to the inevitable pressure from the outside to share the resources of Containment. His final words are a cautionary tale of the possibilities of failure and the destruction of Containment.

THURSDAY NIGHT
EXPERIENCE

❁

Thursday nights during a training week with Michael Harner were used by Michael to give his students an opportunity to see spirits and or sense their presence in some way. On this particular Thursday night Michael started by having us practice a singing journey similar to what some of the shamans in South America do. I found the singing journey to be very refreshing and invigorating after getting the giggles and disturbing everyone around me. Somehow the giggling gave me the energy to be able to see some of what happened after Michael called in the spirits. I did see small green lights moving in the center of the floor but what really captured my attention were glowing white clouds that kept moving just below the ceiling behind Michael and the people in that area. I also felt like something was moving past me or was just off my shoulder. When the drumming stopped and the lights came on I was surprised that more people weren't just jumping inside like I was. They all seemed too calm for me.

I had to get out into the woods. I had taken walks in the mornings to explore the surrounding area and the previous evening Corey Hitchcock and I had gone for a short walk and we had planned to go again this evening. A couple of other people had indicated that they wanted to go as well earlier in the day but when I got over to the community center they changed their mind and weren't going. Corey and I walked over the hill to the east and down the other side. I had been there in the daylight and knew my way around but the moon was up high and almost three fourths full with a big ring around it and the night was not dark. We walked past an old oak tree and on down the trail but as we went further the lights from the freeway became visible again. We decided to go back to the old oak and sit down for a while. When we did that we were looking across a meadow towards the west to the hill that we had climbed over. There was a group of trees along the edge of the meadow at the base of the hill. You could see the dark forms of the trees and the open space underneath them. Where we were sitting there were no lights visible only the moon and the stars. We sat and talked about various things going on in our lives. We were leaning against the old oak and were quite comfortable just sitting there talking.

We had been there a short time when I noticed what looked like a glowing light under one of the trees on the other side of the meadow. I asked Corey if she could see that and she had noticed it as well. We continued to sit and talk and as we watched the area under the trees became filled with glowing moving clouds of light. I kept talking in a lighthearted manner and then I felt a shudder behind me. Corey asked if I had felt that and I replied that yes I had. It felt like the tree moved she said. I agreed. We kept visiting about things in our lives for a while when we noticed that the lights seemed to be moving out into the meadow towards us. About that time we felt another shudder of the tree and looked at each other. It was getting harder to remain calm as we were starting to feel chills around us. We talked a bit and then we decided to head back as it was getting late. We got up and thanked the tree and the spirits and the place and moved back up the trail. The glowing lights were still there. After we came to the top of the hill and were started down the other side, I noticed a glowing cloud on the trail in front of us. Hold up a minute I told Corey and as we waited the form moved to the side of the trail and then dissipated. As we walked past I said thank you and we appreciate it. When we got back to the dorms it was midnight. I figure that we had been sitting for at least forty-five minutes under the tree with the dancing lights being there most of the time.

I have spent considerable time thinking about this. I have come to the conclusion that Michael had called all of these spirits into the room for a demonstration so that the people of the group would have the experience of some direct evidence of spirit. We gave them our attention for a few minutes and then we said thank you and goodbye. I think that the spirits felt that as long as they had gotten together they might as well have a party. Corey and I were fortunate to have wandered into the area where they were dancing under the trees. We never felt threatened or frightened and they had to be aware of our presence. A much bigger mystery to me is the movement of the tree. We both felt it twice. We were leaning against the tree and it felt like someone had shaken the back of the chair that we were in. There was no wind and even if it had been wind the bottom of the tree wouldn't move. It was a solid old oak and now I don't know where to put this experience or how to feel about it. I have felt the spirits of trees on many occasions and when we sat down I felt like the tree was an old friend inviting us to sit there. I remain baffled by the movement, which seems impossible.

This experience lead Corey and I to try journeying to the tree at the same time from our homes in order to meet at the tree to see if we could sense each other's presence. We were able to sense each other and pass information as well. While we were doing this the tree gave us some amazing lessons that inspired us to do some healing for the tree. During one of the times that I experienced when I was connected to the tree, the tree took me down into the roots and at one point my consciousness was in one molecule. This one molecule was a part of the mushroom and a part of the tree as well as being part of the soil. I could experience the knowledge of all three at the same time through this one molecule. I remain amazed at how all things are interconnected. This relationship went on until the land owner asked people to stay off of the trails on their property.

LIFE IS NOT LIKE THAT

Ok, I KNOW THAT YOU are going to think that I am nuts but here is the story as it happened to me. You know that I have been working with a spirit teacher who comes to me and tells me things that I need to know. Well, just the other day as I was talking to him, I happened to make a remark about how well that was what life was like. His reply was, "No, that wasn't what life was like. It was only my limited understanding of life that made me think that life was like that." He then took me on a mind adventure trip to another planet to show me that life is totally dependent on the sun of whatever planet you are on. The planet that he took me to was large beyond our understanding. It was larger than Jupiter. The distance to the sun of this planet was such that the planet was able to support life but the rotational period was extremely long. It took so long to revolve that all of the life forms on this planet had evolved with a strategy that allowed them to live under these conditions.

Basically, there were two types of life that existed on this

384

planet. There were the life forms that lived in the long days and died out during the long nights and were recreated from spores or seeds that survived in the soil during the long night. Some of these life forms became highly developed and built structures that became homes and cities. Each successive generation left instructions for the following generation so that the knowledge was able to be passed on and accumulate so that the cities became more advanced as time went on. These beings sensed when the time of the dark was approaching and they would leave their homes and move into the dark so that they were far enough away from the city when they died away. The carcasses of the beings rotted away over time and left the spores in the soil. These spores would hatch out as the surface of the planet began receiving light again. There was a period of successive stages of growth until the final form developed like an insect out of a cocoon. This last stage had the ability to move into the cities and live throughout the time of light, building and improving the location until they felt themselves growing old and they sought out the dark to begin the process again.

The second series of life forms had developed to follow the light around the planet as the light brought things to life they hunted or gathered the things that they needed. The strategy of continual nomadic life was what allowed them to exist. They were in fear of the dark and kept moving constantly, because every moment of time that they weren't moving meant that they were getting closer to the dark. These beings had developed a hierarchy of position. The families that were at the front of the line had the best resources and they would only leave what they couldn't use or take with them. They had domesticated some animal forms that were herded as food sources. The following groups each had their own way of scavenging or hunting for what they needed, but they were limited to what evolved on the planet and that was left behind from the groups ahead. At the tail end of this continuous parade across the surface of the planet were the various ones who could no longer keep up with progression of the light. They kept losing ground until they were trapped in the dark and passed away.

So I became aware that life is not like that. It can be something so different that we don't even recognize the forms as intelligent such as the forms that first emerged from the spores. Or it can be a being that only knows the light and lives in fear of the dark.

The first faint life that stirs in the soil follows soon after a few stray photons find their way to the surface of the planet. The eternal night is finally becoming day. The passage of time is impossible to describe on this planet. Two factors combine to make the idea of day and night the only division of time that is available to the inhabitants of this strange land. Strange to us who define everything that we do in terms of time. The planet is enormously huge in size and the rotational speed is extremely slow.

As the dawn creeps forward across the surface of the planet, that first faint life is followed rapidly by countless forms that that spring up almost fully formed from the cold dry dust that made up the surface in the dark. If you hiked along the edge of a high mountain snow field in the summer you might see a similar thing as the buttercups and other wild flowers emerged almost at the edge of the snow that was melting away in the summer heat. On this planet's surface, the spores and seeds had lain dormant in the dark and waited for the sun to begin the process again.

Each thing that emerged became more complicated and developed as some things come that began to eat the first things that seemed to be rooted and growing where they stood. As the edge of dawn continued to make its slow deliberate march, behind it grew plants and small animals. At a sufficient distance from the dawn the small animals were completely outclassed by the large dominate species. They were a greedy group of families that spread across the surface of the planet and tried to devour everything that was in their path. Their goal was to leave nothing behind that could possibly help the ones who were following.

These front of the line families were organized in alliances that allowed them to feel secure to each side of their stretch. The stretch of each family was a carefully negotiated responsibility. You had to have the ability to secure that stretch from any attack that came from the rear. No attack could come from any direction but the rear as these beings were at the front of the line. They understood what being at the front of the line meant. Nothing was to be left on the surface that could help the ones who were constantly waiting for a chance to take over the position as first in line.

The adolescent males of the family were assigned the duty of herding the grazing animals that they used for food. The young animals could be ridden and used to herd the rest of the grazers. So you had the young of one species riding on the young of different species. As the grazers who were called wuwubies aged they grew larger and the males were consumed for food while the females were kept to keep increasing the herd. The idea was to maximize the number of grazers to the point that they would devour everything in their path. No sprig of vegetation was left when the hungry herd had passed.

The Trailers were biologically the same as the Fronts but you wouldn't recognize them as the same specie because they had spent their lives in constant hunger compared to the overfed Fronts. The Fronts were what consumption was all about. They were encouraged to have many children and the children were expected to have many children because it was necessary to keep the Trailers at bay and the best way to keep them behind you was to leave nothing behind.

Through the generations of being in front, the Fronts had developed into a powerful society. In the past there had been times when it was possible for a few of the Trailers to make a serious attack on the front. There had been some successful Trailers who in the far distant past had made it to the front of the line after devouring the Fronts ahead of them. This section was the most heavily guarded and these Fronts were the most vehement in their denial of the similarity between the Fronts and the Trailers.

This story was written after spending some time on the surface of the planet among the wuwubies. It is for fun and so you will realize that life is not like that. It is like any and every possibility that that the consciousness of the cosmos can imagine.

Bunyap was an adolescent male member of the Rolling Thunder tribe. They were the third most important tribe of the Fronts. He was proud to be a member of the Rolling Thunder tribe but he was always the slowest of his class to learn the physical skills that you had to master before you could move on to the next position.

Now he was at the rear literally at the rear of the moving column of his tribe. His job was riding herd on the wuwubies that grazed over the surface of the ground. You had to ride a wuwubie to herd them.

The wuwubie was the perfect grazing animal for this job of eating everything. They had a broad flat mouth that extended as they grew older. The mouth parts had sections that slid past the fingers of another part like dozens of pairs of scissors. Hairs grew out from above the mouth that were thick and maneuverable and used to comb the plants into the constantly moving mouth. The wuwubie added sections to its body as it grew, gaining a pair of legs with each section added. Once they went past six legs they were useless for riding and spent most of their time walking forward and grazing constantly. When they were really old they had so many sections that they were almost impossible to turn. The sections just kept walking on, while the head was in the air trying to go the other way.

Bunyap wasn't used to his wuwubie and he had trouble staying centered so he didn't get bounced around. He supposed to make sure that nothing got left behind so his job was to ride back and forth on his wuwubie making sure that it ate everything that was left behind. He was also supposed to make sure that none of the other wuwubies got off of the course. However, he couldn't control his wuwubie and the wuwubie would push ahead in the line of grazing elders so that it could get something more that the scraps of brush that was left at the end of the line. This always provoked a commotion among the wuwubies and led to the other riders noticing that his section was out of line and yelling at him.

This wasn't something that he wanted to do. The other riders seemed to enjoy the time spent on the back of a wuwubie. They couldn't have asked for something better to do and he couldn't think of anything that he wouldn't prefer. The trouble was that choice wasn't an option. Every stage of your life was already planned out and the future was as sure as the past. He was no longer a child and was no longer eligible for the loving care that his mother and teachers had provided. They had another child in the place that he had occupied and when that child came here; there would be another to replace him. That would be the way it was until another younger women took his mother's place as a breeder.

So he might as well get used to the smell of wuwubie dung. He was going to be here for a while. There was no use in thinking. The only thing to do was to control this wuwubie so he didn't get yelled at.

The storms rose in the east and traveled to the west when you were ahead of the sun and rose in the west and moved east when you were behind the sun. The highest temperatures were directly under the sun when it was straight overhead. The storms were mostly wind and dust with little rain. Water was scarce commodity on this planet and most of the life forms were not dependent on the rains or surface water for their needs. The water that was in the soil would gradually thaw as the sunlight came to the surface following the long cold dark. The first things that grew used the water that thawed first and then sent their roots down deeper into the soil as the soil warmed. Each successive form of life either had to get its roots down to the water or use the water from the life forms that it consumed. The surface of the planet was so uniformly level that most of the time there was no place for surface water to accumulate.

The wuwubies did not need to drink as they constantly consumed plant material that contained water. Since they didn't drink water and seldom had rain to contend with they did not like encountering bodies of surface water. There was a genetically carried fear of open water that caused the wuwubies to veer sharply when they encountered surface water. They would not go into the water in any circumstance, so when the Fronts came to any type of pond or lake they had to adjust the stretch of the adjacent families so that they could pass on either side of the water. This always took some doing for even if the body of water was small enough that it was in only one family's stretch there was confusion among the wuwubies when they had to change course. The normal complement of wuwubies were arranged to cover the surface as they passed. The oldest wuwubies were in front and since they had the most sections and the most legs they were the hardest to turn. To complicate matters the oldest as the strongest most powerful of the wuwubies were used to pull the platforms that carried the mothers and their smallest children. These platforms were built on numerous rolling wheels and attached to the wuwubies with a harness.

Each wuwubie had a section of the platform and the platforms could be divided into the sections if necessary to get around a body of water. Normally the sections were all connected so the mother could move about. Some of the largest families had platforms that stretched across the width of fifty wuwubies. The mother was attended by the adolescent females whose job it was to prepare the food. What did these creatures look like? The mature Fronts were much larger than the mature Trailers but they were actually the same species. The trailers were lean and thin throughout their life time but the Fronts grew heavier and heavier as their life progressed. If I had to describe a Trailer as looking like something on Earth, I would say praying mantis. The beings had four legs that they walked on and two legs that they used to manipulate the world as they walked. The creatures were made for walking and the four legs could support the body and keep walking indefinitely. The Fronts with the same basic body structure but with rolls and rolls of flesh surrounding the frame were not as mobile in the long run. They grew up using wuwubies for transportation and never developed the toughness that the continually walking Trailers did. Neither group had what we would consider a face. Their mouth parts made up most of what you saw on their head while their visual organs were located on stalks that could swing to and fro in any direction. Each eye was independent and communicated to a separate section of the brain, so one eye could be watching what was happening up close as they fed and the other eye could be scanning the surroundings to see what was happening in the area around them.

The wuwubies had one large eye that was centrally located in the front of the head well above the mouth parts. It was constantly scanning the area in front for the best plants to eat. The wuwubies did not look behind themselves or concern themselves with anything as long as they were eating. They were controlled by the Fronts whose four legs would wrap around the first section of the body of the wuwubie. This was the part that Bunyap had not mastered yet. He was small for a Front and had difficulty securing his position on the rounded form of the wuwubie. The wuwubies were steered by turning their head while applying pressure on the sides with the legs. Bunyap could not apply the pressure in the proper sensitive spots because his legs were too short. So his wuwubie could ignore him and move in the direction that it wanted.

The continual march forward established the pace. The wuwubies that were pulling the platforms kept walking forward as they fed. They were at the front of the procession and their speed was an even monotonous smooth progression of one leg moving at a time. Each section followed the section in front without pause. The digestive system of the wuwubie went from one end to the other. The green plants went into the mouth and were cut off from the stems right next to the ground by the scissor like mouth parts. The food was then shredded into fine pieces by the rear teeth that acted like grind stones to pulverize whatever passed through them. The digestion took place in a long tube like stomach that went through each section. Each section took what nutrients it wanted and passed the rest to the next section. Young wuwubies left behind manure that was similar to horse manure in that you could see the well chewed remnants of the plants remaining in the manure. Older wuwubies would not have any visible plant parts while really old wuwubies emitted yellow green pelletized manure that had every bit of nutrition extracted.

Why so much attention to wuwubie manures? It was all that was left behind. Everything that came after the fronts had to wait until the manure was broken down and the plants regenerated before there was anything for animals to live on. This was the heart of the front's strategy. If there were no resources for a considerable distance across the planet, then anything following would have to carry all of their resources with them and this would slow them down. The scorched earth policy meant that the Trailers would not have any wuwubies or other domesticated animals to help them transverse the surface of the planet.

All of this Bunyap knew and understood. He knew what his role was and he knew that he was the last line of defense for his people. His job was to get his wuwubie to eat everything that was left behind by the hordes in front of him. Mostly what he had to look at was wuwubie manure and he was tired of it and he had just started his assignment riding the back trail. He would not get another job until someone at the head of the line died. When someone died every one behind him got to move up one position on the trail. In Bunyap's family there were no skips or jumps along the way. Some families would allow favorite sons to jump a position but not Bunyap's. He didn't have a chance of being the favorite son either. With his small size, he was regarded as a throwback to earlier times before the family was as powerful and popular as they were now.

The continual clinging to the back of his wuwubie and the scouting for plant remnants among the wuwubie shit was all he had to look forward to. No wonder that his mind wandered to other things. Such as why did life have to be like this any way? Wasn't there some way to exist that didn't require this constant treading forward? Nothing ever was any different.

Time was not a concept that had been used on this planet.

Everything was rendered in terms of the sun's position. The Fronts maintained their position with respect to the sun by constant migration. We would say that the solar angle would be about 10 to 11 o'clock but they would only know that they were where they were supposed to be. They talked about ahead and behind and since there was no day and night, ahead and behind were all that mattered.

Bunyap knew that he was behind. He was behind his whole family and he knew that he was not going to get ahead of any one who was in front of him. He might as well get used to the endless parade of wuwubie manure piles, because that was what he was going to be looking at until he grew too large to ride the back trail. He wasn't growing as fast as he should either. It was customary for the Fronts to leave prepared food packages for the ones riding back trail but his packages seemed to get lost or forgotten or swiped by the larger more aggressive youths who rode the back trail on either side of him.

He tried to kept his left eye scanning the ground in front of him, moving it back and forth looking for green plants, but his attention kept switching to his right eye which wavered on its stalk as high as he could reach trying to see something, anything, but wuwubie dung. The odor of it was his only companion except for the wuwubie whose back he clung to. His searching right eye was becoming more frantic as he didn't see anything for a long ways. He began to sense that he was behind. He had heard stories about those who fell behind but until now he had only had a reputation as a dawdler. He started to push the wuwubie faster but as he looked up at the sun he had a sudden realization. Now he knew what the stories meant when they talked about losing the sense of direction if you fell behind.

He carefully studied the position of the sun. It was not quite straight over head. If he was careful and kept taking bearings he should be able to gain on the passage of the sun and catch up to the family. They wouldn't miss him or go looking for him. He was an expendable, a male just entering adulthood. There would be no mourning for him on any one's platform. Not even his own mother's. He hesitated to take off at a hard pace. If he pushed his wuwubie too hard, it would not have time enough to eat as it went and if he let it wander looking for food, they would make no gain on the others because the line kept moving continuously forward at the same measured pace that exactly matched the sun. That meant, for the ones living on the platform, that it was always the same, nothing ever changed. There were never any surprises and only a few little rain showers to mar the steady pulse of the light that flowed down to the planet.

He had to start making some gain on the sun and soon. He began to scan the ground for the heavy marks made by the passage of the platforms. The trail in the dirt would give him the direction to head. If he was wrong and went the wrong way he might wander forever until his wuwubie died of hunger. He had to be careful of his wuwubie if he was ever going to catch up with his family. If you didn't show up with your wuwubie then you were sentenced for failure to prevent the wuwubie's body from falling into the hands of the Trailers. The only way to prevent the wuwubie's body from being left behind was to eat it yourself. The time that you spent doing that put you even further behind. If you ate only part of the wuwubie and left anything behind the stories always said that you would be marked by a circle of black birds that would fly over you until you died. No, his only chance was to remain calm and take a deliberate course.

He followed the first trail left by a platform that he came to and quickened his pace a little. The trail is unmistakable. The series of rows of wheels that formed the rolling base of the platform went across plain in an undulating pattern that flowed with the surface of the planet. This platform looked to be drawn by twelve wuwubies so it wasn't his mother's. It probably belonged to one of his younger aunts, who are only starting to produce offspring. The first good sign was a sprig of a live growing plant; his wuwubie quickly ate it and then settled into a steady pace. He could relax they were going in the right direction. What a relief. If he had been only a little slower in stopping to get his bearing overhead he might have been too late. As it was he was lucky. The stories told how once you couldn't decide on a direction because the sun was straight overhead, the smart thing was to sit down and conserve your energy until you could detect a shadow of a stick that you pushed into the ground and get the right direction. The problem was that people were not able to sit still for that long and they would logically decide that the best course was to run in one direction for as long as they could to see if they could get a shadow there. This was foolish of course, as the chance of going in the right direction was slim and the person quickly exhausted themselves running back and forth across the plain in a panic until their wuwubie died and they had to eat it. By the time you finished eating your wuwubie the sun would be casting a long enough shadow that you could never catch up to your family on foot.

That wasn't going to happen to him. He kept the wuwubie

centered on the tracks and kept pushing. Death was behind him. That was the truth of falling behind. Once you were behind the sun you were dead. There was no getting back if you ate your wuwubie. He saw a few more sprigs ahead and his wuwubie dove forward to get them. It was starting to get hungry and he knew that was not good. He had probably wandered off of his course and gotten behind one of his cousins who took their job more seriously than he did. They didn't leave anything ever. He had to get farther up the line to find out how far off from his line he was, but that meant his cousins would know he wasn't doing his job of cleaning the last of the plants from the surface. He would be disciplined for failure to aid the family and would probably be turned back and left to wander. Ostracized from the family and forgotten. He might as well eat his wuwubie now and get it over with.

He focused his right eye on one side of the track and his left eye on the other and tried to sweep the horizon for as far as he could. The left eye definitely picked up more bleeps out on the horizon. If he was correct about the track belonging to an aunt then his cousins had done a good job and his wuwubie would starve to death trying to follow in the track. He canted his course to the left and before too long he was rewarded by a low growing patch of plants that his wuwubie soon polished off. He set a quicker pace and the wuwubie responded well and didn't question his leadership. He was at a slight angle to the course but this would bring him back in line where he felt that he ought to be. He kept up a good pace until a thought struck him. He hadn't checked the sun for a shadow.

Stopping quickly, he found the longest stick of dead twig that he could find and stuck it into the ground. There was no shadow. He had had a slight shadow when he stopped and took the last bearing and then he had found the platform trail and he had started following it and then he realized that he was over behind the wrong family and then he went even faster and he had been traveling for a long time and he was going faster than the sun and there should have been a longer shadow to show how much he had gained not no shadow. There can't be no shadow that would mean he had been going the wrong way. You can't go the wrong way. Nobody goes the wrong way. But he must have. He looked around and saw in the direction that he was going more patches of the green plants that his wuwubie had eaten before. He realized that he had never seen these plants before. They were actually springing up from the ground next piles of manure that seemed to be broken down and dried not like he was used to seeing them. The wuwubie loved the plants and was fighting him to get to them. He began letting the wuwubie circle the stick and eat the plants as he waited for the shadow to show him what he feared. He was going to be behind the sun. He had driven his wuwubie hard there at the end and it was glad for a chance to feed on good green plants. It kept working farther and farther from the stick, until Bunyap lost sight of the stick and started to panic.

He wrenched the wuwubie around and forced it to retrace it tracks until he came to the place where the stick stuck in the soil. There was no shadow. His panic rose almost as fast as his understanding. I was gone from this place for a while and the stick still has no shadow. That means that the sun is still overhead and it hasn't moved far enough to make a shadow. He would have to wait longer. He began to see how one could begin to wander trying to find some way of marking the direction and hoping for the best. He had a minimum of supplies with him but there was a long rope that he could use to tie out the wuwubie and let it browse. When he finished staking out the wuwubie, he came back to check the stick. There was still no shadow. His mind worked over that fact. I am here and I am directly under the sun. My family is in front of me and I should be moving towards them if I am ever going to catch up. If I stay in one place the Trailers will catch up to him and eat him and his wuwubie. Then he would have really let the family down by giving aid to the enemy.

His thoughts wandered again to his wuwubie and as he looked for it he realized a terrible thing. The empty plain was starting to grow with things popping up and the wuwubie was in heaven eating his fill of good green for the first time. It was like being at the head of the line. He realized that they were at the head of the line. They were at the head of the line that began to make it possible for animals to follow the Fronts. New green growth meant that small animals would start appearing and then larger animals and then there would be enough for the Trailer family to subsist on. Because the sun was directly overhead these plants grew quickly and they wouldn't slow down. He was going to have a hard time driving his wuwubie away from here and getting it to cross the plain of barren ground that the Fronts had left behind.

At one time I planned to go back and spend time in one of the cities in the sun to get a feel for the behavior of the creatures that came from the spores. I planned to write another story but I never did.

CHAPTER THREE

❦

Warning! Warning! Warning!

Notice to all sentient beings inhabiting the planet called Earth. The process of planetary recall will begin January 1, 2025.

THE SPECIES THAT HAVE FAILED to care for the planet and spends their time and resources in violence and war have doomed this planet by their greed and unwillingness to care for each other and the planet. Their failure to understand that all life forms are connected means that this planet will be removed and taken to a system where the beings are intelligent and capable of caring for such a delicate and gentle part of creation. The earth was one of the creators' special projects, they expected it to be loved and valued not advertised for sale or seized in war.

Therefore if this planet has not achieved a state of peace and harmony between all beings by January 1, 2025 the planet will be relocated to different galaxy where the beings are more highly intelligent than the simple minded beings humans have evolved to. Those species with the false belief in property rights and ownership will be discarded as the planet is moved. There already are pictures of the beings flying off of the planet in circulation. This was meant as an early warning but wasn't heeded because of the greed of the leaders of the humans.

By order of
Universal Harmony Council

Where do we go from here?

There is a certain fatalism to growing old. Society leaves you behind and casts you aside once you are not earning income. You become fodder to the medical system and the insurance companies. There is always the temptation of the travel industry, but that has lost some of its appeal with the risks of disease and the increasing political instability.

With the experience of our lives we feel that we should have some importance and value but our kids have their own lives and the grandkids are mostly unknown. The opportunities to spend time passing on your knowledge is very limited. Is there much interest in the elderly in fighting climate change?

Here are some resources that you should look up if you wish to learn about how shamanism is able to create the things that happen that seem miraculous.

William S. Lyon Spirit Talkers: North American Indian Powers wmslyon.com

Bill is an anthropologist who spent over forty years working with Lakota shaman and has several books about his experiences. This latest work gives many examples of what they did but also gives an explanation of how they did what they did using an understanding of quantum physics. While the name is similar to the character in Containment I did not meet William Lyon until many years after writing the story. I enjoyed hearing his tales of the Lakota elders some of whom I remembered seeing when I was a kid in South Dakota. You can download some of his work from the internet.

Foundation for Shamanic Studies shamanism.org

The Foundation was started by Michael Harner and remains a source of shamanic education around the world even after Michaels passing. The classes can take you from the basic to the advanced and provide opportunities for experiences you won't get elsewhere. Some of the best and most important experiences in my life happened during a class with Michael Harner. I would not be here writing these words if Michael hadn't opened the door to the experiences.

Here is a different type of non-profit that does a lot of good across the country and might be seen as a model of the way people will work together in the future to work on common problems.

Back Country Horsemen of America www.bcha.org

This is an example of an organization of volunteers that has the right idea. They began with the realization that the Forest Service was not able to maintain trails in the forests and they were losing the ability to ride. The solution they had was to volunteer to maintain some of these trails so that they were available to ride. I am proud to be a member and have helped to clear trails and build bridges. I was president and newsletter editor for the Northeast Washington Chapter of the BCHW at different times. This organization of not that many dedicated people has a huge impact on improving the quality of life for everyone else through the work that they do keeping trails open.

Ideas to think about and work on to move in the direction of harmony:

When the internet first began, we only had a 14.4 modem over a dial up phone line. It worked better than what we have now. The reason was if you went to a site looking for some information that is what you found. The information loaded when you got to the site. Now no site will load the information that you are looking for until numerous ads have loaded. As the information starts to load a pop up will tell you that you need to create an account to see the information. My dream of an idealized internet would be one that banned advertising and included some means of filtering false information and banning anyone who continually expressed false information as true.

Thomas Jefferson said that an educated electorate was necessary to maintain a free society. Allowing the broadcast of false information over the internet gives validity to bad thinking and bad ideas. If there is a dark web allowed by the internet providers currently where criminals have free rein, then we should have a white web where schools, libraries, churches and other community organizations can have a web where they can exchange information without fear of being hacked. I had a web site that was to promote my classes when I was teaching for the Foundation for Shamanic Studies. I had to take the site down after it was hacked and redirected to a porn site.

I have heard that there are a lot of servers becoming available with the crash of the fake currency scams. If you are capable of building a safe web now is your chance. While you are at it include a social exchange program that is not selling people's information and is not a haven for internet manipulators.

I personally stopped going to Facebook for any reason when I learned of the extent of the Russian involvement influencing our elections. I would not contribute my participation to any social medium that allowed the dissemination of false information. If everyone acted and withdrew from any site allowing false information to be spread we could clean up the existing internet to a large degree.

Since all advertising is inherently false banning false information would eliminate most of the band width robbers and it might be possible to get useful information again.

Creating a culture of service founded on individual non-profit organizations is already happening around the world. A lot of this is being done by very young creative caring individuals who had a vision that got them started and then they built on it. The long range goal would be for everyone who wanted to be a non-profit service organization to be and we would fund each other's success by our purchases of services and goods.

My service is to offer ideas to people that they might not think of on their own. In this case the Spirit of Humanity is my big idea. I am offering it to the world as a means of moving forward to a time that we live in peace. The only reason that we have wars now is because the rich people are using the war economy to further their gains. No soldier is better off for having participated in any war. All of the conflicts between nations would end if the politicians were in the front lines.

If we practiced working in harmony our leaders would gather and they would make offerings to appeal to the spirits to help restore the balance of the world. These offerings might start out with stopping all business airline flights. They might require the removal of a string of satellites that should never have been allowed. They could cease all further drilling and exploration for oil. These are all things that the earth would ask for if you took the time to ask her.

The most fundamental rule to live by should be adopted across the board through all levels of jurisdiction and legislation. It is simply this "You can have more when everyone has enough."

The only reason that this world exists the way that it is, is because that is the way the rich people want it to be. Outside of Chouinard who started the company Patagonia you don't see rich people give away their fortune. Most charitable contributions by the rich are another means of control. They control who gets the jobs, the grants, and the opportunities by how their giving is arranged. Then when it is all done their accountant leverages the deductions to get back twice in tax savings as what they donated.

Consciousness is the ether that holds all of the realms of the Universe on the course of harmony and free expression without guilt. Since every cosmic event is following the natural laws of energy and matter there can only be a loving caring benevolent Universe. It is the conscious choice to express love that energizes the dynamic of the cosmos.

Each individual bit of consciousness is just as important as every other bit of consciousness. Each bit of consciousness can imagine a part of what is going to happen. When these parts are connected by working together they are multiplied in their capacity to create. When I was in the program where Michael Harner showed us the Ghost Dance there were forty-six people who each had a part of the vision. When the time came and we acted out the vision it was incredible in how well it worked with the power that the ceremony had to change our lives. Each person's part of the vision was there but each person also had to yield to accept the veracity of every other part of the vision and when we did that the power was palpable in the room with people jumping and spinning in the air as they danced. The power of working together on a shared vision is unlimited.

Diabolica Asking me to Dance

When we traveled in Peru we wanted to learn about as much as we could but we reached a saturation level of looking at another Spanish church full of gold and silver statues so we told our guide in Cusco no more churches, more ruins. When we were at Sacsayhuaman it was one of the places where I was met by a native shaman who came out to greet me. I had walked up to an area where you could see the scratches in the surface of the exposed rock where the large stones were moved down from the hillside to build the walls.

As I was walking up to the upper level the shaman walked across to where I was and we met in this place that looked across the whole expanse of the zig zag walls. He and I talked and he explained that where we were was where the Inca leaders stood to conduct the morning ceremony that energized the work. Virginia and my son Chris walked up as we were standing there. A small natural pool was at the top of the rock where we were standing. The shaman laid out his offering of coca leaves as he made a blessing ceremony for us.

Rocks at Sacsayhuaman

If you looked with your mind open you could see the thirty thousand people standing in rows imagining the rocks moving past them. As the rocks reached the wall they began to turn and roll over each other. It was the chanting of the people creating a hum in the range of a rumble which was accompanied by a higher frequency that caused the rocks to buzz as they were settling into place.

There were horns and pipes and gongs and high pitched whistles made from the quills of condor feathers. The sounds and the empowered imagining continued as the rocks settled into place each yielding a little as the vibrating surfaces became almost liquid as the surfaces closed against each other. A loud drum echoed across the entire area and the chant and the sounds stopped. No one looked at the wall. They would see the marvel that would be revealed tomorrow when they came to do it again.

Working together on a shared vision has enormous power because there is no doubt in the minds of the participants. The most common are music and theater and some sports. We need to begin to expand on that repertoire and build some real successes before attempting total elimination of government owned weapons. It is good to have a goal to work towards. I led our scout troop each year to work the finish line at the Bloomsday Race until we were replaced with electronic timers. At times there were over fifty thousand runners and five thousand volunteers to make it work. I always said "What if all of these people were doing something useful, can you imagine what they could accomplish."

Will the people who live on the planet choose to grow in understanding and become a society of decent people or will they continue to allow money to make the choices that will doom humanity and the planet to destruction? What will be the impact of one wandering spirit from fourteen galaxies away?

I wish you well as you grow in understanding. It is up to all of humanity to decide where they want to grow to in the future.

Leon

ABOUT THE AUTHOR

Leon Sproule has experience in many fields and has volunteered for many causes and has used spiritual powers to solve engineering problems and engineering challenges to further his spiritual growth. An adjunct instructor teaching Hydrology at Gonzaga University at the same time he was teaching Shamanism for the Foundation for Shamanic Studies, designing a water system for a customer and taking care of the farm. His wide ranging experience gives him a perspective shared by few others. Leon rebuilt a generator at Guri Dam in Venezuela in 1973 where he fell in love with South America. He has since been fortunate enough to take brief trips to Brazil, Ecuador and Peru. He greatly admires the native peoples who have mastered the art of living in harmony to nature in a wide range of environments, from the jungles to the high Andes. He has retired from working and has devoted his time to healing and spiritual work and enjoys trying to improve his golf game and hiking.

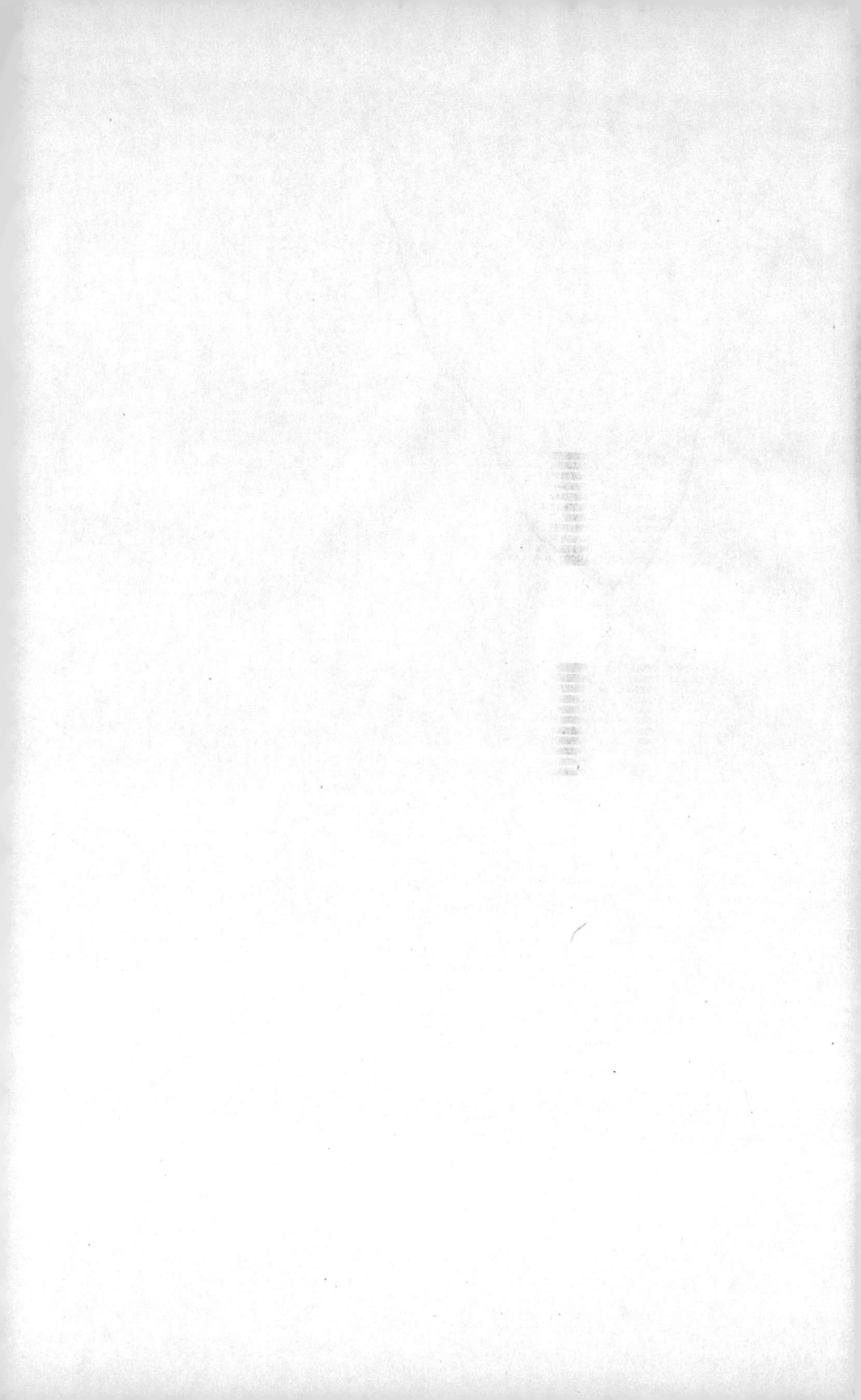